# UNDERSTANDING EARLY CHRISTIAN ART

*Understanding Early Christian Art* integrates the motifs and subjects of early Christian art with the symbols and themes of early Christian literature and liturgy.

The book begins with an analysis of the non-narrative subjects of early Christian art, for example, the Good Shepherd, the praying figure, and fish and birds. The book then explores the narrative images, portraits and dogmatically oriented figures found in Roman catacomb painting, sarcophagus relief sculpture, and early mosaics, ivories and manuscript illumination. The parallels between biblical exegesis as found in early homilies and catechetical documents and images portraying particular biblical figures are also discussed. Finally, the book examines iconographic themes such as Jonah, Daniel, Abraham offering Isaac, and Adam and Eve.

*Understanding Early Christian Art* offers an insightful, erudite, and lavishly illustrated analysis of the meaning and message of early Christianity as revealed in the texts and images of the early Christians.

**Robin Margaret Jensen** is Associate Professor of the History of Christianity at Andover Newton Theological School. She specializes in the history and character of the early Christian Church, particularly as it is revealed in its architecture and iconography.

# UNDERSTANDING EARLY CHRISTIAN ART

*Robin Margaret Jensen*

London and New York

First published 2000
by Routledge
11 New Fetter Lane, London EC4P 4EE

Simultaneously published in the USA and Canada
by Routledge
29 West 35th Street, New York, NY 10001

*Routledge is an imprint of the Taylor & Francis Group*

Typeset in Garamond by Taylor & Francis Books Ltd
Printed and bound in Great Britain by
Biddles Ltd, Guildford and King's Lynn

*British Library Cataloguing in Publication Data*
A catalogue record for this book is available from the British Library

*Library of Congress Cataloging in Publication Data*
Jensen, Robin Margaret, 1952–
Understanding early Christian art / Robin Margaret Jensen.
Includes bibliographical references and index.
1. Art, Early Christian. 2. Christian art and symbolism–To 500.
I. Title.
N7832.J46 2000
704.9'482' 09015–dc21          99–41887

ISBN 0–415–20454–2 (hbk)
ISBN 0–415–20455–0 (pbk)

FOR LIBBY AND BOBBY

# CONTENTS

# ILLUSTRATIONS

# ACKNOWLEDGMENTS

This manuscript has evolved over a long time, from many lectures and bits of articles. I am deeply grateful to the many students and colleagues over the years who have encouraged me to pull all the fragments together into one place. I have learned, from them, that the visual dimension of learning and teaching is effective, fascinating, illuminating, and delightful.

Special thanks must be given, however, to those who have supported my work in particular ways. The Association of Theological Studies provided a grant for a semester's release from teaching in the spring of 1995, which gave me the time to begin this project and provided for my mentoring by Professor Thomas Mathews, who read the original drafts of this work. My doctoral dissertation advisor, Richard Brilliant, has provided some important prodding and always answered my questions along the way. Mary Charles Murray has been an inspiration for more than two decades. Four very valued colleagues, J. Mary Luti, Rosamond Rosenmeier, William Tabbernee, and Mark Burrows, read all or part of this manuscript in draft, making many editing suggestions along the way. Graydon Snyder has given me his support and supplied many photographs, even after many years' worth of friendly arguments about the ways each of us (differently) interpreted some of the same materials. The staff of the International Catacomb Society have been extraordinarily generous with their time, both helping me find illustrations and providing photographs for inclusion here. Sarah Hubbell helped me to index this volume in its final form. My colleagues in the Boston area, particularly those who regularly attend meetings of the Patristica Bostoniensia, have provided lots of ideas and constructive criticism over the years as well.

# ABBREVIATIONS

| | |
|---|---|
| AB | *Art Bulletin* |
| ACIAC | *Congresso Internazionale di Archeologia Cristiana – Atti* |
| AJA | *American Journal of Archaeology* |
| ANRW | *Aufsteig und Niedergang der römischen Welt* |
| ARTS | *Arts Religion and Theological Studies* |
| BAR | *Biblical Archaeology Review* |
| BibArch | *Biblical Archaeologist* |
| BibInterp | *Biblical Interpretation* |
| BR | *Bible Review* |
| CH | *Church History* |
| DACL | *Dictionnaire d'archéologie chrétienne et de liturgie* |
| DOP | *Dumbarton Oaks Papers* |
| EEC | *Encyclopedia of Early Christianity* |
| HistRel | *History of Religion* |
| HTR | *Harvard Theological Review* |
| JAC | *Jahrbuch für Antike und Christentum* |
| JBL | *Journal of Biblical Literature* |
| JECS | *Journal of Early Christian Studies* |
| JEH | *Journal of Ecclesiastical History* |
| JJA | *Journal of Jewish Art* |
| JRel | *Journal of Religion* |
| JThS | *Journal of Theological Studies* |
| LCI | *Lexikon der christlichen Ikonographie* |
| NPNF | *Nicene and Post Nicene Fathers* |
| NTS | *New Testament Studies* |
| PEQ | *Palestine Exploration Quarterly* |
| PG | *Patrologia Graeca* |
| PL | *Patrologia Latina* |
| PTR | *Princeton Theological Review* |
| RAC | *Revista di archeologia cristiana* |
| VChr | *Vigiliae Christianae* |
| ZNTW | *Zeitschrift für neutestamentliche Wissenschaft* |
| ZThK | *Zeitschrift für Theologie und Kirche* |

# INTRODUCTION

At the beginning of *Alice's Adventures in Wonderland*, Alice (who is bored by "sitting by her sister on the bank and of having nothing to do") takes a peek into her sister's book and exclaims: "what is the use of a book ... without pictures or conversations?"[1]

This study is written for readers who (like Alice) want pictures with their prose, and who suspect or believe that a study of ancient art objects or artifacts offer a different kind of engagement with the study of history than texts alone could provide. In fact, even more than merely adding pictures to traditional text-based history books, these persons might argue that nontextual evidence offers an equally valuable testimony to the character of religious or social life in the past, although it may not seem as accessible or apparently eloquent as available written records, especially to historians trained to consult ancient documents for their evidence. Those historians who wish not only to balance their texts with visual images but also to integrate the two will find that such integration offers new depth, or dimension, to their view of the past.

Although this might sound simple or even obvious, the distinct methods and objective goals of text historians and art historians have sometimes undermined efforts that are necessarily interdisciplinary. There are several reasons for this. First, the training of specialists and the practical need for professional focus have contributed to what is often an unfortunate but understandable estrangement between the two scholarly worlds. The data often have been divided between text and art historians, even though separate analyses of material objects and ancient texts miss crucial parallels and relationships between the two fields that would aid in the interpretation of both. This division is understandable, however, because scholars from one field rarely master the vocabulary, tools, or techniques of research belonging to the other, and so each is left to the experts for study and interpretation. Efforts to bring the two fields into dialogue are both time-consuming and also fraught with professional risk, requiring that individual scholars be willing to step over disciplinary lines and daringly enter another's field, often as kind of interested and eager, but hapless, amateurs.

1

Thus while many intellectual historians find visual art beautiful, interesting, and even provocative, they may be fearful of trying to interpret it or incorporate it into their own research. The highly specialized methods and scientific apparatus employed by art historians and archaeologists intimidates them. Alice-like, they might even prefer a book with pictures, but will safely limit their use of those images to mere illustration of the points made in the words on the page, thus unfortunately (and unwittingly) putting art works into a secondary position as service to their own prose.

Art historians, of course, have been trained to analyze material objects as essential and primary (never secondary) monuments of culture. However, because of the restrictions on their time or the emphases in their training, these scholars sometimes have a parallel gap in their understanding of the tools and techniques of text historians, or lack detailed knowledge of the essential documentary sources that might correspond in time and place with the art works they were studying. And even if that were not the case, merely keeping up with new scholarship in the field is nearly impossible.

Beyond the problems of time and training, however, is the slightly more vexing issue of inclination or interest. Scholars working in one field may overlook, or simply be uninterested in, questions that would occur to their colleagues in another discipline, and while preoccupied with their own questions may miss something that appears to be blatantly obvious, profoundly meaningful, or tantalizingly curious from the vantage point of those others.

Thus the need for interdisciplinary research and dialogue makes its case. Questions that arise in one field of study sometimes must be directed to another for consideration and analysis. This is particularly true for scholars engaged in the interpretation of art, in its meaning or significance for the social group or religious community – something broadly labeled the "study of iconography." Those scholars who fit into this category do, in fact, work in the intersection between text and art history and have carved out a distinct field, although in most cases they began with the mastery of a "home discipline" and acquired a broad working knowledge of another.[2] Such interdisciplinary adaptability is getting harder and harder to sustain, for all the reasons stated above. A more practical future model may be that of scholars from different disciplines working as teams, informing and critiquing one another.

But further complicating the matter is the subtle but definite disparagement of images by many of those who come at history through texts. This disparagement may have a philosophical or even theological basis, or it may be nearly unconscious. Church historians' efforts to understand or credit significance of visual art often parallel the famous response of Gregory the Great to the bishop Serenus, who reported a case of iconoclasm in Marseilles in the early seventh century. Gregory rebuked Serenus for destroying images of the saints by asserting that: "what writing presents to readers, a picture presents to the unlearned who view it, since in the image even the ignorant see what they ought to follow; in the picture the illiterate read."[3]

This statement may sum up one traditional Western perspective on religious art – that religious pictures are the "Bible of the Unlettered" – a good thing for those who have no better way to learn the stories of the faith. Although it sounds well-meaning, such a perspective actually views visual art as inferior or subservient to verbal expression and suggests that images are the "food" for childlike minds, whereas theological treatises, homilies, or verbal arguments contain the meat of adult intellectual formation. The function of art in religious contexts is thus seen as primarily didactic and as such dependent on and interpretive of what can be found in written form elsewhere. Not recognizing that visual art can be as deeply theological or intellectually sophisticated as literature consigns even the most refined examples of artistic production to the category of "popular culture" for a mass audience and erroneously opposes it to "higher" forms of theological discourse carried on from pulpits, lecterns, and in the bookstacks of libraries in churches, universities, and theological schools.

This study will provide evidence that visual art often serves as a highly sophisticated, literate, and even eloquent mode of theological expression. Viewers from the past or the present certainly cannot fully appreciate the subtlety of most of the surviving early Christian art objects without at least a basic familiarity with the biblical narratives, liturgical practices, and the common traditions of scriptural interpretation. But in addition, this study also demonstrates the mutual dependence of verbal and visual modes of religious expression. Visual images are neither necessarily distinct nor divergent from images found in written texts. Although the verbal and visual idioms are not equivalent in any sense, art presented as disconnected from literature or theological writing. In fact, early Christian visual metaphors usually have direct parallels in early Christian literature. Viewers, like readers, are allowed, even expected, to be familiar with the many layers of the faith tradition as passed down in different forms, whether homilies, liturgies, dogmatic writings, or pictures.

However, since little documented, theoretical reflection on the use of art exists from the early Christian period itself (unlike the later period encompassing the debate on icons), such a conclusion can only be reached by analogy and comparison. For instance, scholars have studied the theory of creation in the image of God as a basis for a Christian philosophical view of the image's participation in the archetype. Others have undertaken a careful analysis of the theories of vision in the early Church.[4] This study's goal may be somewhat simpler – to demonstrate the concrete points of similarity between verbal and visual reflection on the substance of the early Christian faith. By collecting and comparing the parallel metaphors and typologies, one could then go on to build a theory that would argue that visual and verbal theologies are equally valued and necessarily related to one another.

This work requires an interdisciplinary approach, using the methods of art historians in conjunction with the study of early Christian texts. A critical intersection between these two is in the ways both use metaphors, types, or allegories as ways of indirectly conveying meaning. As such, the function of symbols will be a primary focus of this work, especially when symbols in text and art overlap and reinforce one another. Whether a particular symbol as it appears in a text can be used to interpret a figure in art is a thesis worth testing. However, given the lack of absolutely congruent times and spaces, the work of comparison must be generalized to explore the ways certain symbols worked in texts or in art, not to demonstrate some kind of strict one-to-one relationship.

Each of these scholarly fields (art history and intellectual history) bears a certain degree of healthy skepticism about the other. Text historians may worry about the degree of subjectivity brought to the examination of the artistic evidence. Such work seems to move into "soft fields," which include analysis of symbols and signs as well as their effect on long-dead, relatively silent viewers. Although theological treatises themselves always require subjective analysis and interpretation, so long as words are involved, historians may think they can apply enough scientific analytical tools eventually to discern what the original author meant, or intended. Art, unfortunately, often comes without captions or attached written explanations and, as such, may seem frustratingly ambiguous or dauntingly mysterious.

For different reasons, art historians might worry about over-reliance by a trained text historian on the documentary evidence as a means to interpret something essentially non-textual or to overly apply familiar theological categories as labels on artistic images. These scholars are trained to begin with the images and avoid turning to texts as a primary source for their analysis or interpretation, valuing art objects for themselves, apart from the documents, for their essential beauty and independent significance. However, this often means art historians concentrate on comparative, formal analysis of art-historical materials and thus overlook questions of meaning, or of the relevance of the image to the faith arguably reflected and fostered in the art.

Finally, there are the ever-present problems of point of view (author vs. reader/artist vs. audience), transmission, and tradition – each of which undermines any firm pronouncements about how any extant text or art object might have been received by any particular person or group. Reconstructing the responses of readers or the significance of texts through tradition is a thorny matter and text historians may well wish to avoid the equally vexing problem of theorizing about the perspective of an ancient viewer, a perspective that may seem even more inaccessible than that of the ancient reader.

Looking at art has always been a process conditioned first by the particular situation and the character of the viewer, which is, of course, affected by the object in view. In other words, viewers interpret the art work for themselves, but the object has its own reality by virtue of being seen (over time) by different people with different reactions based on concrete experiences within particular communities. Thus the image can be said to have a presence and power that is both stable in itself and transformed by and through its audience. Both image and viewer are conditioned by their interaction, and may be each time a single viewer returns to the same object. Since multiple messages may be communicated by a single image to a single viewer in a single glance, one might wish to avoid considering what could happen in a room full of viewers, or over a span of generations. As with all history, nothing is ever objectively clear. All we have are slants, angles, and points of view that affect in variant ways the reality we experience.[5]

This is made harder for text historians, because few records exist that record specific responses to art by particular ancient Christian viewers. Neither do we have ancient reviewers offering their perspectives on whether an art object is beautiful or inspirational, or whether it fulfilled its function (as defined by the reviewer, patron, or artist). And although art critics existed in the pagan world, ancient Christian writers apparently made little attempt to interpret specific art works.[6]

Given this state of affairs we must rely on the resources available, and these include the writings that belong to the same *general* context as the images. Texts must be treated as sources of information to aid in interpretation. At the same time we also must consider certain characteristics of the objects themselves. These characteristics include the stylistic aspects of the images, whether the art is expressionistic or naturalistic, and whether of high or low quality. Another characteristic is the composition or content of the works. We might speak of their composition as abbreviated and simple or more detailed and complex. The frequency of a particular theme in an entire decorative program might also be significant, as well as the proximity of other motifs or themes. Once certain images appear together interpreters might begin to speculate about meaning as much as about patterns or motifs. The context of the art is also extremely important. Whether the work was created for a church wall or a tomb wall must have some influence on the choice of subject matter and give us some clues about the meaning of the whole compositions.

But more basic than trying to understand what individual art works meant in late antiquity is the question of how art itself functioned as both constructive and expressive factors in religious belief. We may discover that some images preceded texts and the texts then provided commentary on the visual symbols. However, at the very least visual imagery never merely retold or condensed a text into corresponding pictorial language, but rather made meaning in its own right – by using symbols and allegories already present in written expression (narratives, commentaries, etc.) in such a way as to become a communication mode in itself – one that paralleled, commented upon, and expanded the text, rather then simply amplifying or serving the text. Learning to "read" art works, therefore, means learning to read a visual language, to become familiar with an unfamiliar idiom. Nor is the visual idiom any less historical, contextually determined or theologically sophisticated than the verbal. Any such assumption returns us to the stereotype that art is for the unlearned, while texts are for the elite or belong specifically to the "high culture." Similarly we will need to dismiss the characterization of art as inherently part of "popular" or "unofficial" religion while written documents tend to reflect the "official" statements of the religious authorities. Images and words together constitute sacred symbols, and neither has inherent primacy over the other. Understanding this might require that we transcend modern culture's tendency to disengage symbols and words, and to value words as better or clearer communicative devices.

So how do we begin? By taking into consideration what we can – looking simultaneously at these two modes of communication of meaning, texts and images. We cannot presume that these are inevitably or even often in conflict, and we cannot privilege either word or picture as being prior or more authentic. As I have already said, assuming that the image merely serves the word underestimates the importance of art as a powerful and basic element of communication. But to assume that the word is one or more steps distant from visual expression is to cut off a valuable resource for interpretation. Both word and image must be viewed as evidence of meaning-making either in a culture or in a religious faith, and must be seen as partners in the process.

Visual art has many different functions in the expression and development of the religious tradition. Among these are the decorative, illustrative, and didactic uses of art, but added to these are functions that might be characterized as exegetical, symbolic, liturgical, and iconic. The former are not to be denigrated. Beauty offers glory, and education brings illumination. However, the latter four functions assume that visual art is capable of mediating or even manifesting more complex theological ideas – including the incarnation and the presence of the divine in creation without necessarily being straight-jacketed by the prevailing (authorized) dogma or catechesis. These functions are more subjective or complex in a way that direct discourse might not be. As exegesis, art interprets scriptures on many different levels, from the literal to the allegorical. As symbol, art acts as a bridge between a familiar reality and one that transcends ordinary expression. As liturgy, art may have a performative function and belongs to particular space, time, and ritual actions. Finally as icon, art brings the viewer into direct contact with the holy, providing the mechanism for epiphany.

Another distinction exists between the content of religious images. Although we may make too false a distinction between narrative and iconic expression, these two distinct forms clearly must have divergent purposes. The former may be more directly dependent on memory and familiarity with the tradition (and story) while the latter may be shaped by quite different cultural factors. But the eye and mind must be trained to read certain motifs and this will always be culturally determined, a particular viewpoint we may not be able to recreate across time and space. Although what we see today was, at one time, as familiar to ancient viewers as the most conventional signs or symbols are to us. Narrative images depend particularly on memory and use a kind of sign language to remind us of what we already know. They are not meant to be taken literally, but rather only serve as openings to a far more complex set of layered meaning and significations.

Iconic images are not so related to memory or to textual referents. The icon functions as a kind of stepping-stone or mediator between the invisible realm of the divine and the more direct world of the senses. In a sense the image both presents and protects the divine, in the same way that apophatic theology does. Icons proclaim that the divine cannot be known in its essence, but only in its effect – the way we know without being told. Direct engagement with the divine is difficult to withstand. The icon therefore both reveals and protects both the viewer and the holy mystery.

The following chapters return to these questions and examine them in far more depth. The first chapter raises core questions about the history of scholarship. Chapters 2 through 6 are organized around selected basic motifs characterizing early Christian art. Chapter 2 considers symbols which are not drawn directly from biblical narratives (philosopher, praying figure, etc.); Chapter 3 examines the ways in which biblical narratives are interpreted in both text and image; Chapter 4 considers the development and significance of portraits of Christ and the saints; while Chapters 5 and 6 examine theological or dogmatic aspects of art, especially as the art interprets the crucifixion of Christ or presents a belief in the resurrection of the dead. Each of the motifs discussed is juxtaposed with selected textual or liturgical parallels in an effort to show the relationship or even mutual dependence of picture and word in the construction of sacred symbols.

Thus every chapter of this book in some way attempts to integrate particular textual and visual modes of expression into a coherent discourse. As such, this project is meant to be a demonstration of how this might be done with a number of case studies. The goal of the project is to introduce scholars or students whose view of the past is often mediated primarily through written documents to the power, subtlety, and beauty of sacred images, as well as to counter any belief that art is a substitute "text" for the uneducated or primarily representative of those whose theology remains at the level of "popular religion." By considering texts together with visual images, art historians may discover certain documents or theological treatises that illuminate their understanding of and deepen their appreciation for the monuments they study.

# 1

# THE CHARACTER OF EARLY CHRISTIAN ICONOGRAPHY

## Issues and problems of interpretation

### Introduction

The problem with pictures is that they almost never send just one single, ·
clear message. They take the proverbial thousand words to explain. Perhaps
a skeptic would respond that with printed words on a page, one knows
where one stands – or at least thinks so. But unless pictures come with
printed captions or detailed explanations, their meanings are open-ended
(they are even if there *is* an explanation), and their significance depends on
the viewer's degree of appreciation. The question: "What do you see there?"
can have an infinite number of plausible answers.

To be fair, texts are rarely as clear as they may seem on a superficial level.
The history of interpretation and modern literary criticism (in particular the
practitioners of deconstruction) have taught us that texts also "mean" on
many different levels. The social and historical context of the writing itself,
different visionary slants of writer and reader, the medium-like role of editor
or translator, the relationships among the words themselves, and above all
the competing time and culture-bounded frameworks of original author and
individual interpreter all weigh in to the problem of finding meanings. Like
the great food chain, ideas have already passed through many different
digestive systems before their meaning arrives as nourishment for any particular reader and even then each new reading is both unique and mediated.

So with images. A myriad of considerations and caveats must be laid out
before a single interpreter dare say anything with confidence about meaning.
Each viewer sees an object afresh, but also through the lens of a mediated
tradition, memory, and the culture in which they stand. In the end, all interpreters reveal probably as much about themselves, their values or cultural
formation, as they offer some objective statement about the meaning of a
single image. But that also is the truth of the matter. No one explanation
exists for any image, and the best a self-conscious historian can do is try to
map out the territory, noting the major arteries and bridges, recognizing
that there are different routes to the same destination, and expecting that

other people might find some more scenic or others more direct. Detours are instructive, since they reveal new interpretive possibilities.

So this project begins by laying out some of the main points, with the expectation that others will fill in more details and continue the process of interpretation, often along distinct lines or from entirely different perspectives. These next pages sketch out a few general ways of describing and sorting the data, as well as some of the issues that emerge from such evaluation. Such is a provisional framework to be sure, but one that may provide a useful basis for beginning.

## Preliminary overview of the data

Early Christian art may be characterized in many different ways, according to its formal elements, its functions, its style, or its chronological developments. Broadly reviewing these various aspects of the data, one first notices four ways that the body of Christian art is particularly limited. The first of these is chronological. Christian art as such cannot be dated any earlier than the end of the second or beginning of the third century. Before that date, material evidence of Christianity is scarce, and although not entirely non-existent, often hard to distinguish from objects that belonged to the wider cultural context. Thus it was only in the late second century that carved or painted expressions of distinctly Christian religious beliefs began to appear and to provide later generations with material and artistic testimony of the first believers – visual data that both amplifies and balances the otherwise text-weighted evidence from the first centuries.[1] This limiting factor, of course, applies primarily only to the *terminus a quo*. Once the Christian communities generally accepted the production and use of art (with well-known exceptions during particular periods of iconoclasm), its development and spread was assured and historians can generally divide its development into two main chronological periods: first the late Roman or pre-Constantinian era which includes the third and early fourth centuries; and – second – the early Byzantine period from the mid-fourth century to the early sixth.

One of the questions this relatively late beginning date raises is whether first- and second-century Christians were more faithful to the biblical injunctions against idolatry or, because they believed in a transcendent and invisible deity who commanded abstinence from most earthly luxuries, were more generally resistant to the temptations of a material culture and thus more "spiritual." Constructing the problem in this way raises the vexing problem of the conflict between the image and the word, which is sometimes presented as a battle between popular religion and official theology – conflicts that have a long and complex history in the church.

The second limiting factor of early Christian art is iconographical. Each chronological period has its distinctive themes or motifs, and each is

9

somewhat circumscribed, but perhaps none so much as the early phase. Generally, the subjects of Christian art fall into four distinct groupings: (1) borrowings from the pagan religious world that were adapted to serve Christian teachings; (2) religiously neutral images based on traditional decorative motifs, but which may have been given particular Christian symbolic significance; (3) narrative-based images drawn from favorite biblical stories; and (4) portraits of Christ and the saints. The art of the second and third centuries draws primarily from the first three groupings and shows particular motifs with great regularity, and usually with a fairly consistent composition, among them the extremely common figures of the Good Shepherd and Jonah (Figures 1 and 2) as well as Abraham and Isaac, Noah,

*Figure 1* The Good Shepherd, Catacomb of Callistus.
© The International Catacomb Society. Photo: Estelle Brettman.

*Figure 2* Jonah thrown into the water, Catacomb of Sts Peter and Marcellinus.
© The International Catacomb Society. Photo: Estelle Brettman.

Daniel, and the baptism of Jesus. Compared to later Christian art, the catalog of different motifs or themes is quite small.

This limited field of iconographic types raises the question of why certain images were especially popular and what that reveals about the original community and its beliefs. Similarly, the borrowing of particular pagan themes raises issues of selection and adaptation. In general, however, a limited catalog of motifs requires the images themselves to be both somewhat ambiguous and more expressive than highly specific images existing within a large artistic vocabulary. Their messages are far more complex than their simple identifications, and their language is symbolic rather than precise or specific. Thus, theorizing about what images mean is more analogous to translating than to decoding. The one requires that we look more widely at the culture or context of the message, while the other requires merely that we apply a set of rules – an exercise that might produce a facsimile, but rarely a meaningful equivalent.

The third and fourth characteristic limitations of early Christian art are both the geographical provenance and the specific context of the extant evidence. Most of the artistic remains from the early phase (or pre-Constantinian) derive primarily from the environs of Rome and from funerary settings (catacombs and sarcophagi). Significant exceptions to both of these limitations include the sculptures from Asia Minor or relief carving from Gaul, or the famous fresco-decorated baptistery in the house church at Dura Europos (located in modern-day Syria). Nevertheless, the two most important bodies of pre-Constantinian and Christian art-historical data are the wall paintings found in the Roman catacombs and the relief carvings on sarcophagi, the largest group of which were produced – or at least finished – in Roman workshops. Whether these limitations, of geography and context, arise from the accidents of preservation, or reveal certain key aspects of early Christianity in general – its regional distinctions or theological attitudes toward the visual arts and their appropriate function – is difficult to say. Prominent exceptions neither prove nor contradict any theories, since they bear both clear similarities to and striking differences from the Roman, funerary monuments.

A fifth distinguishing characteristic of early Christian art is not so much a limitation as an observation about technique or style. Most of the earliest examples of Christian art are simple, almost humble, in their manner of presentation or choice of subjects. Extant wall paintings in particular are mostly sketchy and simply rendered, without a great deal of detail or decorative elaboration. And while carved reliefs on late third-century sarcophagi may reveal a high degree of craft and were obviously expensive to commission, their subjects, like those found on the wall paintings, were either simple biblical characters or images drawn from the popular pastoral, bucolic, or maritime images favored by their traditional Roman neighbors. Fish, anchors, and birds appear along with shepherds milking or cherubs harvesting. Praying figures with veiled heads and hands outstretched, or seated readers poring over scrolls are also prominent. These images give the overall impression that the community emphasized traditional Roman – now Christian – virtues of charity, piety, wisdom, and love of nature.

Although each of these points comes up again in the discussion below, they initially demonstrate that Christian art must be studied according to both its forms and its functions. "Forms" are those distinctive iconographical themes or motifs that become the subject of the art itself and are the most overt carriers of its message. The way in which those motifs are presented (their "style") is a second important part of this first consideration. "Functions" are those uses the art served, generally revealed by the contexts and chronological periods in which the monuments have been found (and not found), and which to a large degree shape the kind of message sent. Obviously we must never view form and function as separate or unrelated issues. Style or motif change along with and in relation to time, circumstances, context, or geographical provenance. Determining which is the governing factor in the shaping of the image is often very difficult.

Finally, perhaps the most important influence on the essential design, quality, or character of early Christian art was its audience. This study presumes that the Christian community was both patron and audience – source of vision as well as viewer. Understanding early Christian art requires knowledge of the larger, complex life of the people who were its source. This community may be called the church – broadly defined and not necessarily confined to what some historians might define as a specifically sanctioned institution or organization. More than merely its broader social context, the Christian community was the basis for the existence of Christian art, and the art itself had to have had significant resonance with the teachings, practices, and values of the group it served.

## Aniconism and the conflict between image and word

The theoretical *terminus a quo* (starting point) for Christian art – the beginning of the third century – is now generally accepted by scholars, although earlier art historians tended to date the inception of Christian art as early as the end of the first or beginning of the second century.[2] Modern scholarship's later dating has raised the question of whether Christians created or owned art in the first two centuries, and if they did, what sort of art works they were. Prominent historians of Christianity have often held either that for nearly two hundred years Christians repudiated visual imagery on religious grounds (i.e. obedience to the second commandment against idolatry), or that Christians resisted a practice they associated with the decadent pagan culture, or both, since the attitudes are not mutually exclusive.[3]

To those who espouse this proposition, the emergence of Christian images around the year 200 is the conservative, essentially literate establishment's response to the demands and needs of the practitioners of popular religion. By contrast, those who were "users" of art were the unreformed, former pagans who could not leave their idolatrous past entirely behind them or who misunderstood the anti-material dimensions of their new faith and the invisibility and transcendence of their new God. Scholars have sometimes characterized these producers and/or consumers of art as the illiterate of the society, including the women and the underclasses – groups who were moved or captivated by visual images and symbols more than by the words of the preachers or theologians who represented the authorized "establishment."

However, by the early fourth century a revolution transformed this "establishment" – a revolution that began with the Edict of Milan in 313, and by mid-century the hierarchy included the emperor and his family, who followed the traditional practice of deploying religious symbols as part of their political propaganda. Many scholars have perceived the transformation of Christian iconography during this century as the result of the church's accommodation of imperial, secular culture and its simultaneous adaptation of the symbols and trappings of that powerful force, even supporting certain political aims of the emperor rather than devotional, theological, or evangelical interests.[4] The misguided continuance of pagan practice in the earlier period had come home to roost. Spirituality had become thoroughly tainted by popular culture and pagan idolatry.

13

The first of these widely held characterizations of early Christian art – that it existed in ignorant opposition to a more spiritual form of the faith – presumes that art itself essentially challenges "normative" Christian teachings or tradition. In this case, artistic creation *per se* becomes an almost idolatrous concession to stubborn pagan sensibilities or popular religion by a compromising clergy. The second characterization – that art (as well as religion) became, in the fourth century, a tool to advance secular political interests – presumes that art is a medium easily manipulated as propaganda and thus to be evaluated with a certain suspicion. Both representations also tend to present the message of Christian visual art as distinct from or in conflict with the messages transmitted by literary documents. Or, more simply, sacred image as in conflict with sacred text.

This picture of an essentially aniconic early Christianity, strongly advanced by such eminent art historians as Theodore Klauser in the 1950s and 1960s, came to be widely accepted.[5] Klauser and others portrayed the earliest Christians as proto-Protestants – puritanical, anti-worldly, and opposed to visual art, particularly in worship settings, and cited the writings of the early Christian theologians who were critical of Roman idol worship as evidence of this 'original iconophobia.[6] Many historians of Christianity accepted this explanation rather uncritically, and readily incorporated it into their studies of early Christianity and Roman society. Such a position accords well with a view that Christianity became increasingly decadent or Hellenized in the third and fourth centuries as the church became assimilated to culture.[7] This view, however, relies on far too literalistic a reading of the ancient literature, rather than presenting a picture of early Christianity that accords with the actual archaeological or textual evidence.[8]

Another explanation of the relative lateness of an art that was distinctively Christian suggests that Christians as a group simply lacked the financial resources to patronize artists' workshops, an argument that presumes that most first- and second-century Christians belonged to the lower social classes. A parallel hypothesis proposes that Christians simply comprised too small a portion of the populace to command much purchasing power or make them a viable market for artists' workshops. Such Christians may have purchased art for devotional purposes, but because that art was indistinguishable in style and content from that of their pagan neighbors, it disappeared from historical scrutiny.[9]

The appearance of "Christian" art at the end of the second century may well be the natural result of changing social, economic, or demographic circumstances, rather than the radical abandonment of a fundamental theological principle. Christians always have lived in and engaged with their culture, whether they conformed to or transformed society, or both. The late arrival of distinctive "Christian" art forms certainly is a curious development, given that Christian literature of all genres existed (apology, exhortation, poetry, romance), and that Christian forms of worship were

14

quite well established by the mid-second century. For this literature and these liturgies, Christians did not invent a new language, but rather adopted the literary and regional vernacular. In the same way, Christians adapted the iconographic language around them. Creative ventures with that artistic language emerged only when the converts had achieved significant communities and a certain amount of social status, even a kind of settled respectability. Perhaps the nascent or experimental stages of this creative work have been lost, but clearly the time had arrived in the early third century for the establishment of a material culture and the permanency such a culture implied.

Even though scholars have set aside many of the earlier assumptions about the reasons for the lateness of early Christian art, their re-examination of the matter has reopened the question of the relationship between text and image. In this study we will see that the emergence and development of Christian art in the third century actually parallels certain developments in Christian theology, as revealed in literary texts. Both art and theology do, after all, emerge from the same general culture, and apparently claim to belong to the same religious group. Moreover, the sources themselves reveal no incontrovertible evidence of a direct conflict between image and text (scriptural exegeses, doctrine treatises, liturgies, and recorded homilies). We can no more equate the art of the church with its "official" theology than we can consistently find theology and art in opposition with one another.

Presuming more compatibility between the meaning of visual images and the messages encoded in written texts than previous theorists have allowed, permits us to re-examine the visual evidence for possible interpretative clues suggested in certain contemporary writings. Such an approach assumes the organic emergence of Christian art in a complex but receptive community of believers who saw art as a legitimate expression of religious faith – one not out of step with the teachings or practices of either departed founders or contemporary authorities. Although Christian believers were never an entirely unified community – they had their share of conflicts, factions, and cultural differences – the essence of their differences cannot be based on whether they were essentially visually or textually oriented. We will discover that most Christians used some combination of both expressive modes, and that these modes were compatible.

## The content and categories of Christian art

"Christian art" as a recognizable sub-category of late Roman western art is primarily an iconographic distinction as opposed to an identity based on its context or function. As we have said, the first evidence of a distinctly "Christian" visual or artistic language used to communicate aspects of the faith emerged around the year 200 and is recognized as such by its content or subject matter. The style, technique, and materials that were applied to

Christian art were not essentially different from those used in other art works of that time and region, nor were such works created only to embellish distinctly Christian spaces or objects. Thus their Christian "identity" derives almost exclusively from their themes. The available evidence suggests that before that time, whatever art works Christians created or owned were indistinguishable from those created or owned by their Roman or Jewish neighbors.

The advent of Christian art is set in the time of the Severan emperors, and its first phase generally coincides with the last century of pagan rule, up to the elevation and conversion of the Emperor Constantine. As stated above, that few clearly recognizable examples of Christian art pre-date this period probably ensues from the evidence itself, rather than results from the vagaries of historical preservation. In other words, the art works were not lost or destroyed, they simply have not been recognized as specifically Christian. The fact that little or no evidence of recognizable or distinct Christian material culture of any kind can be dated to the first two centuries CE suggests that Christians either had selectively adapted the symbols of their pagan neighbors or had acquired very little in the way of distinctive material possessions or art works.[10] A late second-century art work classified as belonging to the pagan or secular realm could have been made or used by perfectly devout Christians, but since it has no obvious Christian features (e.g. recognizable biblical characters, style, or provenance), it cannot properly be called "Christian" art. Moreover, no useful information about Christian artists or patrons exists to assist in identification. Two hundred years later, however, if an art object with similarly ambiguous content appeared as part of the decoration of church building or on a liturgical implement, its placement alone could identify it as "Christian."

Christian art first appears during the time when Christianity was vulnerable to persecution, and it was well-established by the time the church was granted tolerance and, soon thereafter, patronage by secular authorities. The distinct shift in Christianity's status in the fourth century, moreover, accounts for the standard periodization, setting the second phase of early Christian art to the years 325–525 CE, beginning with the so-called "peace of the church" and ending with the reign of Justinian. These two eras are often spoken of simply as pre- and post-Constantinian, since Constantine's conversion to Christianity and his promulgation (with his co-emperor Licinius) of the Edict of Milan, both in 313 CE, ended official Roman persecution of Christians. This was a watershed moment for the church and, by extension, for Christian art. In a single stroke the church gained its first imperial patron, and Constantine, in turn, financed the building and artistic embellishment of the first great public Christian buildings.

Thus while the definitive characteristic of "Christian" art in the earlier period is its iconography (i.e. subject matter and themes), the criteria expanded to include context and function during the Constantinian era, when the material, economic, and social situation of Christianity changed so radically. In the third century distinguishable Christian and pagan art works are only just beginning to emerge, identifiable by their "content." However, by the first decades of the fifth century, the culture was so permeated by Christian interests that the categories "secular" and "sacred" were less sharply defined, and the appellation "Christian art" came to be as much defined by setting, function, or patron as by content.

Those Christian subjects that characterized Christian art in the earlier (pre-Constantinian) period were actually fairly limited, and generally can be separated into three broad categories: first, those derived from classical, pagan prototypes that had been adapted to express aspects of the Christian faith; second, religiously "neutral" images of essentially decorative quality, but that were probably understood to carry particular Christian symbolic significance; and third, narrative-based themes or cycles that were drawn from favorite biblical stories. Portraits of Christ and the saints are rare in the pre-Constantinian period.[11] Clearly, these are subject categories, based upon content rather than function or context. Generally sarcophagus reliefs and catacomb paintings reproduced the same catalogue of figures or themes, although certain images appeared earlier or more frequently on one than on the other.

The first category encompasses a series that are related to scriptural themes, or in some other way symbolically and recognizably Christian, but are not exclusively derived from particular biblical narratives. In general these figures also tend to be among the earliest appearing images in Christian art and include the Good Shepherd, a fisherman of men, the philosopher, the person praying (orant), meal scenes, and scenes of harvesting – either grapes or wheat. Most of these motifs, more than the biblical subjects in the first category, have direct Greco-Roman artistic parallels, or even prototypes, so that classifying them as Christian is sometimes problematic and even controversial. Such categorization often depends on the subjects' proximity to or juxtaposition with other figures found in the more clearly Christian category of biblical themes. Also included in this category are certain more overtly "pagan" borrowings such as the representation of Christ in the guise of Orpheus or Apollo/Helios. The more "generic" praying figure, as well as a type commonly identified as a seated philosopher, are religiously neutral images that may have been intended to serve as portraits of or references to the deceased.

The second category is less figurative and more decorative, sometimes even more symbolic, although its contents may be recognizably Christian, especially when found in compositional proximity to biblical subjects. Even so, their pagan roots or parallels are undeniable, and their decorative aspects suggest caution against over-interpretation. One person's meaningful symbol may be another's lovely decoration, and nothing more than that. Doves, peacocks, twining vines and grapes, fish and other sea creatures, boats, lambs, and olive or palm trees may symbolize the resurrection, refer to the sacraments, or amount to cryptic references to the cross. Depending on context, however, these same images may also have little to do directly with the faith of the deceased beyond suggesting the beauties awaiting in paradise. Christians clearly used or adapted themes familiar to them, with no qualms about the propriety of figures so well known in the social world around them. Alternatively, certain symbols seem specifically adapted for Christian purposes, such as a dove with an olive branch in its beak, a chalice with fish or loaves, or an anchor flanked by two fish (Figure 3).

A related group of images also belongs to this category, since it contains elements that are purely decorative and have no specific Christian (or pagan) significance, although some of these motifs have parallels in the second category described above. These decorative items, including flowers or fruit in urns, garlands, birds and little cherubs (*putti* or *genii*) picking flowers or

*Figure 3* Anchor and fish from a titulus in the Catacomb of Priscilla.
Photo: Graydon Snyder.

carrying garlands, look just like those in contemporary pagan tombs. The fact that these subjects are also common in domestic decor suggests that they may be religiously neutral, having no other purpose than to beautify the space.[12]

In fact, at first glance, most catacomb paintings and sarcophagus reliefs are intrinsically decorative, and in this respect they are like their pagan counterparts. Both Christian and pagan tomb decoration might include geometric designs, masks, grapevines, urns, floral garlands, birds, and images of a shepherd with one or two of his flock. Some entire compositions are neither clearly pagan nor wholly Christian. Two third-century sarcophagi in the Vatican Museum are cases in point. One exceptionally well-carved monument known as the Via Salaria sarcophagus has two immense rams' heads at either end and a centrally placed figure of a shepherd carrying a ram over his shoulders (see Figure 6). The other figures, including a male reader and a praying female (*orant*), provide no definite Christian associations despite the presence of the shepherd. The second Vatican Museum sarcophagus shows three shepherds standing on pedestals ornamented with Bacchic masks. The shepherds are surrounded by a decorative scene of small cherubs harvesting grapes and milking ewes (see Figure 16). Such imagery might have eucharistic associations, or as in the case of other similar examples, it might simply be traditional Roman funerary decoration employing lovely bucolic and garden motifs with similar vintaging cherubs.

The third category of subjects, the most clearly "Christian," contains biblical subjects or personalities and includes images from both Old and New Testament and Apocryphal narratives. Included in this category are portrayals of Jonah, Abraham offering Isaac, Noah in the ark, Moses striking the rock, Daniel with the lions, Jesus' baptism, Jesus healing the paralytic, and the multiplication of the loaves. These subjects may have more or less distant Greco-Roman artistic parallels, but their specific compositions are unique and their narrative source – the scriptures of the early church – is clearly recognizable.

Although these images clearly are tied to textual sources, they should not be understood as mere illustrations or picture bibles for the unlettered. Certain themes were vastly more popular than others and often present an abridged style that suggests that they functioned more as composite symbols than as narrative illustrations. Many of the most popular motifs disappeared altogether or were subsequently replaced by others. Particular figures often were grouped together as if they made a new or particular statement in relation to one another.[13] Each of these aspects of composition – selection of individual elements, position within the larger whole, and the general context of the monument itself – contribute to the meaning conveyed to the viewer and to the success or failure of such visual communication.

After the time of Constantine, the range of Christian subjects increases in all three categories, but perhaps most dramatically in the third category, with the appearance of many new scriptural themes and especially with the inclusion of episodes from the story of Christ's nativity and passion as well as the representation of Jesus as law-giver, teacher, and enthroned king of heaven.[14] Other popular figures gradually disappeared from the iconographic programs, among them representations of the Good Shepherd, the *orant* (praying figure), and Noah and Jonah. In the meantime saints, martyrs, and apostles began to figure more prominently in post-Constantinian art, especially Peter and Paul. Other popular subjects included martyrs processing with their crowns of martyrdom, and an empty cross surmounted by a wreath of victory.

## The context or setting of early Christian art

As stated earlier, with some significant exceptions, early Christian art in the pre-Constantinian period comes predominantly from the Italian peninsula, especially the environs of Rome. Furthermore, the particular context for this art was funereal. In fact, the first significant examples of Christian image-making, the very basis for setting the beginning date, are frescoes on the walls of the Christian catacombs along the Via Appia Antica in Rome itself. The oldest of these tunnel-like burial grounds, the Catacomb of Callistus, was named for an early bishop of Rome (*c.*217–22) who, while still a deacon of the church, was put in charge of this first subterranean Christian cemetery.[15]

Of these two contextual limitations (geography and setting), neither is absolute. Exceptions to the Roman-Italian dominance of extant pre-Constantinian Christian art include the Cleveland marble sculptures, generally dated to the third century, and assumed to have come from a Christian family tomb in Asia Minor. Possible third-century frescoes have been found in catacombs in North Africa and Thessalonica. Most significant, perhaps, are the frescoes from the house-church baptistery in Dura Europos. Additionally, many surviving examples of early Christian relief sculpture on sarcophagi may have been produced by ateliers in Gaul, although the influence of Roman workshops is apparent in their technique and style.[16]

To a great degree, the limited geographical provenance of early Christian art is an accident of history and, unlike the lack of pre-third-century data, not a characteristic inherent in the evidence. Moreover, the fact that existing artistic data derive from Rome is not positive proof of Roman superiority in the crafts or dominion within the church at this early date. Although Rome was the political center of the empire, it would not be accurate to presume that all data from outside Rome were little more than local adaptations of Roman models. Evidence of early Christian artistic activity in other parts of the Roman empire, from Spain to Syria and the Tigris-Euphrates region, and from the British Isles to North Africa, refutes such assumptions. Much of the other non-Roman material, which must have existed, has been lost, presumably to wars, outbreaks of iconoclasm, or the continuous urban renewal of cities and towns. However, given the concentration of extant evidence in Rome, some historians have speculated that all early Christian art derived from, or was influenced by, that city's workshops and its particular styles, tastes, and catalogue of subjects.[17]

The funereal context of surviving early Christian art monuments also may be due to an accident of history. Almost all existing pre-mid-fourth-century art work was specifically created to decorate tombs or coffins. In fact, only two basic types of artistic evidence exist before the fourth century: catacomb frescoes and the relief sculpture on sarcophagi. Documentary sources, however, reveal that third-century Christians built or converted buildings or parts of buildings for their assemblies, and that they owned liturgical implements as well as scripture books. These buildings or objects were probably decorated, but like data from areas beyond the Italian peninsula, these examples of material culture have been lost or destroyed over the centuries, perhaps even during the persecutions of the third and early fourth centuries. With certain notable exceptions – such as wall paintings in the mid-third-century baptistery in Syrian Dura Europos, pavement mosaics in the Christian basilica in Aquileia, and (perhaps) the marble Jonah statuettes now in the Cleveland museum – almost no examples of non-sepulchral religious imagery remain from the early period.[18]

Whether these non-funeral examples were, in fact, exceptions to the rule or remnants of a large, but lost, repertoire will stay an unsolved problem unless archaeologists make a phenomenal discovery. For instance, we have no way of knowing whether at Dura Europos the walls of the assembly hall were decorated like those of the baptistery, or left plain. Until some new evidence emerges, no good way to compare artistic content from one context to another is available. Historians cannot say, for instance, whether or not the subject matter of paintings on the walls of the catacombs paralleled the subjects that decorated early Christian worship spaces. Such comparisons would either support or refute theories that iconographic programs in funerary contexts specifically referred to aspects of Christian belief about death and afterlife, and were not simply generic selections from a widely popular corpus of images.

## Private and popular vs. public and official

The sepulchral provenance of early Christian art often has caused art historians to classify it as essentially "private" or "unofficial" rather than "public" or "monumental." These terms suggest that individual patrons selected the decor for these tombs with little oversight or control by church officials. While the wall paintings certainly were created for specific persons or families (and may have been privately financed and personalized to a large degree), the establishment of a Christian iconographic language should not be seen as the work of individuals, but rather as a part of the gradually emerging public "face" of a religion that was developing its identity – and making it visible. There may be some differences between the funding and oversight of catacomb frescoes and the more costly carving of marble sarcophagi, which would have been limited to wealthy patrons; nevertheless, neither artists nor patrons were solely responsible for the images that characterize third-century Christian art. On the one hand, Christians relied on the standard repertoires of the (mostly pagan) artisans and workshops that executed the work. On the other, the art's content reflected the faith and values of the whole Christian community.[19]

Nor can the inclusion of certain carved or painted symbols on underground tomb chambers be explained as an effort to disguise or hide their Christian identity from Roman officials. Although the third-century emergence of Christian art coincided first with sporadic and later with imperially sanctioned persecution of Christians, the logistics of excavating and decorating these catacombs must have made their construction a fairly public activity, undertaken with the full knowledge of the secular authorities. Moreover, their existence signaled that the local Christian community had achieved both the capital and the right to own property and to bury their co-religionists in a space purchased specifically for them. Despite the often-applied term "crypto-Christian" to such supposedly disguised symbols as the fish-*Ichthys* or the cross-anchor, no evidence suggests that these symbols functioned any differently from the way they do today – as shorthand references to certain aspects of the Christian faith, widely understood but not particularly esoteric or deliberately clandestine identification marks of secret worship spaces.[20]

Scholars who attempt to distinguish "popular" or "private" art versus "official" and "public" art do so for sometimes opposite purposes. Theodore Klauser's portrayal of first- and second-century Christians as purist and aniconic (see above discussion) presumes that when Christian art finally appeared, it was pioneered by the theologically backward or Hellenized rank-and-file who were among those converted to the new faith around the beginning of the third and fourth centuries. According to this view this group had difficulty giving up its pagan habits and needed a kind of devotional crutch or "illiterates' Bible," while the more spiritually adept or theologically sophisticated either continued to resist the temptation to syncretism or "visualization" or, out of pastoral concern, indulged their weaker sisters and brothers. J. D. Breckenridge expresses the Klauser thesis succinctly:

> What we would suggest, then, is that the expansion of Christian art in the later third century was not the result of a change in the attitude of the Church toward religious images, but of the

enfeeblement of its ability to enforce its rules ... an unchanged official position which ... was in reality impossible to maintain in the
face of popular interest in the portrayal of the objects in their
worship – an interest all the stronger in view of the mountainous
wave of new converts from idolatrous paganism following the Edict
of Toleration.[21]

However, other scholars who argue that Christian art belongs to "popular"
religion in contrast to official or "high" forms, present the anti-image eccle-
siastics as elitist, authoritarian, theologically adept, and anti-material.
Ordinary, simple Christian folk, women especially, are thus seen as recipients
of official censorship by a repressive hierarchy that refused to value their
delight in images or understand the need for visual articulation of religious
beliefs, personal piety, and life experiences. Close study of Christian art is
proposed as a way for historians to "hear" from this silenced group.[22]

Both perspectives presume that art was the medium of the common folk,
created against the will and teaching of church authorities who were icono-
phobic well into the fourth century. However, such arguments rely on a
literal reading of certain early church documents that appear hostile to art,
and on contrasting textual evidence (the ideal or theoretical) with material
evidence (the real or practiced). But the relevant texts were written with
purposes quite different from the condemnation of figurative art *per se* and
find no widespread literary tradition of Christian iconoclasm. Christian art
from the beginning must have required both community and clerical
approval.[23] The cemetery of the deacon (and soon-to-be-bishop) Callistus, a
primary source of examples of early Christian art, is an example of official
ecclesiastical sponsorship. Given the general consistency of the images in
this catacomb, as well as the duration of its use, we must assume that church
authorities at least tolerated if not approved both the decoration and the
content of the iconography on its own property over a fairly long period of
time. Moreover, as the study will make plain, Christian iconography neither
provided idols for worship, nor represented the divine essence. In these
respects visual art responded to the concerns of theologians or apologists
who worried about possible idolatry or blasphemy.

In sum, Christian art of the third and early fourth centuries primarily is
distinguished as "Christian" by its themes or subjects, and secondarily
demonstrates its limited geographical and contextual scope; these characteristics set it apart from what follows in the era after the "peace of the church."
Although it seems not to have emerged before the third century, it cannot be
understood as aberrant, essentially private, or cryptic in any general sense.
Nor is it particularly "from below" (i.e. the product of the laity in opposition to the convictions of clergy or theologians). In the second era of early
Christian art, from the Constantinian era to the early Byzantine, most of the
art is unquestionably official and made for the public realm – whether

church architecture or liturgical objects. Funereal settings cease to be significant sources of Christian art by the fifth century and both wall frescoes and sarcophagus relief carvings give way to mosaics, manuscript illuminations, and ivory and metal work as the primary media. Despite the change of settings, however, certain themes are carried over into this "official art." Such transferability may be evidence of the conservative nature of iconography, but it also must keep us from being too categorical in our distinctions between "public" and "private" art works.[24]

## Style and quality

While most of the few examples of pre-Constantianian Christian sarcophagus carving are of fairly high quality, Christian catacomb paintings seem to reflect a lower standard of workmanship. Although similar to the interiors of some Roman houses of the same era, they appear hastily or even carelessly painted when compared with the better examples of Campanian fresco painting. Walls were divided into pictorial compartments by frames of decorative lines of red or green, mostly filled with small figures from one of the three or four categories mentioned above. Most likely because of the sepulchral context, or possibly because most early Christians had limited financial resources, the oldest images are neither stylistically sophisticated nor even well-painted. Details are two-dimensional, often rendered awkwardly, without extraneous details, paying little attention to setting or landscape. Occasionally paintings of much higher quality appear on the catacomb walls, but more often they are poorly done and crammed together in a small area, with little obvious relationship to one another.

However, this apparently careless execution, haphazard composition, and lack of detail in the paintings actually lends an expressive quality that challenges any conclusion that this imagery was primarily decorative. In character with other Roman paintings in an "impressionistic" style, attention is drawn to the message rather than to the esthetic qualities of the artwork. Because of their terse lack of detail, the compositions are abstract and referential rather than illustrative. These expressive figures function better symbolically than decoratively. Those who commissioned these works must have intended this symbolism. Rather than being straightforward evidence that most Christians were of modest social status and unable to afford better, this kind of sketchy composition suggests that communication was valued above artistic quality or refinement and that the emphasis was on the meaning behind the images more than on their presentation.

Sarcophagus reliefs tended to be of a different quality of craftsmanship. Normally carved on only the three exposed sides of both lid and base, the front of the coffin was the center of the focus, while the lid and two ends were sometimes given more cursory treatment. Since this form of burial was extremely expensive, we can assume that only the most wealthy Christians afforded such work and could employ highly skilled artisans capable of fine carving and finishing work, and that most of the commissions were to some degree personalized or individually designed rather than selected "off the shelf."

Sarcophagi were carved with drills and chisels in white marble, but occasionally also in limestone. They were sometimes painted lightly to make them polychrome but the use of color was normally restrained. In the earlier era, most sarcophagus figures were portrayed on the same level or register, and by the end of the third century designs began to become more detailed, even crowded with smaller figures and multiple scenes. In the early fourth century, double-registered sarcophagi gave more structure or order to the multiple images. The quality ranges from high relief with beautifully polished details to flatter and less finely carved work, often in a lower grade of marble or softer limestone.

Extant Christian sarcophagi, sarcophagus fragments, and less expensive grave-slabs that predate the time of Constantine are consistent with the frescoes in sharing imagery with the pagan world. Many of the scenes on these sarcophagi are standard for funeral art, including grape-harvesting cherubs, the seated philosopher, a shepherd bearing a ram or sheep over his shoulders, and praying figures (hands outstretched). Decorative elements are taken from the then-universal catalog of maritime and bucolic themes which were also perfectly appropriate for Roman domestic decor. Biblical themes also appear on these sarcophagi, however, helping us to identify them as Christian. The most popular were scenes from the story of Jonah, followed in frequency by Noah, Adam and Eve, Daniel, the offering of Isaac, and the raising of Lazarus. These biblical scenes were presented in shorthand, or abbreviated fashion, much like the catacomb frescoes, and may have been drawn from the same prototypes. Thus, like the catacomb frescoes, the sarcophagus carvings combined familiar and new images. For the artisans who were commissioned to carve the marble coffins, these presented both well-practiced and challenging assignments.

After 325 CE, the quality of work, the variety of contexts, and the compositions themselves were improved or expanded. The decoration of churches and baptisteries, gospel books, and liturgical objects was fueled initially by the patronage and donations of the Emperor Constantine and sustained by the changing social, economic, and political status of the Christians themselves. Wealthy Christians were not only motivated but also positively encouraged to add their patronage to that of the Emperor, decorating the walls and floors of local churches with beautiful mosaics, and purchasing objects of ivory, precious gems, gold, silver, and glass adorned with Christian iconography that reflected the wealth and values of the new Christian upper classes. Meanwhile, throughout the fourth century and until the early fifth, Christians continued to decorate their coffins and the walls of their underground tombs, yet gradually even these art works evolved to more detailed and elegant forms. An evolution of style and taste was under way.

## Iconography and historical context

As noted above, the art of the third and fourth centuries both reflects and parallels the change of fortunes both of Christians and of the institutional church over time. The Christian religion, although certainly focused on divine laws, transcendent issues, and other-worldly expectations, was lived out amidst and in reaction to political and cultural circumstances. To a large degree, even transcendently theological debates about the nature of God had this-worldly stimuli and ramifications. Similarly Christian art developed in and responded to particular social shifts and historical events. And even while it must bear evidence to its circumstances, as a product of a living religious community, visual art was also affected and shaped by contemporary theological debates, methods of scripture interpretation, and liturgical practices. In other words, Christian art evolved in an integrated environment and evolved in relation to external historical pressures as well as internal theological developments.

The end of the second and beginning of the third centuries was the age of Clement of Alexandria, Hippolytus of Rome, Irenaeus of Lyons, and Tertullian of Carthage. Origen was probably born in the year 185. In the last quarter of the second century, sporadic outbreaks of locally instigated pogroms had martyred Christians in Lyons, Carthage, and eventually Alexandria. The refutation of gnosticism, Montanism, and monarchianism was a main goal of theological writing. External persecution by secular authorities and internal repression of non-conformists were not the church's only problems, however. Power struggles divided the church in Rome between the adherents of Hippolytus and Callistus. Schism and strife returned in the mid-third century following the Decian persecutions, as well as the problems of disciplining apostates, defining the authority of confessors, and the evaluating of the sanctity of sacraments administered by bishops who had lapsed.

The Roman empire itself was extremely unstable during the era between the Severan dynasty and the ascent of Diocletian with his establishment of the tetrarchy. Invasions of Persians and Goths threatened the security of the empire's borders and emperors came and went at an alarming pace. In the fifty years between 235 and 285 CE, twelve different men ascended to the purple, frequently raised up by the armies they commanded in some outlying region. The economy spun out of control and the currency was devalued and debased. Inflation ran rampant. Plagues destroyed whole villages, and natural disasters wiped out crops. The secular state was near collapse.

All these events are the unseen background of early Christian art. We

26

cannot know just how much they influenced the selection of themes and the composition of images, but we cannot discount their influence entirely. As noted above, the change in political, economic, and social context of Christians following the conversion of the emperor Constantine was radical, and scholars have argued that these events transformed the art produced by and for the Christians of that era. The preceding century's events were arguably no less influential on the content as well as context of Christian iconography in the earlier age.

Some historians have identified the persecutions of Christians during the third century as a formative influence on the content of the catacomb iconography in particular. Analysis of the imagery turns up what appears to be an emphasis on safety, security, or deliverance from immediate danger, particularly danger perpetrated by the secular authorities. For example, scholars have interpreted figures of Daniel and the three youths in the fiery furnace as early Christian references to the plight of the martyrs and the wicked persecution of the godless government. Susannah represents anyone falsely accused and condemned to death. Isaac and Noah are characters "at risk" who are delivered from danger.[25] Sometimes, however, an "historical" explanation is contrasted, unnecessarily, with a theological one. Thus, for instance, some scholars have disallowed any Christological significance of the scene of Abraham offering Isaac in the pre-Constantinian era because they understand the "deliverance" and "sacrificial" motifs to be mutually exclusive.[26]

Certain motifs appear with great regularity and predictability, suggesting that they were deliberately selected and popularly reinforced. Viewers therefore logically conclude that the earliest known Christian images were not accidentally chosen or pulled out of some artist's grab-bag. An extended study of this art leads the student to expect certain standard types and to be surprised by innovations or inventions. The very clear message seems to be that certain subjects were appropriate for specific contexts, and that the suitability of these subjects was well understood by the community. The consistency of the iconographic programs from tomb to tomb indicates that individual taste or personal whim played little role in the decoration of these places. The historian's challenge is to discern what that community, as a whole, understood by those images.

## History of interpretation

The great scholars of Christian art and archaeology in the nineteenth and early twentieth centuries, including those associated with the "Roman school," tended to interpret early Christian iconography in terms of literary sources from the patristic era.[27] These scholars often dated artifacts too early and inappropriately harmonized the material evidence with later theological and liturgical developments. Meanwhile, text historians often viewed evidence of Christian art as merely illustrative of written sources and not as an independently constructed data field that might provide a wealth of information apart from literature. Thus, art-historical materials were deemed to be supplementary and supportive, rather than autonomous and sometimes divergent sources of data regarding the faith and practices of early Christians. It was as if art contained a canon of static symbols that was a relatively simple tool for expressing basic theological truths as contained in catechism or creed.[28]

This style of interpretation had obvious problems, including the assumption that Christian material or physical remains should corroborate the history as presented in documents, and that what would emerge was a fairly unified or "catholic" form of Christianity that could be viewed as mainstream or normative in some sense. Thus both text historians and art historians presented material and literary remains as being more or less in agreement with one another. Where these two kinds of evidence contrasted or diverged (or the historians simply did not like what they found), written documents were usually presumed to be more accurate historical data than art-historical evidence, and the latter was often explained away as unrepresentative, unreliable, or unofficial ("popular" or "heretical"). When interpreters therefore deemed dogmatic issues to be overriding and respectable art subservient to the writings of theologians and promulgations of church councils, different images or symbols were interpreted accordingly. In addition to making assumptions regarding aspects of early Christian tradition that would make it harmonize with later teachings (e.g. the centrality of the Virgin Mary in the work of salvation, or the particular blame given to Adam and Eve for the fallen human state), these interpreters also saw Christian art as a distinct departure from contemporary pagan iconography.[29]

Scholars writing in the latter part of the twentieth century have tended to be very critical of this approach, partly in an effort to make the field of early Christian art and archaeology more objective and less confessional in its approach. In the 1930s Paul Styger argued for a scientific dating of the catacombs and was one of the first to reject the early, pre-third-century dating of the frescoes. Erich Dinkler was extremely critical of the habit of attributing later theological developments to earlier periods, and the over-interpretation of certain images, particularly the cross symbols found on inscriptions in the Roman catacombs.[30] Echoing earlier writers like Ludwig von Sybel, and unfettered by a need to create a Christian apologetic, such scholars as Theodore Klauser and Ernst Kitzinger reemphasized the continuity and parallels between pagan and Christian iconography.[31]

Correcting what they saw as an often abusive manipulation of evidence, the innovative approach of Klauser and Kitzinger pushed the separation or distinction of written sources from archaeological ones. This distinction was perceived as more scientific and respectful of the non-literary evidence, since it was purer in some respects, and less likely to be corrupted by the biases inherent in the documents, especially with regard to theological polemics and ecclesial politics. On the negative side, the fact that the art was produced for a community of Christian believers began to be lost in an effort to remain objectively detached from the religious context of the evidence.

More recently, certain scholars have suggested that the material evidence is more reflective of the faith of the common folk than literature, which is perceived as being primarily representative of the aristocratic and educated male clergy. Moreover, the tendency has been to stress the derivative nature of Christian art, emphasizing its pagan or even its Jewish prototypes. Art, it is sometimes suggested, is a window into popular religion, or the beliefs of the forgotten or lost folk, including those individuals who may have been out of step with the orthodox faith as presented in the surviving written sources. Recovery of the material evidence is thus seen as a means of getting a more balanced view of the history of Christianity, a more direct or representative body of data.[32]

So while the earlier style of interpretation presupposed that the archaeological data required coordination with the written sources, the later group argued for an almost radical disjunction of the two. At least this approach called for a much more critical approach that treated texts with skepticism and, in some cases, even suspicion, wanting to reject their "elitist" presentation of the faith. This disjunction, it might be argued, mirrors the division in the social world between the upper and lower classes, or between clergy and laity, orthodox and heretic. The difficulty with such a presentation is that one of the dimensions of historical perspective was lost along with a key tool for interpretation – the literature of the community.

A third and related movement is characterized by the works of Franz Dölger and Erwin Goodenough, who analyzed Christian imagery with the methods of the history of religions school and emphasized the continuity of Hellenistic and Christian iconographic themes.[33] Dölger particularly emphasized the funerary context of early Christian art in his analyses, as well as the place of pagan and other religious imagery in the development of Christian iconography. Goodenough, well known for his work on Jewish symbols, differs from Dölger in his more generous interpretation of the symbols themselves, seeing in them perhaps more than Dölger would have permitted.

Without doubt these more recent scholarly trajectories have served as important correctives to an earlier method of "reading in" the texts to the artworks, or asking the art to serve as mere illustration of the continuity and truth of tradition. Yet, the time has surely arrived for a further reconsideration of the relationship between sacred image and sacred writing. Christian art was not created in a vacuum, having no reference to pressing theological, doctrinal, or liturgical issues within the community – the same issues discussed in the literature. Since works of art were costly, they were unlikely to represent the faith or values of lower classes or common folk in a way that texts do not. Moreover, without some recourse to written documents, much of the imagery is at least ambiguous, and at worst indecipherable.

## Conclusion

Taking all these issues into consideration, the proposition that the interpretation of early Christian art works may be advanced by considering contemporary written documents and visual art synoptically seems only common sense. Moreover, students who undertake such synoptic consideration also should do so without presumption that one body of evidence is the more accurate or reflects one or another group within society. By synthesizing texts and images from comparable geographic and chronological contexts, trained text historians may achieve more than superficial harmonization of symbols with certain doctrines or pictures with particular text narratives while art historians may recognize the high degree of resonance between Christian literature and visual art and appreciate how a broad familiarity with the documents may contribute to an understanding of the visual evidence. In addition to casting more light on the historical and theological situation of the early church, this dialogical process also may reveal the kind of relationship that exists between theological treatises and sacred image — two modes of communication or speculation about the nature of divine and human existence. Rather than beginning with the presumption that visual art and literary texts represent divergent belief systems, theological sophistication, or the varying taste of different social groups, this study proceeds from the proposition that written documents and art objects emerge from the same or similar communities, and have common purposes or outlooks. This proposition does not mean that images and texts will always be in complete accord, or that they will present aspects of religious faith in parallel form, but rather that one mode of discourse may help to elucidate another and give historians a better understanding of ancient symbol systems.[34]

Those writers who expounded their understanding of the Christian faith in words frequently illustrated their prose with metaphors, and scriptural illustrations whose parallels appear in visual form in the paintings, mosaics, sculpture, and other crafts of the early church. Many of these metaphors remain constant through centuries and have their parallels in the writings of theologians living in other parts of the Roman world. Such durability of imagery, as well as their variety of presentation (both literary and visual) suggests the existence of a certain common tradition, in spite of acknowledged chronological evolution and regional specificity. Moreover, this common tradition probably cut across social class and gender distinctions. After all, the liturgy, the homilies, and the images expressed therein were more or less available to everyone — rich and poor, male and female, literate or not. The only limits on appreciation seem to have been in the imagination of the reader, hearer, or viewer.

As the following chapters will demonstrate, central religious images, both visual and literary, balance and reinforce each other, as well as sensitively responding to the changes in the social or religious environment. Historians cannot give pride of place to texts, assuming they speak more clearly or accurately for a particular community than do material objects. In isolation, textual data only give a partial view of things. No matter how frustratingly enigmatic they may seem to those primarily trained in interpretation of words, visual images provide an extraordinary testimony to aspects of the hopes, values, and deeply held convictions of the early Christian community. Art is neither simply illustration of texts, nor is it necessarily challenging to them. Images are articulate and complex modes of expression that make no sense in isolation and have no meaning apart from ideas that emerge in a local community and engage that community's values. The historian's task is not unlike the artists – to make those ideas three-dimensional, having both surface and depth.

# 2

# NON-NARRATIVE IMAGES

## Christian use of classical symbols and popular motifs

### Introduction

Some common iconographic themes from Christian art of the pre-Constantinian era lack a clear connection with any specific biblical narrative. This absence of narrative reference indicates that these images are more generally symbolic and arguably less illustrative than others that portray an episode from scripture. Their symbolic import is of long standing, since many such figures were common in non-Christian or pagan contexts, although often known by other names or changed in certain ways as they moved into Christian settings. Since they are not exclusively Christian, both their signification and their meaning depend on their juxtaposition with other clearly Christian figures.[1]

Because they lack direct textual references, these simple, usually single images seem less complex but are in many ways more difficult to interpret. They invite viewers to apply their own meanings and values, making precise interpretation impossible. Two of these, the shepherd and the praying figure (orant), were extremely popular and appear in early Christian art more frequently than any biblical subject, including the extremely common image of Jonah. Like Jonah, however, these two figures peaked in popularity in the third and early fourth centuries, and had lost their dominant place in Christian art by the beginning of the fifth.

Despite the lack of direct narrative textual reference, most of these images have thematic counterparts or parallels in theological or exegetical writings of the early church. Asserting that such figures are the exact visual representations of literary metaphors would go too far, but in many cases the relationship between idea and image is a close one and examination of the parallels suggests that a broad symbolic system existed that had its expression in a variety of forms, both visual and verbal. In fact, the relevant writings often seem to provide the missing link between pagan and Christian significance for these characters.

*Figure 4* Adam and Eve, peacock, and orant, Via Latina Catacomb.
© The International Catacomb Society. Photo: Estelle Brettman.

The first of the two frequently appearing images is the somewhat enigmatic praying figure (orant) – a standing female with head veiled and hands
up or outstretched in prayer (Figure 4). The second is the representation of
the shepherd – a male carrying a sheep or ram over his shoulders, usually
with sheep or rams at his feet (Figure 1). This symbolic figure also has
metaphorical parallels in biblical texts. Another common type, often seen
with the praying figure and the shepherd is the seated philosopher or teacher
(Figures 5 and 6). The fish and fisher (Figures 13b and 13c), may be
grouped together, although the fisher, like the shepherd, has biblical parallels. Yet another very frequent subject, the banquet scene (Figure 14), is
included in this category, although it too might seem out of place, since it is
sometimes identified with a specific biblical narrative (the feeding miracles,
or the Last Supper) or as an illustration of an actual Christian eucharist. This
particular scene also has more than one figure and a number of props.
However, the meal scene's pagan parallels are well attested and its identification will be reconsidered in the discussion below. Finally we include images
of the grape and wheat harvest in this category (cf. Figure 15). These
symbols may be associated with scriptural metaphors, but they also carry a
weight of symbolism beyond any particular text. And, like the others, they
have significant parallels in contemporary Greco-Roman art.

*Figure 5* Jesus teaching, late fourth-century sarcophagus now in the Musée de l'Arles Antique (Arles).

Photo: Author.

*Figure 6* Rams' head sarcophagus from the Via Salaria now in the Vatican Museo Pio Cristiano, *c.*250–75.

Photo: Author.

## The orant

The term "orant" was adapted by art historians from the Latin word *orans*, meaning a praying person. The orant is a universal and popular figure of late antique art, almost always shown as a veiled woman, standing, facing front, gazing heavenward, with her hands outstretched and slightly lifted (*expansis manibus*). Both her posture and appearance are characteristic of classic prayer images (cf. 1 Timothy 2:8) and are not specifically Christian. Best known from funerary art, the orant also occurs as one of the many personified virtues among the reverse types on Roman coinage throughout the second and third centuries. The praying figure shown on these coins often appears with a flaming altar, and sometimes a small stork, symbol of familial piety. These coins appear with such accompanying legends as *pietas aug* or *pietas publica* and probably referred to the piety of the emperor toward his deceased parent or predecessor, or the extension of this filial value to the entire Roman state.[2]

The term also referred to the honor and obedience given by the ruler and/or people to the gods. Descriptions of characters like Aeneas as "pious" connote a dutiful individual, devoted to family and nation. Justin Martyr used the term "pious" to refer to religious activity or worship, whether Christian, Jewish, or pagan. Other Christian writers, however, applied the word to correct or orthodox faith or behavior, in opposition to heretical beliefs or immoral acts.[3]

However, figures of *pietas* on coin reverses, or the uses of the term "pious" in literature may bear no direct relation to the meaning of orant images in funerary contexts, whether the deceased was pagan or Christian.[4] Various controversial interpretations have been offered. Given the funerary context of most of the orant images, some interpreters have proposed that they represented the deceased's soul in paradise. Other scholars, citing the secular meanings of the image and its rare appearances in non-sepulchral settings, have argued that it simply refers to filial devotion, and in the case of Christians, their devotion to their new family – the church. When these figures are found in non-Christian contexts, they might serve as quasi-portraits, referring to the deceased person's pious behavior in life – his or her honor to the gods, whether state or domestic.[5]

Interpreting the orant figure as representing the soul of the deceased is supported by the fact that the soul was traditionally spoken of as feminine, thus accounting for the figure's feminine attributes. However, since Christians similarly spoke of the church, or *ecclesia*, in feminine terms (as bride), perhaps adapted from Jewish metaphorical language for Israel, this image has also been interpreted as a symbol of the church.[6] Occasionally the orant figure is so specifically portrayed as to indicate that it is a portrait and not simply a generic allusion to piety, the soul, or the church itself. Possible examples of such use are the image in the catacomb of Priscilla known as *donna velata*, and the orant with doves on the Roman sarcophagus called *della Lungara*. Art historians have identifed a few sarcophagi with the faces of these images left blank, as if prepared to receive a portrait likeness.[7]

Many orant figures appear in paradisical or bucolic settings, near representations of the Good Shepherd, suggesting to some interpreters that the orant is being represented as having arrived in heaven. Considering the presence of the shepherd, the iconography, taken together programmatically, thus represents human salvation and its two principal actors – the savior and the one saved. The orant image is then asserted to be a portrait of the already-saved deceased whose prayer is one of thanks (*eucharistia*), rather than a petition for a yet hoped-for deliverance.[8]

In addition to possible portraits of the deceased, several central biblical characters also appear as orants, including the sailors with Jonah, Daniel, the three youths in the furnace, Susannah, Noah, and in one rare instance, Abraham and Isaac. In a few of these images male characters are shown wearing the dalmatic robe of the female orant. These figures might be seen to be praying for (or giving thanks after) divine deliverance from threatening circumstances.

Although the possibility that the orant's posture subtly suggests the sign of the cross seems far-fetched, it is supported by textual evidence. This nearly universal praying posture of late antiquity (today ordinarily reserved for clergy celebrating the eucharist or proclaiming a benediction), was described by Tertullian as having the appearance of Christ on the cross: "We, however, not only raise our hands, but even expand them; and, taking our model from the Lord's passion, even in prayer we confess to Christ."[9] Minucius Felix, writing in the late second or early third century, also compares the image of a person praying with outstretched hands to the cross-shape, a motif nearly ubiquitous in the world (e.g. the mast of a ship or the shape of a plow).[10] Thus, an iconographic figure well known to Christians and non-Christians alike might have been adapted to a Christian context with little or no change in appearance apart from occasional prop changes (scripture rolls exchanged for the pagan altar, or doves for stork), and given a specific Christian meaning.

By the mid-fourth century, the stance and gesture of the orant figure was employed in a host of full-length portrait representations including Mary, the saints, bishops, and martyrs. Thus the image successively progressed from the realm of the purely symbolic personification of a virtue, to the portrait of a specific but ordinary individual, and finally to the conventional type of the Virgin or a saint in intercessory prayer. To some degree, with this development the symbolism of the image returned. For instance, in later Byzantine art, when the Virgin assumes this posture, she often also encloses the Christ Child in a mandorla on her breast. This familiar icon, sometimes named "The Sign," represents the dogma of the Incarnation, or in the words of Vladimir Lossky, "an iconographic revealing of the Church personified by the Mother of God, Who had confined within Herself the unconfinable God."[11]

## The Good Shepherd

The shepherd carrying a sheep or ram was another popular figure in Greco-Roman art. He is usually youthful and beardless and wears a short belted tunic and boots. Sometimes he carries a shepherd's purse, a set of pipes, or a bucket of milk, but nearly always has an animal of the sheep family (usually a ram) over his shoulders (Figures 1 and 6). Related images show the shepherd with his flock or milking a ewe (Figure 7). The sheep-carrying figure had an antecedent in Hermes the guide to the underworld (*psychopomp*), a character associated with hopes for a blessed afterlife and particularly appropriate in a funereal environment. However, in late antiquity, the image of the shepherd could have developed a more generic meaning of philanthropy, or humanitarian care. In any case it is not always possible to identify a single image of the shepherd definitely as Christian or pagan, since both communities valued charity and were concerned about the afterlife.[12]

*Figure 7* Shepherd milking (lower center, below the portrait medallion), with Moses striking the rock (left) and Jesus raising Lazarus (right) on a fourth-century sarcophagus now in the Vatican Museo Pio Cristiano.

Photo: Author.

Because of the ubiquity of shepherd imagery in both Old and New Testaments (cf. Ezekiel 34 or John 10), the shepherd was a symbol Christians could easily incorporate and endow with specifically Christian meanings. Such a figure appeared more than 120 times in extant Roman catacomb frescoes alone.[13] In addition to frescoes and sarcophagus reliefs the shepherd also appears as small statuettes, on innumerable lamps. However, whether the shepherd was an early metaphor for or a representation of Jesus is debatable.

Some scholars take the identification of Jesus and shepherd for granted, seeing the parallel as so obvious that it hardly needs challenging.[14] Other historians, however, refuse to allow this possibility before the Constantinian period, citing the image's widespread use in Roman society as evidence that the Christian significance of the figure must be more general and compatible with a broader cultural symbolism. Some interpreters have argued that the shepherd represented the safety or caring of a Christian community in the midst of a time of persecution and danger, and that the shepherd was a personification of *philanthropia* rather than a symbolic representation of Jesus.[15] Aside from the fact that personifications of the virtues are ordinarily accompanied by identifying captions and normally portrayed as female, such an argument begs the question of how limited an abstract metaphor must be, and why the shepherd figure could not represent both Christ's most characteristic virtue and (thus) him as well.

Support for this solution comes from parallels in the literary evidence. Obviously the biblical texts, including John 10:1–19 in which Jesus calls himself the Good Shepherd who lays down his life for the sheep (v. 11); and Luke 15:3–7 (with its parallel in Matthew 18:12–13, the parable of the lost sheep), are starting points. However, the biblical citations do not prove that early Christians would have necessarily associated the image of a young man carrying a full-grown ram over his shoulders as a type of Jesus. Evidence of this association, however, can be found in the writings of early Christians, including Hermas, one of the apostolic fathers, who described his vision of a man "of glorious aspect, dressed like a shepherd, with a white goat's skin, a wallet on his shoulders, and a rod in his hand," a description that corresponds to the artistic images.[16] Later, at the end of the second century, Tertullian reports that Christians depicted Jesus as the Good Shepherd on cups, to show forth the figurative meaning that the "flock is the people of the Church, and the Good Shepherd is Christ."[17] Similarly in the "Hymn to Christ the Savior," attributed to Clement of Alexandria and found at the end of Clement's treatise on Christian instruction, Jesus is three times addressed as a shepherd.[18]

The autobiographical epitaph of a late second-century Christian bishop from Hieropolis, Abercius, now in the Vatican Museum, describes its author as a "disciple of the pure shepherd who feeds his flock on hills and plains, with large eyes that look into everything," while the editor of the "Passion" of the North-African martyr Perpetua recounted one of her visions in which paradise appeared as a beautiful garden, tended by a tall white-haired man who was dressed as a shepherd and milking sheep and who offered her sweet milk (or cheese) to eat.[19]

The milk in Perpetua's vision echoes certain lines in Clement's hymn where Jesus is addressed as a shepherd, but also as "heavenly milk, pressed from the sweet breasts of the bride." Clement's next lines speak of "small children sucking at the nipple of the logos."[20] The milk of wisdom (*sophia* – which may refer to either the divine Son or the Holy Spirit) is a well-known theme in early Christian literature, and finds a liturgical parallel in the milk and honey offered to neophyte Christians immediately after baptism (cf. 1 Corinthians 3:1–2; Hebrews 5–12; and 1 Peter 2:2).[21] These textual and liturgical symbols may have visual counterparts, or at least parallels, in late second-century artistic representations of the shepherd carrying a bucket of milk, or a shepherd milking a ewe (Figure 7).

In addition to the catacombs and sarcophagi, however, the image of the Good Shepherd appears above the baptismal font in Dura Europos (Figure 28), and in the later, early fifth-century baptistery of S. Giovanni in Fonte, Naples. The shepherd's particular aptness for a baptismal context may parallel its function in the funerary setting. J. Quasten's extensive discussion of this context notes the connection of the twenty-third Psalm with the baptismal liturgy in Naples and concludes that the suitability of the pastoral theme has something to do with the fact that shepherds branded their sheep, just as the neophytes are given a sign (*sphragis*) in baptism.[22]

Quasten's argument, however, fails to take account of the fullness of the twenty-third psalm's associations with aspects of the baptismal rite. The font represented the still waters, and the table and the cup figurations of the eucharistic meal. The shadow of death was part of the rite itself. The candidates, then, were the lambs, and the flock the church, all being led to salvation by the shepherd. The psalm may have been sung as part of the baptismal liturgy in many places besides Naples, possibly as the neophytes processed from the baptistery into the nave of the church after the rite was complete.[23]

The orant's frequent juxtaposition with the Good Shepherd justifies explaining the pairing as a convention of early Christian funerary imagery. The two figures balanced each other. Perhaps one represented the deceased's prayers for salvation and the other the one who could fulfill those prayers. This suggestion raises a possible parallel between Hermes the guardian of souls and guide to the underworld, and the Good Shepherd (Jesus) as the Christian *psychopomp*.[24] If the composition represented the soul in paradise, the shepherd could signify the bucolic bliss and pastoral care of the next world (guaranteed in baptism). That the two simply represent the universal and multi-faith virtues of piety and humanitarianism is also possible, but pushes aside the textual evidence to the contrary.

The Good Shepherd begins to disappear from the catalog of Christian types during the post-Constantinian era and is almost completely gone by the beginning of the fifth century, a particularly surprising development given the near ubiquity of the shepherd in the earlier era. Apart from a few exceptions, the figure did not reappear in Christian art before the late Middle Ages. The possible reasons for this disappearance might include a shift in emphasis away from more symbolic imagery and toward more representational, dogmatically oriented, and majestic portrayals of Jesus as enthroned Lord and (eventually) crucified and resurrected savior.[25] These new artistic emphases on specific manifestations of Jesus' divinity might have been difficult to integrate with indirect or symbolic visual references to Jesus' general qualities. The shepherd image had little relevance to a church struggling to affirm the full divinity of its savior. While an image of a loving shepherd reminded viewers of the protection of God the Son, along with his compassion and mercy, these aspects of his nature were no longer in the center of theological debate and formation of doctrine.

Boniface Ramsey considered the fifth-century mosaic of the Good Shepherd in the Mausoleum of Galla Placidia to be a kind of transitional Christological composition as it shows the shepherd with a golden cross, gold tunic and purple mantle rather than shepherd's crook and rustic garb.[26] According to Ramsey, by the fifth century, a visual reference to God's safe deliverance of his "flock" from danger would have been essentially anachronistic in an age when Christians had arrived on or near the seats of secular power. Ramsey interprets the Good Shepherd as a fairly general symbol of humanitarian protection, gentle guidance, and loving kindness; and although he cites the shepherd's signification in Christian baptism and expectations for life after death, he argues that this role was displaced in the fourth and fifth centuries because it lacked "sufficient dogmatic content."[27]

A fourth, and last, consideration regarding the disappearance of the Good Shepherd is the treatment of the image in the literature from the late fourth to the sixth centuries. Despite the diminution of artistic portrayals the patristic writers continue to comment on the parallels between Jesus and the shepherd, and even go on to incorporate the parallels into their Christological speculation, distinguishing between titles that represent Christ's nature from those which refer to his works.[28] The shepherd as a tender and loving figure was more appropriate for describing Jesus' works and accorded less well with some with some emerging presentations of Jesus as pre-existent Son of God, triumphant and enthroned Lord. Yet, these later writers also make much of the fact that the shepherd also lays down his life for his sheep – a characteristic that leads into discussions of the passion and is associated with images of Christ as the Lamb of God.[29] Augustine makes this point quite clearly:

> The sheep, of course, is under the shepherd; yet he is both shepherd
> and sheep. Where is he a shepherd? Look you have it here. Read the

Gospel: 'I am the good shepherd,' Where is he a sheep? Ask the prophet: 'As a sheep he was led to the slaughter.' Ask the friend of the bridegroom: 'Behold! The Lamb of God. Behold! He who takes away the sin of the world.'[30]

## Christ as Orpheus or Helios

The figure of Orpheus may parallel the Good Shepherd, since Orpheus (as a Christ metaphor) is shown as a shepherd, surrounded by both wild beasts and a flock of sheep. Images of Orpheus playing his lyre have been found on a number of third-century Christian sarcophagi, third- and fourth-century catacomb paintings (Figure 8), and in ivory on at least one fifth-century pyxis. In most of these compositions the central figure is shown frontally and playing his lyre, wearing a long or short tunic, and sporting his distinctive Phrygian cap. One or more sheep gaze calmly at the musician. Thus the shepherd figure is transported into a mythological setting, arguably in order to emphasize Jesus' ability to tame the wild or evil hearts of humanity and to bring them to himself. This Christ–Orpheus parallel was used by early Christian writers in both apologetic and exhortatory literature. For instance, Clement of Alexandria contrasts Orpheus and Jesus, "my minstrel ... the only one who ever tamed the most intractable of all wild beasts – man."[31] Here Clement speaks in particular of the ability of the baptismal water to transform "wild animals" into faithful Christians.[32]

*Figure 8* Orpheus, Catacomb of Domitilla.

© The International Catacomb Society. Photo: Estelle Brettman.

The existence of a comparable Jewish figure of David (identified by his label) playing a lyre, discovered on a fifth-century pavement in a Gaza synagogue, opens the possibility of a parallel Jewish David/Orpheus association, although certain reliable scholars have questioned whether an identification was intended, or whether the Orpheus prototype merely provided a handy iconographic model for an ancient musician-figure.[33] Archaeologists found a similar Orpheus figure in a church at Huraté in Syria, but identified as Adam, it offers another intriguing parallel.[34] An entirely different image, found on a cylinder-shaped amulet or seal, shows a crucified man with the legend "Orpheus Baccichos." Recent scholarship has dated this inscribed gem to the fourth century and shown that it may have pagan or gnostic origins. In this case, Orpheus (or Bacchus) is presented as Christ, not Christ as Orpheus.[35]

Unlike Hermes *criophorus* imagery, which developed as the Christian Good Shepherd in large part because of direct support from symbolic metaphors in scriptural texts, the Orpheus image was transferred to the new religion almost purely by virtue of its signification in Greco-Roman tradition. A similar process of adaptation, without direct scriptural parallel, also explains the rare third-century mosaic usually described as "Jesus-Helios" discovered in the Vatican necropolis, mausoleum of the Julii (Figure 9).[36] Such a representation is not evidence of Christian syncretism but rather of symbol conversion or appropriation. In these cases, the suitability of a composition had more to do with its symbolic functionality than with its original source. Portraying Jesus as the Sun God may have directly challenged the cult of Sol Invictus by appropriating its iconography and transferring it to Sol's replacement in the new Christian cult, or such iconographic transference simply may have been a way of communicating attributes or virtues of the deity in the visual language of the surrounding culture.[37]

As with the shepherd and Orpheus, such a possibility is supported by textual and liturgical evidence that metaphorically links Christ with the rising sun, the Lord's day with the day of the Sun, and Easter itself with the rebirth of the Sun.[38] Scriptural references to Christ as the "light of the world" (Matthew 4:16, a citation of Isaiah 9:2; and John 1:4–5, 9; Ephesians 5:14 based on Isaiah 60:1–3) as well as "sun of Justice" (Matthew 5:45, following Malachi 4:2) may be important scriptural sources for such images. Pliny the Younger's correspondence with Trajan referred to Christians gathering at dawn to sing hymns to Christ.[39] Tertullian felt he needed to defend the Christians against charges that they worshipped the sun because they prayed toward the east and made Sunday their feast day.[40]

Clement of Alexandria described Christ as the "Sun of the Resurrection" (*helios tas anastasis*), the "one begotten before the morning star, who gives life with his own rays," a description that could have served as a caption for the Vatican mosaic, apart from the irony of the fact that a good portion of the treatise is directed against the work of artists.[41] In another section of his treatise, Clement describes Christ as a charioteer ascending into heaven and

*Figure 9* Christ as Helios, Mausoleum M (of the Julii) beneath St Peter's Basilica, Rome.

©The International Catacomb Society. Photo: Estelle Brettman.

bringing dawn and eternal life with him: "Hail, oh light ... for he who rides over all creation is the 'Sun of Righteousness' who ... has changed sunset into sunrise, and crucified death into life."[42] The endurance of the parallels between Christ and the Sun god is demonstrated by an ancient prayer taken from an Armenian liturgy for the Feast of Epiphany; it reads:

> Come and see how the radiant Helios
> Is baptized in the waters of a wretched river.
> A mighty Cross appeared over the baptismal font.
> The servants of sin descend,
> And the children of immortality rise up.
> Come then and receive the light![43]

As this prayer attests, from early days Christian baptism was commonly spoken of as "illumination," and many aspects of the baptismal rite and setting were symbolic of dawning light.[44] Baptisteries constructed in the fourth to sixth centuries were often eight-sided to symbolize the "eighth day" which is the Day of the Sun, and sometimes oriented so that candidates would enter the building and/or font from the west, and emerge towards the east. In some early baptismal rites, upon arrival at the baptistery, candidates were instructed to turn toward the west to renounce Satan and toward the rising sun to proclaim their faith.[45]

In summary, these adaptations of Roman iconographic models serve less as clear evidence of religious syncretism, than of the continuity of symbols in the culture. They may even reflect a degree of overt competition with figures from pagan religion and myth. These were familiar images from the surrounding culture that, with a little recasting and placement in context, could communicate aspects of the Christian faith or particular attributes of Jesus Christ, and as such appeared in both literature and visual art.

## The seated philosopher/teacher

A third, less common figure sometimes joins the company of orant and shepherd (Figure 6). This seated male is normally shown in profile, reading from a scroll, barefoot, and dressed in the philosopher's *exomis* tunic and mantle and showing a partially nude torso. Sometimes a small person is shown kneeling at or apparently kissing the feet of the seated figure (Figure 10). In pagan contexts, this composition may have been a standard way to portray the deceased (whether pagan or Christian) in the flattering guise of the intellectual or scholar, and in this respect it might share a portrait function with the orant figure.[46]

*Figure 10* Figure in cape kneeling at the feet of the seated philosopher. To the left Jesus holding a scroll of the law. Fragment of a fourth-century sarcophagus now in the Musée de l'Arles Antique, Arles.

Photo: Author.

However, the occurrence of the philosopher in Christian contexts might also allude to Christianity as the true philosophy, or to the place of wisdom or reason in Christian teaching. This tradition, exemplified by the apologists, especially Justin Martyr (a self-proclaimed teacher of Christian philosophy), went so far as to posit certain classical philosophers as proto-Christians (especially Socrates) whose teachings, although in error about some things, paved the way for Christian revelation to the Gentiles. Tertullian, comparing Christianity to other sects and philosophies claims: "And yet, the truth ... is that which these philosophers pretend to know, and which Christians alone possess."[47]

Certain other biblical figures also appear in philosophical garb (sometimes the shorter tunic of the itinerant cynic), including Daniel, Job, Moses, and John the Baptist. The appearance of these characters in philosophical dress echoes Justin's representation of certain Hebrew Bible patriarchs and heroes who lived according to "reason" and thus could be considered forerunners of Christ himself, or at least "pre-Christian" Christians.[48] Job, the devout sufferer who was eventually vindicated, might be regarded as a type of Christ or a figure of the resurrection.[49]

As with the orant and the shepherd, however, nothing particularly distinguishes this figure as Christian apart from the surrounding images. In fact, as we have seen, the Good Shepherd, orant, and seated philosopher appear together in several sarcophagus compositions.[50] The proximity of these three images in several significant Christian monuments suggests some connection. Perhaps they symbolize three aspects of the church's ministry: prayer, study of scripture, and pastoral care. Or, like the shepherd, the seated philosopher might be an indirect representation of Christ (supported by the occasional addition of the person kneeling at his feet); but his particular appearance (or lack thereof) makes this a better candidate for a portrait of the deceased and/or a more general symbol for the church or its teaching, than a specific reference to Jesus.

A different philosopher type began to emerge in the late third and early fourth centuries which may be more assuredly identified as Christ. The first may be a kind of transitional image. The facial features and philosophical dress are similar, although the figure is now shown facing front, holding up (rather than reading) his scroll, and making a gesture of speech. The juxtaposition of this with an identical person (judging by his facial features) shown performing healings helps us identify the former as Jesus. This figure is related to a later type of Jesus representation that shows Jesus passing a scroll to his apostles (Figure 11). All of these compositions show Christ surrounded by his disciples, who appear to be receiving a lesson from the master. A parallel to both later images is a late fourth-century Syrian mosaic that presents a balding and older Socrates among six other sages – to the first by virtue of the philosopher's appearance, to the second because of the arrangement of the figures in the composition.

45

*Figure 11* Jesus as philosopher, Catacomb of Domitilla.
©The International Catacomb Society. Photo: Estelle Brettman.

These developments in the iconography suggest a parallel theological development concerning Christ himself as the philosopher/teacher rather than the more general presentation of the Christian faith as true philosophy. Artists of the later, post-Constantinian era showed Jesus also surrounded by his disciples, holding a scroll and making a gesture of speech – the image described above and commonly known as the *traditio legis*, the "giving of the New Law" (Figure 33).[51] Like the orant or the shepherd, this iconography first passed from the wider religious environment and carried with it a commonly understood significance, even as it appeared in a Christian setting. The teacher/philosopher type, however, subsequently developed, changing over time so that it came to be uniquely Christian, even suggesting Christianity's ascendance over its religious competition.

## The fisher and the fish

Several different images belong in the category of the fisher and the fish – the single fisherman with a line in the water; a man wrestling with a large fish; several fishermen in a boat casting their nets (which might actually be a narrative reference); and the fish as an emblematic symbol, by itself or in conjunction with a chalice, loaves, or anchor (Figure 12; also 3 and 13c). These various figures, at least one of which might have a scriptural narrative source, belong together partly because of their iconographic parallels, but also because of their possible interpretative connections.[52]

Although discussed here with "non-narrative images," just as the Good Shepherd, these figures also could have a general scriptural source, or specifically refer to a number of different Bible stories – the calling of the apostles to be "fishers of people" (Luke 5:1–11; Matthew 4:18–19; Mark 1:16–17), the apocryphal story of Tobias and the miraculous fish (Tobit 6:3–9), the story of Peter and the fish with the coin in its mouth (Matthew 17:27), or the post-resurrectional story of the miraculous catch of fish (John 21:1–8). Supplying a textual reference for some of the images is easy, others are more obscure. The fish, when it occurs alone or with other simple objects, could be anything from a reference to the two miracle stories of the multiplication of the loaves and fishes (Matthew 14:15–21; Mark 6:35–44; 8:1–8; and parallels) to a Christological symbol. By itself, the iconography is ambiguous.[53]

Like other figures in this chapter, the popular fish/fishing iconography was not specifically Christian, and has parallels in Greco-Roman art. More generally, fish served and still serve as an important symbol in many cultures both ancient and modern. The dolphin, a convention common in Roman art – one that is associated with the iconography of Apollo, Aphrodite, and Poseidon, and especially connected to the cult of Dionysus and the promise

*Figure 12* Fish and loaves, Catacomb of Callistus.

© The International Catacomb Society. Photo: Estelle Brettman.

of a blessed afterlife, also appears in Christian art programs.[54] Maritime themes in general were quite popular in late antiquity, and boats with sailors or waters teeming with all kinds of sea creatures were especially chosen for mosaic pavements. Some of the imagery is purely decorative, some mythological, some of it quite realistic and detailed. Compare, for example, the fishing scenes and sea life depicted on North African mosaics of the third, fourth, and fifth centuries CE with the fourth-century mosaic floor of a Christian basilica in Aquileia, demonstrating how the Christian Jonah cycle generally belongs to this category of maritime art. Christian iconography, apparently, made use of these popular motifs and adapted them to its own uses, imbuing them with a somewhat different meaning.

In addition to the probability that, in a Christian setting, these compositions had a general biblical source, fish and fishing images also might have functioned as broader symbols, for example as symbols of the sacrament of baptism.[55] Often the presence of water seems to unify the artistic motifs. For instance, the late third-century sarcophagus in Sta. Maria Antiqua combines images of fishers, baptism, Jonah (tossed overboard and reclining), along with the Good Shepherd, philosopher, and orant (Figures 13a–c). The water that unites the figures in this composition flows first out of the jug of the Jordan River god at one end of the sarcophagus, across the front to serve as the water of Jesus' baptism, and to the other end where the fishermen cast their net.

The proximity of other biblical scenes that are either directly or indirectly baptismal in theme supports the baptismal interpretation of the fishing images. These scenes include portrayals of Jesus' baptism, scenes from the Jonah narrative, Moses striking the rock, the healing of the paralytic, the woman at the well, and the raising of Lazarus. A man fishing can also be seen in the late third-century mausoleum of the Julii, near to both a Jonah figure and, of course, the better-known Christ-Helios representation (Figure 9). Chamber 21 of the Catacomb of Callistus in particular contains two parallel combinations of scenes that include Moses striking the rock, a man fishing, the paralytic carrying his bed (referring to the Johannine story which mentions an angel stirring up water for a healing purpose), a baptism, and a banquet scene.

Literary evidence confirms these connections. New Testament stories that refer to the miraculous healing or transforming powers of water were often treated as baptismal typologies – stories that prefigure later events or community rituals. These include the stories of the woman at the well, the healing of the paralytic, and the wedding at Cana.[56] Christian writers, moreover, particularly underscored the parallels between the fish, fisher, and baptism. Tertullian opened his treatise on baptism with these words: "Concerning our sacrament of water by which we are liberated to eternal life ... we, little fishes, after the example of our *ichthys* Jesus Christ, are born in water, nor in any other way than by permanently abiding in water, are we

*Figure 13a* Sarcophagus of Sta. Maria Antiqua: front frieze. Rome, late third century.
Photo: Graydon Snyder.

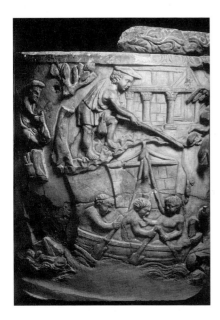

*Figure 13b* Sarcophagus of Sta. Maria Antiqua: right end.

Photo: Graydon Snyder.

*Figure 13c* Sarcophagus of Sta. Maria Antiqua: left end.

Photo: Graydon Snyder.

safe."[57] Origen's commentary on the Gospel of Matthew draws a connection between calling the "fishers of people" (Matthew 4:18–19) and the story of Peter with the fish that had the coin in its mouth (Matthew 17:27): "But this coin was not in Jesus' house, but was found in the sea, and in the mouth of a fish of the sea – a fish which jumped up of its own goodwill, having been caught on the hook of Peter, who had become a fisher of people." Origen goes on to suggest that the fish in the story is a type of the convert, caught by Peter, one of the commissioned fishers.[58]

A century later, Cyril of Jerusalem, speaking to catechumens preparing for baptism, mixed the fish symbolism with the baptismal rite's metaphorical death and rebirth: "You are fish caught in the net of the church. Let yourself be taken alive: don't try to escape. It is Jesus who is playing you on his line, not to kill you, but by killing you, to make you alive."[59]

Tertullian's and Cyril's lines differ about whether Jesus is the fisher, or the fish itself. Cyril's metaphor finds parallels in a "Hymn to Christ" by Tertullian's contemporary Clement of Alexandria, which hails Christ as the "fisher of men, of those saved from the sea of evil, luring with sweet life the chaste fish from the hostile tide."[60] By contrast, however, the late second-century Abercius epitaph seems to agree with Tertullian that the fish is Christ and even goes on to speak of eating the fish along the pilgrimage of conversion: "Everywhere faith led the way and set before me for food the fish from the spring, mighty and pure, whom a spotless virgin caught, and gave this to friends to eat, always having sweet wine, and giving the mixed cup with bread."[61] Thus Abercius, who describes himself as a "disciple of the Good Shepherd," and speaks of Christ as the fish the "Virgin caught," also refers to the sacrament of eucharist (literally eating the fish in the form of the bread and wine), and perhaps also baptism, since the fish is "from the spring" and because the sacrament of eucharist is first offered to the neophyte Christians after baptism.[62]

Neither Tertullian nor Abercius, however, made a direct association with the acrostic made of the Greek word for fish (ΙΧΘΥΣ), each letter of which represents a word in the divine name: Jesus Christ, Son of God, Savior. Later Christian writers, including Augustine and Maximus of Turin, did make an explicit connection between the fish image and that acrostic that is first recorded in the Jewish-Christian Sibylline oracles.[63] Even so, both Abercius' and Tertullian's phrases seem to accord with the acrostic.[64] Moreover, Tertullian's description of Christ as the "big fish" recalls the story of Jonah and the "big fish." Tertullian's hinting at the Jonah story could simply have been intended to reinforce a baptismal metaphor but also presents a more intriguing possibility – that Tertullian knew of a Jewish tradition that posits the beginning of the Messianic age as corresponding with the eating of the great sea creature, Leviathan (Psalms 74:14; 104:26; and Job 3:8; 41:1ff.).[65]

Christological, eschatological, eucharistic and baptismal symbolism are finally so merged in the fish symbol that it becomes impossible to factor them out. For example, a Christian epitaph from the Catacomb of Callistus (the so-called stele of Licinia now in the Museo Nazionale in Rome), shows two fish and an anchor above which are the words "Fish of the Living" (ΙΧΘΥΣ ΖΩΝΤΩΝ). Beginning in the fourth century, western baptismal fonts were often called "fish ponds" (*piscinae*), a play on words graphically illustrated in a font from Kélibia in Tunisia, where fish are portrayed in the mosaic design of the pool. In the late fourth century, Optatus of Milevis elaborated on the associations between the Greek word *ichthys* and the Latin word for the font, *piscina*:

> This is the fish, which in baptism is put into the waters of the font by the invocation so that what had been called water is also called *piscina*, from the word *piscis*. This word, *piscis*, in its Greek form, contains in its individual letters a multitude of sacred names in one title, ΙΧΘΥΣ, which in Latin reads, *Jesus Christus dei filius Salvator.*[66]

A later (fourth-century) Greek inscription, the epitaph of Pectorius, found in southern France, uses language similar to that found in the Abercius epitaph, identifies Christ as the fish, and alludes to both baptism and eucharist within five lines that simultaneously form an acrostic using the Greek word *ichthys*. An English translation of the epitaph's text reads approximately:

> Divine child of the heavenly Fish, keep your soul pure among mortals, since you have received the immortal spring of divine water. Be cheerful, dear friend, with the ever-flowing water of wealth-giving wisdom. Take the honey-sweet food from the Savior of the saints. Eat with joy and desire, holding the fish in your hands. Give as food the fish, I pray, Lord and Savior.[67]

Thus the fish symbol has many possible meanings, and it is probably impossible as well as unwarranted to distinguish them. As we have seen, multiple references are suggested by single images, both in literature and in artistic compositions. The proximity of meal or baptism scenes, or representations of Jonah, Noah, the woman at the well, or the healing of the paralytic, also combine with these symbols to form possible sacramental cycles or overall programs with composite meanings, beyond the symbolism of any one image taken alone. Jonah, especially, serves the double function of symbolizing both Christ's death and his resurrection – the "sign" of Jonah (Matthew 12:39 and parallels), and the baptism of each believer.

## Fish and meal scenes

In early Christian art fish and meal scenes go together. Fish is a menu item almost never lacking from the representation of a banquet or meal whether painted or carved in relief (Figures 14 and 15). This fish in the scenes, however, complicates the question of what these figures are meant to represent and whether they are purely symbolic, based on scripture narrative, or represent some actual meal in early Christian practice.[68]

*Figure 14* Banquet, Catacomb of Callistus.
©The International Catacomb Society. Photo: Estelle Brettman.

*Figure 15* Banquet on sarcophagus fragment now in the Vatican Museo Pio Cristiano.
Photo: Author.

These banquet scenes – among the most common in early Christian funerary art – have significant parallels in earlier and contemporary Greek and Roman funerary iconography.[69] The Roman images seem to be of two basic types. The first depicts a diner reclining on a couch (*kline*) in front of a three-legged table laden with loaves of bread, cups of wine, and sometimes a variety of other foods (Figure 15). Another diner may appear in the scene, often a woman (spouse of the deceased) seated on a straight chair. Servants commonly appear in the scene, often in the foreground. The second and less common type shows a number of diners seated around a sigma-shaped table (*stibadium*), sharing a convivial banquet meal.[70]

The Christian banquet scenes generally have one basic composition, and that is related to the Roman *stibadium* type since the images typically show seven diners reclining on couches around the half-circle table set with cups of wine, platters with one or two large fish, and loaves or baskets of bread.[71] The bread often appears as individual round loaves marked with a *chi*, or cross, but more frequently in baskets of smaller loaves. Five or seven loaves or baskets seem to be the norm, but we sometimes see six, eight, or ten.

A related type of Christian banquet scene shows a man stretching his hands over a small three-legged table laid with bread and fish. An orant figure stands opposite, on the other side of the table. Just such a scene, in the Catacomb of Callistus, appears adjacent to a meal depiction as described above. Moreover, a combination of table types occurs on several sarcophagi and on frescoes in the Catacomb of Peter and Marcellinus, which show a tripod with a platter of fish positioned in front of the sigma table.

Given the very specific composition of the meal scenes, many scholars have presumed that they must illustrate a particular biblical narrative. Therefore, these images have been variously identified as scenes of the Last Supper, a reference to the gospel narratives of Jesus feeding the multitudes (Matthew 14:13–21; 15:32–9; Mark 6:34–44; 8:1–10, 14–20; Luke 9:11–17; and John 6:5–13), or as portraying one or another post-resurrectional meal.[72] By contrast, other interpreters have proposed that the blessing of the food on the tripod table depicts an actual liturgical action rather than a scene from a story.[73]

Following this, still other viewers have seen all the banquet scenes as illustrations of various liturgical meals – funerary banquets, agape meals, or eucharists. This last option lies behind the scenes' common identification as representing the *fractio panis*, a caption applied by J. Wilpert specifically to a meal scene in the Cappella Graeca of the Catacomb of Priscilla.[74] This fresco shows the usual seven figures seated behind a sigma table on which is set a cup, a platter with two fish, and a platter with bread. Seven baskets of bread are also shown in the image. The person (a woman?) seated at the "head" (the right end) of the table is making a gesture that looks like the breaking of a loaf.[75]

Early agape meals or eucharists conceivably may have included fish along with the bread and wine shown in these meal scenes, although no clear literary evidence reflects such a practice. Several early Christian sources include milk, honey, oil, cheese, olives, and salt as elements of sacred meals.[76] Tertullian claimed the followers of Marcion considered fish the "more sacred diet," but does not actually suggest that they ate it in place of eucharistic bread and wine.[77] The epitaphs of Abercius and Pectorius sometimes have been cited as evidence for the use of fish as a eucharistic food. As we have seen above, both the late second-century supposed bishop of Hieropolis and his Gallican counterpart spoke of eating the fish: "Eat with relish, holding the fish in your hands. May I fill myself with fish, I long for it, my master and my savior."[78]

These enigmatic inscriptions do not, however, offer convincing evidence that early Christians commonly included fish in their eucharists. In fact the passages cited more likely refer symbolically to Christ as fish and to an eschatological, rather than an earthly banquet. An excerpt from the work of an unknown author that goes under its Latin title: *"Narratio rerum quae in Perside acciderunt,"* strengthens the case. Probably dating from the fifth century but drawing upon an earlier tradition, the text conflates the Virgin Mary with the Goddess Hera and both with the fountain of life: "For the fountain of water flows ever with the water of the Spirit, having the one and only fish, taken with the hook of divinity, which feeds the whole world, as if dwelling in the sea, with its own flesh."[79]

The late fourth-/early fifth-century monk and then bishop Paulinus of Nola associated both fish and bread with Christ and described his congregation at an abundant banquet – one modeled on the stories of the miraculous multiplication of the loaves and fishes. In one excerpt Paulinus doesn't seem to be describing an actual experience but rather an anticipated future meal: "I see the gathering being divided among separate tables, and all the people being filled with abundance of food, so that before their eyes there appears the plenty bestowed by the Gospel's blessing and the picture of those crowds whom Christ, the true Bread and the Fish of living water, filled with five loaves and two fishes."[80]

Identifying these meal scenes as portraying actual Christian eucharists, moreover, is refuted by liturgical and textual evidence. By the third century, the eucharistic liturgy was quite formal and would have included the whole community, not a small representative number reclining at couches.[81] The ancient agape meal remains a possible candidate for the image's model, but since the term is rather indefinite and seems to cover a wide variety of table-fellowship occasions (including the eucharist), it may not be specific enough to be applied to so fixed an iconographic tradition.[82] Two possible exceptions, nevertheless, occur in the Catacomb of Peter and Marcellinus. These scenes, both showing fewer than the traditional seven guests, also have captions that record commands ("mix me wine," "bring the warm wine") to "servants" named "Irene" and "Agape."

The names of these "servants" give credibility to another option – one favored by many interpreters – that these scenes represent the funeral meals that Roman Christians translated from their former religious and social environment to their new faith community. These compositions appear commonly in funerary contexts (i.e. catacombs and sarcophagi), just as the earlier and contemporary pagan images did. Attributing a specifically funerary significance to them seems like nothing more than good common sense. Christians, after all, adapted many symbols present in the surrounding culture as their own, and through them communicated similar if slightly modified religious messages. For example, while pagan banquet scenes very likely reflected on the deceased's past domestic comfort as symbolized by the sumptuous feast – and perhaps hope for similar paradisical banquets – Christian banquet images more likely illustrated future heavenly banquets, since their expectations of the afterlife are far more important and well-developed than pagan thinking on the matter.[83]

Finally, a most interesting banquet scene was found in the small catacomb of Vibia on the Via Appia Antica in Rome. Vibia probably was not a Christian (her husband is elsewhere identified as a priest of Sabazius), but even if she was pagan, the imagery in her tomb is worth considering as an important contemporary parallel. Adjacent to portrayals of Pluto carrying Vibia off to the underworld and her subsequent judgment by him, is a banquet scene showing six diners waiting for the deceased woman to make up the seventh at their party. To the left of the scene a figure identified as an *Angelus Bonus* conducts Vibia through a gate into paradise. The meal of fish, bread, and wine takes place in a bucolic setting, and is attended by four servants. The diners also carry the identification: *Bonorum Iudicio Iudicati* ("those approved by the judgment of the good"). Vibia's fresco clearly continues the Roman tradition of symbolizing the deceased's happy afterlife via the symbolic banquet. And although this banquet's particular composition – seven guests at a sigma table – suggests possible Christian influence, the usual direction of borrowing was from pagan to Christian. Common cultural symbols may be adapted for distinct theological purposes in any case. Although tracing the direction of the borrowing in this case may be a chicken and egg question, the image's meaning seems unambiguous – a meal of the departed in a paradisical garden.

Like many other ancient people, Romans practiced the custom of eating banquet meals at the gravesite of their dead relatives, on the day of the funeral, at the end of the nine-day mourning period, on particular days established for honoring ancestors, and on departed loved ones' birthdays. In time, this custom was transferred from family members to other special dead within the Christian community (saints or martyrs), and of commemorating the day of death (rebirth by martyrdom) rather than birthdays. Such meals were distinct from either eucharists or agape meals.[84]

Certain distinctive pieces of furniture have been discovered in the catacombs, such as small altars or offering tables, and even stone chairs or

benches that may have served dining functions. The chairs, sometimes identified as seats for presiding clergy during a worship service, were probably
designated seats for departed souls.[85] Underneath the church of S.
Sebastiano archaeologists have found the remains of a mid-third-century
open courtyard that must have served as an open-air banquet hall (*triclia*).
The inscriptions found at the site (dated as early as 260 CE) give evidence
that this early picnic shelter was probably built to serve the faithful who
came to feast in honor of Saints Peter and Paul.[86]

In Roman custom, the dead had a share of the food set apart for them,
and graves were often provided with a table-like structure (*mensae*) including
basins or pipes to receive libations of the food or drink. The foods commonly
associated with these offerings are wine, bread, cakes, oil, fruits of all kinds,
and eggs. Several of the archeological finds show depressions in the shape of
the foods offered. Some of these depressions are, in fact, in the shape of fish –
evidence that fish also may have been offered at these occasions. Similar
receptacles have been found in Christian tombs, but it remains unclear
whether Christians believed the dead were in some way actually present at
the meal itself, or already departed and either in Hades awaiting the general
resurrection (a *refrigerium interim*) or in paradise at a parallel banquet. The
existence of several Christian epitaphs that wish the deceased a good
"refreshment" (*refrigerium*), or suggest such a meal held on their behalf
complicates the case.[87] However, scholars generally agree that the *cubicula*
within the catacombs were probably used for this purpose (and not for
regular worship and/or celebration of the eucharist), and we have records of
church officials trying to curb the practice, since it was too closely identified
with pagan practice and often got a bit out of hand.[88]

Nevertheless, the possibility of a textual reference cannot be entirely
dismissed. In the same way that fish and fishers have prominence in biblical
stories, fish as a food figures prominently in meals described in the New
Testament. Jesus multiplies baskets of food (loaves and fishes) and feeds the
multitudes, stories that are among the most commonly portrayed in early
Christian art. Jesus ate a piece of broiled fish in one of his post-resurrectional
appearances (Luke 24:41–3), and in another, grilled fish on the beach after
the apostles hauled in their miraculous catch (John 21:1–14). The prominence of fish in these texts may not be an accident of history. Fish may
already have had a deep symbolic significance in the culture, and thus were
specifically mentioned in the narratives.[89]

The tripod that appears in many of these paintings points to an
intriguing possibility. E. A. Goodenough and others noted that similar
presentations of a tripod set with a platter of fish occur on contemporary
Jewish gold glass fragments.[90] These fragments seems to represent a special
meal within Jewish tradition, perhaps a Sabbath or other ceremonial meal.
According to at least one ancient source, the type of fish eaten at the
Sabbath was the tunny, a particularly large fish, which might be that fish we

see in the Christian art as well as on these glass fragments.[91] Scholars have tried to connect this meal with the *cena pura*, known to Tertullian and others as one of the Jewish festivals – a special meal eaten in anticipation of the future messianic banquet.[92]

The fish served at a Sabbath meal may itself be rooted in Jewish messianic expectations and legends about the eating of Leviathan. Although not the centerpiece of a messianic feast in the Bible, later Jewish tradition connected the eating of the monster-fish with the inauguration of the messianic age. According to the tradition, God, with the help of the Angel Gabriel, will catch the Leviathan, dismember and cook it, and serve it to the pious remnant at the messianic banquet. These accounts come mostly from Jewish apocalypses in the Pseudepigrapha but also may be found in the Talmud.[93]

Although the most important biblical sources for the linking of the destruction (but not eating) of Leviathan and the Day of the Lord are Job 41 and Isaiah 27, the Book of Jonah makes a natural parallel, telling the story of another great fish. For both Jews and Christians, the tale of Jonah had messianic significance. A few Christian writers may have been aware of the Jewish prophecy that Leviathan would be eaten at the messianic banquet. Origen and Jerome both cite the tradition that the Messiah will destroy Leviathan, and understand Jonah as a type of Christ. Thus the eating of Leviathan may have the force of prefiguring the Christian heavenly banquet following the resurrection.[94]

Such traditions and interpretations recall the inscriptions of Abercius and Pectorius, where eating the fish is a symbol for the Christian eucharist – the faithful dining on the Messiah himself. Thus it seems quite possible that the meaning of the fish in these Christian images developed from Jewish traditions.

Even so, a specific biblical reference still eludes us. The amount of bread or number of fish on the platter (usually two fish, and five or seven loaves or baskets of bread) may have been intended to recall the miracle stories of Jesus' multiplication of loaves and fishes that often start with five or seven loaves and two fish and end with either seven or twelve basketsful of leftovers. Apart from the fact that other, common, and more directly illustrative portrayals of Jesus multiplying baskets of bread were painted and carved in the catacombs and on tombs, the rest of the banquet image in no way conforms to this or any other text narrative.

Nor can the images, which regularly depict seven diners and prominently feature the fish, be intended to depict the Last Supper. However, beginning in the sixth century and continuing through the Middle Ages, Last Supper scenes frequently incorporate a sigma table and a platter of fish. An early example of this composition occurs in the church of S. Apollinare Nuovo in Ravenna, where Jesus is shown reclining at the head of the *stibadium* with his twelve apostles. On the table are seven small loaves of bread and a platter bearing two large fish. The two large fish, not mentioned in the scripture narratives, may have an eschatological significance. In other words, the unexpected element in the iconography was perhaps intended to carry the meaning of the image. Like Abercius, the apostles are being asked to "eat the Fish." Another possibility is that by the fifth century the fish had become a standard element of the iconography. A roughly contemporary manuscript illumination from a fifth-century copy of the Aeneid (the *Vergilius Romanus*, now in the Vatican Library) shows Aeneas and Dido at table with a platter of fish set before them.

Finally, the shape of the tables and the number of diners may be as significant as the food served in the scenes. Based upon examination of non-funerary images in Roman painting, it appears that the sigma-shaped table (*stibadium*) was commonly used for outdoor banquets or hunters' picnics. When the sigma table appears in the funerary context it is often shown with hints of an outdoor setting, details which might be a reference to paradise.[95] In fact later artistic portrayals of the miracle of the loaves and fishes (an outdoor event) show the diners seated around a sigma table.

Although the Greco-Roman banquet scenes show different numbers of guests around the table, most of the Christian scenes depict seven diners. Although there are exceptions (some of the earliest Christian images show five diners), the significance of the number is clear by its consistency. Martial, in a discussion of Roman table manners, offhandedly says that seven is the right number of guests to be seated at a sigma-table in one place, but suggests eight in another.[96] Apart from following table custom, the seven diners most commonly seen in the earlier banquet images might possibly represent the seven deacons appointed to serve tables in Acts 6:2–3. Later on, the deacons were appointed to distribute the eucharistic elements to the congregation and carry away a portion to those absent from the meal.[97]

Another possible explanation involves the post-resurrectional meals of Jesus with his disciples, which are much closer in both menu, setting, and number of diners, and thus could be a narrative source for the artistic compositions. In the Lukan version of the post-resurrectional appearances, Jesus eats a piece of broiled fish, perhaps to demonstrate his fleshly reality. In the post-resurrectional seaside meal described in John's Gospel, precisely seven disciples dine, and grilled fish is the main course.

Augustine makes an important Christological point of this story in his exegesis of this Johannine pericope:

> Now the Lord said: bring the fish which you have just now caught
> ... and of these he prepared a dinner for his seven disciples, namely,
> of the fish which they had seen laid upon the coals, to which the
> Lord added bread which we are told that the disciples had also seen.

The fish roasted is a figure of Christ's suffering; and he himself is also the bread that comes down from heaven.[98]

Thus, given the compositional details of the scenes, the meals should not be identified as actual agape meals or eucharists, although they may symbolically be related by virtue of the basic theme of eating together with Christ. The New Testament texts that seem most relevant are not narratives of the miraculous feeding or even the Last Supper, although these are obviously connected. The key texts are those that refer to the heavenly banquet (Luke 13:29; 14:15–24; Mark 14:25 and parallels) or describe Jesus' post-resurrectional meals. Moreover, given the sepulchral setting of the paintings – not an insignificant matter – the eschatological significance of these post-death meals not only fits the context, but simultaneously connects the images most closely with the tradition of the funeral banquet.

We must conclude that these scenes are a symbolic combination of post-resurrectional meal, messianic feast, and actual funerary banquet, meals to which the Christian agape and eucharist are not unrelated. After all, the Christian eucharist is a sacrament that looks forward to the messianic banquet, a meal in paradise granted to the baptized (the "little fishes"). Since the eucharist is celebrated on the Christian Sabbath or Lord's Day – the day of resurrection – the meal asserts that this future banquet is also partially accomplished in the present. Like the art works, the actual liturgical meal points to a partly realized eschatology that is proclaimed by Christ's resurrection, reenacted in every convert's baptism, and celebrated by eating and drinking with the risen Lord.[99] This rather complex interpretation finally unites imagery found in the biblical narrative with the liturgical practices of the early church, and (last but not least, given its sepulchral setting) incorporates Christian visions of the afterlife.

## The vine and the wheat

Nearly countless other symbols appear in Christian art, including a variety of birds (especially peacocks and doves), animals (deer and dolphins), and plants and trees (palms, acanthus, and laurel). Among all these symbols, however, two in particular also appear as metaphors in the gospels, and have significant parallels in theological writings – grapevines and bunches of wheat.[100]

Grapevines arguably are one of the most popular decorative motifs in Roman art, and as such also are common in early Christian contexts. We also find these themes quite naturally associated with Dionysian themes in Roman art, iconographic traditions that may have directly influenced Christian imagery.[101] In addition to these associations, however, harvesting motifs often served as allegories for the seasons spring (the grain harvest) and autumn (the grape harvest) along with figures of small children (*putti*) picking olives or carrying flower garlands. In Christian art, grapevines loaded with bunches of ripe fruit are common, also often being harvested by children (Figure 16). Wheat is slightly less popular, but often appears in Christian art harvested along with the grapes. Bunches of wheat also appear in images of Adam and Eve, indicating the consequences of disobedience – back-breaking labor in the fields in order to produce food to eat.[102]

The vine and the wheat alone or shown with vintaging and harvesting children are general symbols of abundance or fertility, whether pagan or Christian. As neutral decoration, they are as appropriate for a Roman dining room as for a Christian mausoleum. The beautiful vault mosaics in the Mausoleum of Sta. Constanza with their scenes of grape-harvesting and wine-making are complemented by lush presentations of other fruit, grain, flowers, birds and cornucopiae suggesting the beauty and abundance of paradise, and have nothing that specifically restricts them to a Christian context or meaning. Such images also have been found in Jewish art of the same period.[103]

Christians no doubt appreciated the decorative qualities of these motifs and took them over from pagan art, but in time must have added new significance to the symbols.[104] Jesus, after all, speaks of himself as the "true vine" (John 15:1–5) and the "bread of life" (John 6:35ff.). At the Last Supper Jesus spoke of the wine as the "fruit of the vine" and the loaf as his body, promising to renew the banquet in the Kingdom of Heaven (Mark 14:22–5 and parallels).

Connecting the Christological symbol from John 15 with the wine at the Last Supper, the text of the *Didache* speaks of the cup of wine as "the Holy Vine of David."[105] Clement of Alexandria also saw the grape as both a Christological and a eucharistic allegory, a grape "bruised for us" in order to produce blood that when mingled with water brings salvation.[106]

*Figure 16* Grape harvest with Good Shepherds. Fourth-century sarcophagus now in the Vatican Museo Pio Cristiano.

Photo: Author.

Subsequent commentators on the symbolism of the vine also saw it as a eucharistic metaphor.[107] The alternation of wheat, grapes, and pomegranates over the font in the baptistery of Dura Europos (Figure 28) might have been intended to refer to the eucharist following baptism. The sacraments are, after all, the foretaste of the new life after death, promised by Christ and symbolized in the rites of baptism and eucharist.

In addition to the sacramental signification, however, according to Jesus' allegory the vine is Christ and its branches represent the apostles and by extension the church. This symbolism is also used by early Christian writers. Irenaeus cites Hosea 9:10, in which God finds Israel as new young grapes, imperfect but full of promise for a plentiful vintage.[108] Origen elaborates on the need of the branches to stay firmly attached to the "true vine" since they cannot produce the fruits of virtue apart from it.[109] Later, Basil of Caesarea developed this theme at some length, beginning by asserting that "every one who is grafted by faith into the church are branches, urged to produce abundant fruit, lest infertility should condemn us to the fire."[110] Back in the third century Hippolytus explained the vine and harvest as symbolizing different "branches" of the church, its apostles, saints, and martyrs. Hippolytus' description seems to have assumed experience with such visual images on sarcophagus reliefs or in mosaic:

> The spiritual vine was the Saviour. The shoots and the vine branches are his saints, those who believe in him. The bunches of grapes are his martyrs; the trees which are joined with the vine show forth the Passion; the vintagers are the angels; the baskets full of grapes are the Apostles; the winepress is the Church; and the wine is the power of the Holy Spirit.[111]

As all these texts make clear, the symbolism of the vine as the church is complete only in light of the harvest. In the Gospel of John, Jesus says that those branches that do not produce fruit will be gathered up and thrown into the fire. This threat is echoed in other gospel texts, such as the parable of the wheat and the weeds (Matthew 13:24–30), in which the coming of the Kingdom is compared to the gathering of the wheat and the burning of the weeds. Because the motifs themselves show the harvest, we cannot overlook the significance of these texts. Probably more than simple references to the eucharist, or to the church and its many "branches," these harvesting scenes may serve as pictorial references to the eschatological harvest, perhaps partially realized among those already dead. Given the fact that we see only fruitful vines and ripe bundles of wheat, the viewer is reassured that the deceased have been safely gathered in.[112] Thus, like the fish and the banquet scene, these images reflect upon biblical texts, liturgical practices, and expectations for the afterlife.

## Conclusion

Early Christian art employed different kinds of visual language from fairly simple symbols to more complex or sequenced narrative scenes. Of these two types of imagery, the symbolic may have been the most theologically broad, encompassing central values, themes and ideas of the church as well as contributing to its self-identity. However, as symbols, these figures were also multi-faceted and ambiguous. Their meanings defy simple translation or one-to-one relationship with single ideas. The figure of a shepherd, orant, philosopher, or fisher may have had several different significations – sometimes simultaneously – depending on context, overall composition, and viewer. Used over time, the symbols may be more unequivocal in their meanings, as they become a kind of visual shorthand for particular abstract concepts, perhaps even being reduced to decorative evocations of favorite themes.

The fact that many of the most popular early Christian images have clear parallels in contemporary pagan imagery argues for a less distinct separation between "Christian" and "pagan" imagery in the third and early fourth centuries. Christians plainly made use of popular symbols and figures from their surrounding culture, adapting them for their own contexts and seeing in them specific Christian meanings, without being overly self-conscious or apologetic for the borrowing. However, if we consider the examples of the orant, the Good Shepherd, the philosopher, the banquet, and the vine – or even the more particular analogies to Helios or Orpheus iconography, these specific Christian meanings need not be radically different from the connotations of their non-Christian counterparts. All these images emphasize the human virtues of piety, philanthropy, and the love of wisdom (and by extension the deceased's possession of those virtues). They also speak of general hopes for an afterlife that offers those of such virtue a caring guide into the next world and a community of cherished friends once there. Non-Christian Romans may not have had the same expectations of death and afterlife that their Christian contemporaries did, nor did they necessarily understand their future rewards to be based on faith in a particular savior god or initiation into his or her cult. Nevertheless, the optimism expressed in pagan funerary imagery was almost effortlessly carried over into early Christian art and became joined with a larger canon of images or symbols that expressed a more particular belief in a resurrection of the faithful to an eternal life of peace and joy among the community of saints.

This almost graceful transition from pagan imagery to Christian symbolism in the early period has its parallels in many of the writers of the second and third centuries, including Justin Martyr and Clement of Alexandria – apologists and theologians who also emphasized the similarities and even continuity between Christian teachings and late Hellenistic philosophy, especially with regard to human virtues and the character of the divine being. To do this they chose to speak with a vocabulary that would have been familiar to their audience. Such vocabulary carried their ideas very effectively, and clearly was intended to smooth the transition from old religion to the new – to make conversion seem as natural as growing up and leaving home. The very real clash between Christian and pagan that may have been happening "above ground" is hardly sensed here, and the differences between Athens and Jerusalem are diminished.

The similarities would and could not last, however, and as the next generations of Christians refined and distinguished their faith from a surrounding (and diminishing) pagan culture, the themes or motifs of their art works concurrently became more particular or distinctly Christian, even as they drew upon other aspects of the society for models or inspiration. The time came for the religion to assert itself as distinct, but not ever as entirely foreign to the culture in which it grew and became established.

# 3

# PICTORIAL TYPOLOGIES AND
# VISUAL EXEGESIS

## Introduction

Thematically distinct from artistic compositions that had parallels in traditional Roman (pagan) iconography, many early Christian images referred directly to particular biblical texts and are the most distinguishably "Christian" in content. Unlike such non-narrative images as the praying figure or the seated philosopher, the textual sources of most of the subjects usually are obvious, but the reasons lying behind their selection and arrangement are more elusive. Examination of both the kind of setting as well as overall artistic program in which particular scenes appear may give some clues about their particular significance in context, while background analysis of the textual tradition of the source narratives themselves may provide information about the hermeneutical function of these images as "types." Initial study of specific characteristics of individual scenes – their frequency of appearance, specific compositional details, and their placement in relation to other figures – will provide some basic data for consideration.

Even a superficial study of the subjects portrayed in early Christian art reveals that certain biblical figures appear with greater frequency than others, both before and after the Constantinian period. The use of biblical themes generally underscores the prominent place scripture stories played in the faith and daily life of Christians, especially in an era when theologians were preoccupied with doctrinal formulation and refutation of heresy, and apologists attempted to give Christianity a philosophical pedigree as well as an intellectual justification. However, beyond the general use of biblical themes, the observer will note the popularity of certain biblical stories in particular and may begin to see some patterns in these images' frequency of appearance.

To modern eyes some of the more popular subjects may seem odd choices, while other arguably more prominent biblical scenes appear lacking. For example, among the Old Testament subjects in the pre-Constantinian era no extant portrayals are found of Moses crossing the Red Sea (and even after Constantine they were relatively rare), while numerous frescoes and sarcophagus carvings depict Moses striking the rock in the wilderness (Figure 17). Similarly, we find dozens of representations of Abraham offering Isaac, Jonah, Noah, and Daniel flanked by lions, but not a single third- or early fourth-century instance of Jacob, Joseph, Joshua, David, or the major prophets.[1] Of course, our modern expectations are conditioned by the emphases of contemporary biblical imagery and the theology implied by these emphases. However, by examining the subjects that do appear in early Christian art we can speculate about the connection between the popularity of different biblical narratives and theological emphases in antiquity.

Similar to Old Testament subjects, certain New Testament subjects also are distinctly popular, including the baptism of Jesus, the raising of Lazarus, the multiplication of the loaves and fishes, the healing of the paralytic, the transformation of water to wine at Cana, and the woman at the well. Thus, while specific healings and miracles appear frequently, other scenes from Jesus' life – including Jesus with the elders, his temptation, or cleansing of the temple – are entirely missing from the early iconography. Certain other images appear surprisingly late, given their relative popularity in the entire history of Christian art, including representations of Jesus' nativity, transfiguration, Last Supper, passion, and resurrection.[2]

*Figure 17* Moses striking the rock (upper right) with Noah, Lot and the multiplication of the loaves and fishes, Catacomb of Peter and Marcellinus.

©The International Catacomb Society. Photo: Estelle Brettman.

In addition to the frequency of certain subjects, their composition also may seem strikingly odd to modern observers. An image may be condensed (such as Noah floating in a box-like ark, but without Mrs Noah or all the animals that we have come to expect – Figure 18), or show unexpected, non-textual features (Jesus using a magician's wand to change the water to wine at Cana, or the presence of the river deity in scenes of baptism, for example). The first instance may be an attempt to capture the essence of meaning in a simple, almost formulaic reference to a familiar narrative. This practice demonstrates the symbolic as opposed to illustrative value of the scenes. In other words, the image's significance has more to do with its referential power than with its narrative details. The second compositional character-istic – the addition of extra-textual props or figures – graphically demonstrates the adaptability of this iconography, to expand beyond literal readings of texts and to add elements of meaning not strictly in the narrative source.

Each of these issues – the frequency or compositional peculiarities of certain images – are important interpretive clues as such, and even more important if they can be juxtaposed to similar patterns that appear in contemporary documents. However, a third significant issue that needs consideration is that of context. In other words, we can speculate that certain figures are juxtaposed or given proximity to one another in order to suggest an overarching meaning. A single subject may be part of a unified program

*Figure 18* Noah, Catacomb of Peter and Marcellinus.
© The International Catacomb Society. Photo: Estelle Brettman.

rather than an isolated figure, and the theme of that unified program is only revealed by the character of its composite parts. Any single part could also play a part in a different composition, with a different meaning. Like any complex symbol system, early Christian iconography cannot be served up as a catalogue of images with simple definitions. For example, a portrayal of Abraham offering his son Isaac as a sacrifice (Figure 19) might be part of a simple message of deliverance in one context, particularly if it is juxtaposed to other scenes that might relay the same meaning (Daniel in the lion's den and the three youths in the fiery furnace, for example). But a nearly identical presentation of Isaac's sacrifice could also serve as an early Christian type of Jesus' sacrifice in a different programmatic context – one that might include the raising of Lazarus and the "sign" of Jonah.[3]

*Figure 19* Abraham and Isaac, and Balaam with his ass, Via Latina Catacomb.
© The International Catacomb Society. Photo: Estelle Brettman.

67

The message imparted, whether by individual compositions or by whole pictorial programs, must also be related in some way to their physical setting. Almost all of these scenes function, at least contextually, as cemetery art. Since little non-funereal evidence remains for comparison with the art of the earlier period, we may never know for certain how or even if this imagery differed from the decoration of other spaces (e.g. churches and baptisteries). Still, we cannot ignore the fact that these subjects were painted on the walls of a tomb, or carved on a marble coffin, and thus must have reflected to some degree Christian beliefs about death and afterlife, the nature of salvation, and the community's hopes in that regard. Such significance was apparent in the representations of the banquet, or the grapevine, for instance and it is no less applicable to these narrative-based images.[4]

As already noted, after Constantine, the funeral context ceases to be the primary origin of Christian iconography. The practice of decorating catacombs died out by the early fifth century, except for the occasional embellishment of the tomb of a saint or martyr. While the carving of sarcophagi continued for a time in Ravenna, even there it was essentially discontinued by the early sixth century. In the interim, new iconographic subjects appeared on fourth- and fifth-century sarcophagi and in catacomb frescoes, but the new themes also found new venues – on church apses and nave walls. The most notable examples of these new themes are the presentations of Jesus seated on a throne, and the empty crosses of victory that emerge in the fourth century in both church and sarcophagus iconography.[5]

Thus, the art works, when examined apart from the documents, can be assessed according to the frequency and repetition of certain figures, the details or peculiarities of their composition, compositional patterns (e.g. regular proximity or juxtaposition to other subjects), and finally their physical setting. This data will give clues to the symbolic message of a tomb's overall decoration, as well as to the possible meaning of any single subject. However, by themselves, the images are still ambiguous and non-self-interpreting. The keys to their significance will continue to depend on the clues we find in the written documents, including theological treatises, liturgies, homilies, and exegetical works. The most relevant documents will interpret the biblical stories cited above, as allegories, typologies, or moral figures that give the "hidden" meaning or significance behind the narrative.

## Popularity of Old Testament themes: external explanations

Returning to the first apparent character of early Christian iconography, i.e. the frequency of certain images, several interesting points arise. First is the general dominance of scenes from the Hebrew scriptures over representations of New Testament subjects. In fact, Old Testament subjects occur as much as four times more often than New Testament themes in the Christian art of the second through the fourth centuries. This predominance surprises those who assume that Christian art logically would show preference for purely Christian themes. Instead, the story of Jonah is an overwhelmingly favorite subject, usually presented in a two- or three-part cycle of images: Jonah cast overboard and being swallowed, Jonah disgorged by the sea monster, and Jonah at rest again on dry land, under his gourd vine (Figure 20). Slightly under one hundred Jonah figures are found in the catacombs or carved on sarcophagi dated to the pre-Constantinian era alone.

After Jonah, Noah in the ark is a distant second favorite, with a dozen or fewer third- or early fourth-century examples, followed by Moses striking the rock in the wilderness, Abraham offering Isaac, Adam and Eve, and Daniel in the lions' den, each with less than ten third- or early fourth-century examples. Of the New Testament scenes, only the representation of Jesus' baptism and the raising of Lazarus are comparably popular, with around six representations each. The woman at the well, the healing of the paralytic, and the multiplication of the loaves and fishes are known in two or three versions.[6]

Several theories have tried to account for the prevalence of Old Testament subjects, including the hypothetical existence of an earlier or synchronous Jewish iconographic tradition that could have served as a prototype for Christian artistic output.[7] At various points in his extensive study of Jewish symbols, Erwin Goodenough suggested a Jewish influence on Christian catacomb art, particularly seeing parallels between paintings in the Dura

*Figure 20* Jonah under the gourd vine, Catacomb of Callistus.
©The International Catacomb Society. Photo: Estelle Brettman.

Europos synagogue with the Roman frescoes.[8] However, the style and content of these two bodies of evidence bear little, if any, similarity. One has to struggle even to posit parallels between the decoration of the synagogue and the Christian baptistery in Dura, two buildings both chronologically and geographically linked. Admittedly, Dura's baptistery iconography has parallels in the Roman catacombs, but this admission gets us no further toward finding an external source for the iconography. This Jewish-source thesis seems particularly flawed.

Kurt Weitzmann's more recent thesis, that Christian iconography was the direct heir of an Antiochene- or Alexandrine-Jewish tradition of biblical illumination, specifically of an illustrated (and now lost) manuscript of the Septuagint, is equally problematic.[9] No evidence of such a tradition has been found, and although not entirely implausible, the hypothetical "lost manuscript" would represent the work of a hellenized first- or second-century Jewish community somewhat outside the mainstream of rabbinical Judaism.

The existence of an early Jewish iconographic tradition has, of course, been amply demonstrated by the discovery of the third-century synagogue in Dura Europos with its richly figurative wall-paintings, as well as by a number of fifth-century Palestinian synagogues with decorative and figural mosaic pavements. Scholars can no longer claim that Jews were rigidly aniconic in the early centuries of the common era. However, apart from the problem that the thesis is an argument from silence, the proposition that sources for this iconography were ancient illuminated Jewish manuscripts skirts the fact that the known Jewish iconography from this period is neither strictly narrative (illustrating the biblical text), nor purely canonical. Like Christian catacomb imagery, the scenes seem to have a different purpose, perhaps more related to theological, exegetical, or liturgical elaborations on biblical themes.[10]

Moreover, the hypothesis that Christian iconography was derived from this lost Jewish illustrative tradition is further weakened by the lack of similarity between the art of the early church and the supposed missing link – the paintings in the Dura Synagogue. Early medieval Christian manuscript illumination unquestionably shows similarities to both the Dura paintings and later Jewish manuscript painting, but reading medieval traditions back into late antiquity is a dubious practice.

Positing the derivation of Christian art from Jewish sources may be problematic at another level. As mentioned above, the dominance of Hebrew scripture images in early Christian art might surprise those who presume the Christians would favor purely "Christian" themes. Implied in this surprise is a distinction between scriptures that is suspiciously Marcionite in that it discounts the importance of the Hebrew Bible (especially in its Greek translation, the Septuagint) to the early church. Apart from such heterodox teachers as Marcion, for the first two centuries of its existence the church regarded the Jewish scriptures as its own and read them in every assembly, while the gospels or "memoirs" of the apostles were only gradually included in collections of sacred books. In fact, the very way Christian clergy and theologians treated the Hebrew Bible goes beyond mere acceptance or adoption to approximate a kind of literary despoliation. Christian thinkers, eager to establish a link between the old and new covenants in the sacred history, deftly identified prophetic figures or types in the Old Testament that bore out their claims of divine providence and anticipated the coming of Jesus as Saviour.[11] Thus, the offering of Isaac is the prefigurement of Christ's sacrifice on the cross, and Moses striking the rock in the wilderness probably should be understood as a type of Christian baptism.[12]

An alternative explanation for the frequency in early Christian iconography of certain motifs (and of Old Testament themes in general) in early Christian art, like the "lost manuscript theory," regards Jewish sources as key, but not direct artistic precedents. In this case the sources are not artistic prototypes, but liturgical texts. The tomb frescoes portray particular biblical heroes who are cited in ancient Christian prayer cycles (cycles perhaps originating within Judaism) that ask for deliverance of the living from danger or salvation of the soul after death. The prayer calls upon God for help, citing the precedents of those others God delivered in former times, including Enoch, Elijah, Noah, Abraham, Job, Isaac, Lot, Moses, Daniel, the three youths in the fiery furnace, Susannah, David, Peter, Paul, and Thecla. Proponents of this theory argue that many of these same figures are found in the Christian catacombs because the deceased or the family wished to give their prayers visual form and extend the prayer for salvation to life after death.[13]

Unfortunately, the most often cited Christian prayer, the *ordo commendationis animae*, which contains just such a list of biblical paradigms, cannot be dated before the fourth century, while the only known Jewish parallel, the "Prayer for the recommendation of the soul," dates from the ninth century. Moreover, the coincidence of characters is slim. Not all of the ancient heroes who appear in the *ordo commendationis animae* actually make it into the catacomb catalogue (e.g. Enoch, Elijah, Lot, and Thecla); and, conversely, some of the most popular biblical characters or scenes on the walls of the catacombs are unexplained by this thesis (e.g. Adam and Eve, Lazarus, Jonah, the multiplication of the loaves, and the baptism of Jesus). Earlier lost prayers could be models for these later examples, of course, ideally with cited figures more parallel to those in the iconography. The argument's strength lies in its acknowledgment that the funerary context of the art is significant. Its weakness, like the previous theory, is its dependence on hypothetical evidence.

On the other hand, certain early Christian iconographic analogies may have had liturgical parallels. In the early decades of the twentieth century, Victor Schultze noted a pattern of citations in the fifth book of the *Apostolic Constitutions*, a compendium of miscellaneous materials that may have originated in Syria in the third century.[14] These citations appeared to correspond to the painted subjects on the walls of the Christian catacombs. In the first section of the fifth book, concerning the martyrs, the resurrection of the faithful is demonstrated by recalling the examples of Enoch and Elijah, but also the creation of Adam, the raising of Lazarus, Jairus' daughter, and the son of the widow of Nain. The text further cites the deliverance of Jonah, Daniel, and the three youths; the legend of the phoenix; the trials of Job; the harvesting of wheat; the healing of the paralytic and the man born blind; and the miracles of the multiplication of the loaves, the changing of water to wine at Cana, and the coin in the mouth of the fish (Matthew 17:27). All these wonderful events or works, along with Christ's passion, death, and resurrection, are given as lessons to the faithful, and signs of their own salvation.[15]

Coming from a different perspective, we might ask whether certain subjects were chosen or represented in particular ways primarily because existing artistic prototypes from the Greco-Roman world provided helpful aids for the artisans who painted or carved the scenes. This view has practical merit but, as an explanation, is incomplete and unsatisfying. Certain images do, in fact, have direct parallels in pagan art, but even these parallels may exist for reasons other than simple artistic convenience. For instance, the representation of Jonah reclining nude under the gourd vine (Figure 20) has been recognized as a Christian version of a sleeping Endymion, to whom Zeus granted blissful sleep for eternity.[16] Assuming the viewers were familiar with both stories, this particular presentation of Jonah could have inherited significance from the Endymion symbolism as well as having conveyed a secondary Christian meaning given to the Jonah story. Therefore, this figure could refer both to the expected resurrection of the Christian dead (cf. Matthew 12:40: Jesus' use of the "sign of Jonah") as well as their interim wait for that resurrection, in a state of blissful repose. Moreover, such symbolism is certainly more fitting for a funereal context than the pictures of the threatened destruction or ultimate conversion of the sinful Ninevites.

The subjects of Greco-Roman art undoubtedly influenced both the specific appearance as well as general composition of Christian artistic images. For example, particular artistic conventions led to the rendering of Daniel as an heroic nude (Figure 21), the representation of prophets in philosophical garb, and the appearance of typical Roman altars in the scenes of Abraham offering Isaac. Although such influences seem quite natural, their effect on Christian religious symbolism might be more significant than at first appears. Rather than being neutral cultural transferences, these anachronisms or peculiarities heighten the significance of an image and lend it a particular meaning or significance that is not apparent in more literal or illustrative artworks.[17]

Rejection of the Jewish illustrated source hypothesis, for instance, does

*Figure 21* Daniel and lions, Catacomb of Peter and Marcellinus.
© The International Catacomb Society. Photo: Estelle Brettman.

not conversely argue that Christian art was created *de novo* in any sense. Rather, the most obvious source for much of early Christian iconography is the one closest at hand – the surrounding Greco-Roman environment with its familiar themes and types. Since the workshops that produced the earliest Christian images must have been most familiar with subjects from the pagan repertoire, it was undoubtedly natural for artisans simply to adapt whatever was at hand. Sometimes this meant using available models but changing their identity and context, as in the Endymion-Jonah pattern, or the ascension of Elijah as a reworking of the Roman image of apotheosis.[18] Other examples include the mere "lifting" a prototype from the pagan context intact and attributing Christian meanings to it, as was the case with the Good Shepherd, or Christ in the guise of Orpheus or Helios, already discussed in Chapter 2.

That certain images are borrowed with little change in detail or style (the Good Shepherd, Orpheus, etc.), serves as evidence not of religious syncretism but rather of core cultural values – values which transcend the specificity of dogma and find their parallels in certain artistic symbols. This is where the literary sources have proved useful. For example, without recourse to some other corrobative evidence, we cannot know whether the dolphin's appearance as a Christian symbol represents an importation of Dionysiac theology as well as its visual symbolism. However, if we find examples of homilies or liturgies in which such an image plays its part in the newly emerging Christian tradition, we can at least assert that the church was self-conscious of the significance of these pagan symbols (e.g. resurrection), and intentionally provided them with new, Christian, significance. The intrinsic nature of symbols is that they are adaptable to new and multiple meanings. Christian art has always made use of available symbols but imbued them with new significance. A dolphin may be approximately as "pagan" as the Christmas tree. Even the most unsophisticated viewers understand that something has been borrowed from a non-Christian source in order to enhance the message of the Christian story – i.e. life and light (evergreen and candles) in the midst of death and darkness (the season of winter). In some cases, however, borrowings from the surrounding non-Christian culture appear to have amounted to a deliberate and direct announcement that the new God had come to replace the old gods. In these cases the parallel of symbolism was all the more critical to the success of the arguments.[19]

## Popularity of Old Testament themes: theological explanations

Leaving aside the issue of specific artistic models or literary sources (real or theoretical), a more general explanation for the dominance of particular Old Testament or Apocryphal stories in early Christian art simply asserts that these subjects were selected and popularized because they, in particular, represented God's deliverance from danger, especially in a time of persecution. Related to the theory that the images were drawn from familiar prayers for deliverance, this proposal takes seriously the social context of the paintings and assumes that in a hostile, threatening environment Christians understandably drew upon stories that suggested security and safety. Those scholars who take this view assert that after the "peace of Constantine," Christians no longer faced the danger of persecution and martyrdom, and so dropped some of the most popular of these themes, the Noah and the Jonah cycles in particular. Certain motifs were retained if they could be recycled for other uses: Abraham offering Isaac (becoming a "type" of the crucifixion) or Moses striking the rock (transformed to Peter baptizing his Roman jailers).[20]

One facet of this theory is its presumption that most of the subjects in the early Christian iconographic repertoire are comprehensible by one over-arching motif – desire to be delivered from immediate and present danger. Once the danger goes away the imagery must change to accommodate new concerns that are then translated into new symbolic or iconographic language. Moreover, this theory is based on the false premise of "early empire-wide persecution." Christians were always vulnerable, but on the whole tended to live in harmony with their neighbors during the third century (apart from brief periods of persecution).

A second aspect of this theory is its elevation of this-worldly concerns over a next-worldly focus that might be more fitting for the funereal context of this imagery. Thus the hypothesis must assert that the iconographic programs are not distinctly sepulchral, nor was their context particularly significant for the choice or interpretation of their decor, an argument that seems simply illogical.

A third feature of this theory is its assertion that iconography functions on the symbolic level as much as (or more than) on the illustrative or literal levels. The biblical story is a source for the iconography, but the figures from the story have transcended the narrative to become symbols of God's stead-fast protection, and prototypes of Christian heroes. This aspect of the arguments is, in fact, supported to a degree by the textual tradition, as will be demonstrated below.

Recognizing that artistic figures often overstep their own stories and become symbols allows an interpretive shift. Even a cursory look at the artworks reveals that they were not intended to be merely narrative or didactic. The limited view that these images are primarily illustrations of particular biblical stories and function didactically for the most part reduces the work of interpretation to simple labeling and cataloging.[21] A more inte-grated viewpoint sees these images as chosen, composed, and put into certain contexts to serve a second, and perhaps a third, level of meaning. This perspective accounts for certain unusual themes that are selected or portrayed with abridged compositions. Representations of Noah, for instance, only require those iconographic markers that make the meaning clear. Mrs Noah and the animals are unnecessary either because they are taken for granted, or because they are superfluous. All the observer needs to see is Noah safely in his ark, floating on the waters of the flood.

In the case of the Jonah imagery, we have already noted that the iconog-raphy concentrates only on elements of the story that convey the central message: Jonah into the sea, into and out of the belly of the fish, and finally reborn onto a new land. Other narrative details, the sins of Nineveh, for instance, are omitted. Whatever is communicated by these pictures does not require the artistic representation of auxiliary details. A man carrying a bed frame signifies the whole story – or conflates both the synoptic and Johannine versions – of the healing of the paralytic. The entire Lazarus narrative is represented by the moment when the shrouded figure emerges from his tomb (Figure 22). God delivered Moses and the Israelites on many occasions, some of them even the direct result of cultural persecution, but the only Moses image that pre-dates the Constantinian era illustrates the story of Moses striking a rock and receiving water to give the thirsty Israelites during their travels in the wilderness. This selectivity both in subject and composition must have a purpose and that purpose is most likely symbolic.

Finally, considering the whole program or composition may aid the interpretation process, assuming that individual catacomb paintings were parts of

*Figure 22* Jesus raising Lazarus, Catacomb of Peter and Marcellinus.
© The International Catacomb Society. Photo: Estelle Brettman.

a unified agenda, rather than isolated scenes. Furthermore, the funerary context plays a similar role in determining the meaning of an artistic program. In other words the first step is discovering what all these images might have in common, and the second step is determining why they might be appropriate for a cemetery.[22] The hypothesis that the iconographic program was derived from intercessory prayers for the dead (see above) meets both criteria, but unfortunately the tenuous match between existing texts and early Christian iconography is further debilitated by a lack of chronological congruity.

## Scriptural images as visual exegesis

Since the artistic themes are mostly drawn from biblical stories, we must assume that they serve an exegetical function – that is, they are commentaries on the texts as well as references to them. As such, we might examine the methods that guided much of early Christian exegesis, especially exegesis that was delivered orally and would have been familiar to the faithful from the homilies they heard or catechism they learned while being prepared for baptism. This guiding methodology often reasoned that scripture was not meant to be understood purely on a literal or historical level, but that its true, or higher, meaning was imparted symbolically or metaphorically. Seeking this secondary level of meaning often meant finding the figures or types in the text – symbols that referred to something hidden at the obvious or literal level.

This particular tradition of biblical exegesis had earlier roots in Hellenistic Judaism, with the writings of Philo of Alexandria, whose work in turn influenced the great third-century Alexandrine exegete, Origen. Origen's system varied somewhat in different writings, but basically outlined three levels of interpretation, each corresponding to an aspect of human existence. The first level is the literal or historical meaning of the text, the simple or plain "facts" that are known purely through the human bodily senses. The second surpasses the first and uncovers the meaning of the text at the level of the human soul, gaining insight into its typological or moral significance. This level often deciphers the message of the text for Christian conduct, but sometimes also identifies symbols and prefigurations of the Christian gospel also hidden within. The third level, corresponding to the human spirit, is the highest and penetrates both the lower levels of meaning to find the allegorical and transcendent message hidden in the story. Similarly dependent on the discernment of symbols, this level often points out the eschatological import of any text.[23]

Origen's system was extremely influential even though allegory was less popular in some regions of the Christian world (e.g. Carthage and Antioch). However, it certainly gained some of its momentum from the strong assertion (perhaps in response to Gnostic claims) that the Hebrew scriptures and the Christian gospels were mutually dependent: one the prophecy, the other the fulfillment of God's plan. Thus, every Old Testament story has hidden within it some kind of prefigurement of Christ, the church, or the Christian sacraments. Herein lies the mysterious unity of the two "testaments" for early Christian exegetes.

This type of interpretation appears in the earliest Christian literature. According to the gospels, Jesus himself spoke of Jonah as a paradigm of his own death and resurrection (Matthew 12:39; 16:4; Luke 11:29). The text of 1 Peter 3:20-1 associates Noah's salvation with baptism, just as Paul (1 Corinthians 10:1-5) indicated that "our fathers" were all "baptized into Moses in the cloud and the sea," and the supernatural rock from which they drank in the wilderness was "the rock of Christ." Some of the allegories most familiar to us come from John's Gospel, Christ as the "Lamb of God," the "true vine," or the "bread of life."

This metaphorical or symbolic rhetoric has definite visual qualities. One literally "sees" a truth in an image. As such it is a natural artistic device. The paintings in the catacombs must have functioned as visual rather than verbal typologies and allegories and conveyed messages hidden behind the literal or illustrative level. This explains why certain subjects were so often portrayed in abbreviated or unexpected ways. The viewer had already moved beyond the literal meaning of the narrative to its deeper messages. Christians would see for themselves, in pictorial form, the interpretations or symbolic associations they were regularly hearing in their weekly homilies and their baptismal catecheses. Just as most modern Christians understand that a single lamb with a cross is a symbol of Jesus and his sacrifice, so early Christians must have understood Jonah, thrown overboard and regurgitated, as an image of death and resurrection.

With an exegetical function in view, the question of the common link between the variety of motifs in the catacombs and on the sarcophagi can be revisited. We should not think that all the images (or even all the examples of one subject) function the same, symbolically. As discussed above, a number of figures seem to refer to God's deliverance from trial (Daniel, the three youths, Susannah and the elders). These images might have been intended to reassure viewers suffering persecution in their own time, or the deliverance alluded to might have been less worldly and more spiritual. Other representations of Old Testament stories seem to be visual prefigurations of events in the life of Jesus. Some of these are more clearly typological or formulaic, and some less strictly bound to a controlled system and thus should be understood to be allegories.

This latter category includes the offering of Isaac as a prefiguration of Christ's sacrifice, or the story of Jonah as a sign of Jesus' death and resurrection. Even a New Testament story, the raising of Lazarus, appears to function as a symbolic precedent for the death and resurrection of Jesus.[24] All of these are appropriate for a funeral context since they at least indirectly refer to the hope of salvation or future resurrection of the Christian faithful.

Thus, early Christian art proceeds along the same paths as much of early Christian literature, at least with respect to its exegetical function. Although written or spoken interpretation is functionally different from visual presentations of textual narratives, these two forms may have parallel goals and, in fact, similar methods. This does not mean that we can find precise parallels or direct aids for the interpretation of art images in texts, but it does mean that they share a common function – the construction of meaning from the biblical source.[25]

This proposition returns us to the value and potential yield of considering literary documents in conjunction with art objects. Commentaries and homilies on biblical texts are two sources that assist in discovering how visual images also function hermeneutically. These sources may be nearly contemporary with and from the same geographic region as particular works of art, or they may span centuries and distance, yet indicating the broad use of certain images in the evolving traditions of the early church. Stressing the parallels between visual and textual narrative interpretation of scripture does not, however, indicate that the Bible was the only source for the themes of early Christian art any more than canonical scriptures were a proof text for every aspect of the church's tradition more broadly. As the previous chapter has shown and as subsequent chapters will demonstrate, the subjects as well as the compositions move well beyond what is strictly biblical either in source or in message.

The ancient interpreters of texts rarely limited themselves to the literal or historical sense of the narrative but found in the stories (from both New and Old Testaments), figurations, or symbols that had deeper or wider signification. The literature gives many clues regarding the frequency of certain themes, or why they appear in a particular context. The texts will demonstrate the durability of some of these themes across time and space. One vivid example of this is the portrayal of the three youths in the fiery furnace. Another set of examples are particular themes that may be interpreted as references to either baptism or eucharist.

## The three youths in the fiery furnace

The three youths in the fiery furnace (Daniel 3) regularly appear both in catacomb painting and among sarcophagus reliefs of the third through the early fifth centuries. Beginning with an early third-century fresco in the Catacomb of Priscilla, the compositions have a remarkable consistency – nearly all of them show the three standing with hands lifted in prayer, almost always in a particular kind of open brick oven, with arches across the front allowing us to see the leaping flames (Figure 23). The youths are dressed in short tunics, and usually wear phrygian-style caps on their heads,

*Figure 23* Three youths in the furnace, Via Latina Catacomb.
©The International Catacomb Society. Photo: Estelle Brettman.

probably intended to signal their eastern (in this case Babylonian) origins. A somewhat less common image – that of the three youths shown refusing Nebuchadnezzar's orders to bow down and worship the idols – also appears in the artistic repertoire of the late third and early fourth centuries. These scenes include figures of soldiers as well as the person of Nebuchadnezzar, whose face is exactly identical to the visage of the idol, placed on top of a column.[26]

Many of the "fiery furnace" scenes are juxtaposed with a figure of Noah, at sea in his box-shaped ark, and about to receive the dove with the olive branch (Figure 24). The frequent connection of these two biblical images suggests that they should be understood as belonging together. The scene of the youths' (or Daniel's) refusal to worship idols often appears in conjunction with scenes of the magi bringing their gifts to the Christ child, perhaps to suggest the contrast between true and false veneration of the divine being, or perhaps to suggest the victory of true wisdom and worship over sorcery and idolatry (Figure 25).

Most interpreters of this scene propose that the three youths in their fiery furnace represent prototypes of the early Christian martyrs. Since the three faithful Jews were put into the furnace because they refused to bow down and worship the god of the Babylonians, they logically prefigure early Christians who stood up to religious persecution of secular authorities on

*Figure 24* Three youths and Noah on the front frieze of a fourth-century sarcophagus, now in the Vatican Museo Pio Cristiano.
Photo: Author.

*Figure 25* The three magi presenting gifts to the Christ child on the front of a fourth-century sarcophagus now in the Vatican Museo Pio Cristiano.
Photo: Author.

similar grounds.[27] Early Christian writers also saw this significance in the biblical story, beginning at least as early as the late first-century epistle known as 1 Clement.[28] Subsequently, both Tertullian and Cyprian interpreted the story of the three youths as a moral exhortation to the ambivalent and an encouragement to the courageous during the times of persecution during the early to mid-third century. These North African writers particularly emphasized the three youths' refusal to venerate pagan idols and remain faithful to God.[29] Cyprian's use of the story of the three is nothing less than exhortatory:

God in His goodness has allied with you in glorious confession young boys as well; to us He has made manifest deeds such as those illustrious youths Ananias, Azarius, and Misael once did. When they were shut up on the furnace, the fire drew back from them and the flames yielded them a place of refreshment, for the Lord was present with them proving that against His confessors and martyrs the heat of hellfire could have no power but that those who believed in God would continue ever safe and in every way secure. I ask you in your piety to ponder carefully the faith which those boys possessed, a faith which could win God's favour so fully.[30]

In a later epistle Cyprian remembers to add that the "dignity of the youths' martyrdom was in no way diminished merely because they emerged unscathed."[31]

Undoubtedly, then, the images must to some degree reflect on the theme of martyrdom. Yet, their frequent placement next to Noah suggests two other possible interpretations – one that parallels the destruction of the sinful race by means of water and fire, and the other that places emphasis on Noah's and the youths' salvation, or rescue from death, rather than their willingness to undergo it.[32] The former interpretation, seeing this image as a reference to the eschatological judgment day, opts for a moralistic emphasis: out of destruction, the righteous (and only those) shall be rescued.[33] As visual parables of judgment these subjects are related to the harvesting scenes described above (Chapter 2). Interestingly, these scenes of Noah juxtaposed with the three youths often appear on opposite sarcophagus ends (cf. Figure 26), just as the grape and grain harvests are juxtaposed on other monuments.

The second alternative interpretation that emphasizes rescue as resurrection, rather than the salvation of the righteous alone, seems less threatening and more hopeful – especially given the funereal context of the art. The story of the three children in the furnace is a demonstration of the preservation or resurrection of the physical body and seen along with Noah in his ark, both images serve as typologies of baptism (which itself contains the promise of physical resurrection).[34] Here we turn more to the typological tradition within the New Testament itself than to early Christian literature, beginning with 1 Peter 3:20–1, Noah's watery travail was often understood by early commentators as an Old Testament figure of baptism.[35] The dove serves as a connecting symbol – the dove arriving at the ark in the scenes is a twin to the dove which descends on Jesus in portrayals of his baptism. Like Noah, the three youths are also figuratively baptized since martyrdom was considered a "baptism of blood," a tradition that may reflect the imagery in

*Figure 26* Three youths on sarcophagus end now in the Vatican Museo Pio Cristiano.

Photo: Author.

the epistle known as 1 John 5:6–8, which speaks of three witnesses to Jesus Christ: the Spirit, the water, and the blood. Moreover, when John the Baptist announces the coming of Jesus, he says that while he (John) only baptizes with water, the one to come will baptize with the Holy Spirit and with fire (Matthew 4:11–12). This last text, it should be noted, returns us to the theme of judgment since the fire that John describes consumes the earth at the end of time. Irenaeus had already summed up this complex symbolism in his reflection on several gospel passages concerning judgment (Matthew 3:10; 7:19; 12:18–22 and parallels):

> He gives to those who believe in him a well of water springing up to eternal life, but he causes the unfruitful fig tree immediately to dry up; and in the days of Noah he justly brought on the deluge for the purpose of extinguishing that most infamous race of humans then existent ... and it was he who in the days of Lot rained fire and brimstone from heaven upon Sodom and Gomorrah, "an example of the righteous judgment of God," that all may know, "that every tree that does not bring forth good fruit shall be cut down and cast into the fire."[36]

All these interpretations share the common theme of triumph over evil and victory over death – a theme appropriate for decorating a tomb or sarcophagus. At the end of the fourth century, John Chrysostom, sounding much like the earlier writers Tertullian and Cyprian, frequently used the three youths as models of courage, nobility, and steadfastness in the face of death, evil, or temptation. In more than one place Chrysostom speaks of the youths' escape from death as the equivalent of the Christian's escape from the devil and winning a wreath of victory, first through baptism and then by continually resisting evil. Thus Satan departs from the scene "fearing he should be the cause of our winning more crowns."[37]

## Scriptural images as sacramental symbols

Scholars have long noted that many of the figures painted in the catacombs or carved on the sarcophagi appear to be symbols or references to baptism and eucharist. Certain chambers in the Callistus catacomb even have been labeled "chapels of the sacraments."[38] This interpretation is especially attentive to the issue of program, or the relationship of adjacent images. For instance, chamber 21 contains representations of the baptism of Jesus, Jonah at rest and cast into the sea, Moses striking the rock, a fisherman, seven young men eating a meal, the resurrection of Lazarus, and the Good Shepherd. Chamber 22 similarly shows scenes of baptism, Moses striking the rock, a fisherman, the healing of the paralytic, Jonah tossed into the sea and back on dry land, the miracle of the loaves and fishes, a banquet scene, Abraham's offering of Isaac, the Good Shepherd, and the Samaritan woman at the well. The so-called crypt of Lucina, older than and originally separated from the Callistus catacomb, contains the often-reproduced facing figures of fish and loaves (Figure 12), as well as representations of the Good Shepherd and the baptism of Jesus.[39]

But Callistus wasn't the only catacomb to have sacramental programs painted on its walls. The catacomb of Vigna Massimo's "Loculus of the Epiphany," probably painted during the early to mid-fourth century, shows Jesus healing the paralytic, raising Lazarus, and multiplying the loaves, the adoration of the magi, Moses striking the rock, Tobit and his fish, Noah in the ark, Daniel with his lions, and the reclining river god (Jordan). Similarly, sarcophagi also seem to have been designed with unified sacramental programs. Consider, for example, the design of the Sta. Maria Antiqua sarcophagus, in which the iconography is unified by a water flow, beginning on the left with the Jordan River emptying his jug and continuing with portrayals of Jonah's boat, an orant, a seated philosopher, the Good Shepherd, John baptizing Jesus, and a group of fishers on the right end (Figures 13a–c).

Some of these subjects are manifestly sacramental (e.g. representations of the baptism). Scenes of the multiplication of the loaves and fishes and later on the wedding at Cana may have been eucharistic figures. The enigmatic meal scene, although variously interpreted as a representation of a eucharist, agape meal, funerary meal, and the Last Supper, and finally as the Messianic Banquet, must in any case have sacramental significance.[40]

Some of the most popular early Christian images clearly had more than one meaning. As we have already seen (above, ch. 2), the fisher, and especially the fish, serve both as eucharistic and baptismal typologies. Old Testament stories often became typologies of baptism or eucharist. Jonah's plunge into the sea and his re-emergence to new life, for instance, can be as much a symbol of baptism as a prefiguration of Jesus' death and resurrection – especially given the paschal significance of baptism in general (cf. Romans 6.3–4). In Ravenna's church of S. Vitale and at S. Apollinare in Classe, scenes of Abraham serving his three visitors and nearly sacrificing his son are joined with portrayals of Abel's and Melchizedek's offerings as types or prefigurations of the eucharist. Likewise, Lazarus' raising may be a type of Jesus' resurrection, a general reference to the death and resurrection undergone by neophytes in baptism, or a specific reference to the resurrection of the deceased (promised in baptism).[41] And as discussed above, the scene of the three youths in the fiery furnace may refer simultaneously to martyrdom, to salvation through baptism, and to the final judgment. Interpretation of many other images as either baptismal or eucharistic relies on a receptive sensitivity to symbolism supported by the evidence of allegorical or figurative interpretations by early Christian writers.

As stated above, Paul identifies the Israelites passing under the cloud and through the sea as a figure of baptism and interprets Christ as the Rock that provided the supernatural water (1 Corinthians 10:1–5). The text of 1 Peter 3 represents Noah's being saved "through water" as corresponding to baptism. The tradition continues into and beyond the apostolic age, however. Justin Martyr also cites Noah's rescue as a prototype of baptism.[42]

In his elucidation of the rite of baptism, Tertullian provides a whole catalog of biblical "types" of that sacrament, including the flood, the crossing of the Red Sea, Jesus' baptism, the miracle at Cana, Jesus walking on the water, Pilate's washing his hands, and the water from Jesus' wound on the cross.[43] Cyprian adds the stories of Moses striking the rock and the Samaritan woman at the well to the list of baptismal figures and then expands even more to claim that as often as water is mentioned in scripture, baptism is proclaimed. Ambrose includes the story of the flood and the healing of Naaman the Syrian in his list of scriptural prefigurations of baptism.[44]

Thus, any image incorporating miraculous water, the water of life, or the healing properties of water may symbolically refer to baptism. Mid-fourth century representations of the healing of the paralytic and the man born blind, as well as stories of the woman at the well, and even the wedding at Cana, are cases in point. In the Johannine stories of Jesus healing the paralytic (John 5:1–15) and the man born blind (John 9:1–12), the characters that need to be healed are the victims of sin, and each healing involves a sacred pool. Rare early illustrations of Jesus healing the leper should cause us to remember the healing of the leper Naaman by means of his sevenfold plunge in the Jordan River (2 Kings 5:1–14). Similarly, the woman at the well is represented as a sinner in need of the water of life, provided by Jesus. Significantly all these stories were texts particularly associated with the preparation of catechumens for baptism in the early church.[45]

Taken at face value, the representation of Jesus transforming water into wine at the wedding at Cana (Figure 27) might be explained as a eucharistic figure, given the place of the wine in the story. However, since the miracle includes a transformation of water and the symbolism of the wedding party – both aspects of early baptismal liturgies – it may have (at least) a dual symbolic value.[46] Additionally, the Cana wedding text often was read during the season of Epiphany, when Jesus' baptism by John was also celebrated. Epiphany was thus the festival that commemorated Jesus' nativity, his baptism, and the first miracle of his public ministry. As such, Epiphany was an appropriate baptismal season in many parts of the world, and some eastern churches added a rite of sanctifying holy water for the faithful to carry away with them.[47]

*Figure 27* Jesus changing the water to wine at Cana with orant figure (far right), with Moses striking the rock and the arrest of Peter (left and center) on a late fourth-century sarcophagus now in the Vatican Museo Pio Cristiano.

Photo: Author.

The stories of Noah and Jonah reveal the life- and death-giving properties of water, and visual representations of these figures may remind viewers that baptism is a type of death and rebirth.[48] The iconography of Moses' rock miracle suggests that this story, like the crossing of the Red Sea (and later the crossing of the Jordan), signified the "baptism" of the Israelites. Paul himself first suggests this particular interpretation (1 Corinthians 10:1–5) followed by the assertion that Christ is the rock, the source of living water.[49] Cyprian expands Paul's symbol and suggests that Christ (the rock) was "struck" by the spear at the crucifixion, and the life-giving fluid is the blood and water that flowed from his wound.[50]

Two of these "sacramental" catacomb images also appear in the Dura Europos baptistery: the woman at the well and the healing of the paralytic. The other scenes that archaeologists found and identified in that space include Christ walking on the water (or stilling the storm), the five wise brides and their lamps (or the women arriving at Jesus' tomb), David and Goliath (probably), and – over the font itself – a figure of the Good Shepherd and his sheep above a smaller painting of Adam and Eve (Figure 28). Adam and Eve were the perpetrators of the fall, which Jesus, the New Adam (and the Good Shepherd), reverses. Christians re-appropriate original human nature and begin their pilgrimage back to Eden beginning with the rite of baptism.[51]

In addition to the fact that the sacramental interpretation gives the images a great deal of programmatic consistency, it accounts for the context, composition, and selection of the art itself. Decorating a tomb with symbolic references to eucharist, or especially baptism, is not surprising considering the belief that these sacraments are essential – especially to the dead and dying – as assurance of eternal life. Such assurance is arguably even more important than reminding viewers of God's previous interventions in times of crisis. As Paul's letter to the Romans 6:3–4 states so clearly, baptism represents the Christian's participation in Christ's death and resurrection. Moreover the use of abridged compositions demonstrates the transformation of certain narrative scenes into metaphors or types which direct the viewer to a secondary meaning. Even the sometimes baffling selections and compositions become intelligible when one understands these figures as symbols pointing to something other than the plain sense of the story.

Finding sacramental symbolism in early Christian art, of course, does not rule out other interpretive possibilities. As noted above, some figures, including the three youths in the fiery furnace, Daniel in the lions' den, and Susannah, seem to refer primarily to danger and deliverance. Their sacramental meanings are less obvious, but not necessarily absent.[52] Similarly, no overt sacramental significance can be found in the images of Jesus healing the woman with the issue of blood, or the arrival of the magi.[53] These other subjects may be useful reminders that interpretive systems cannot be applied

*Figure 28* Reconstruction of the interior of the Christian baptistery at Dura Europos (*c.*245).

Photo: Rights and Reproductions Department, Yale University Art Gallery.

immutably. Moreover, the nature of symbols is never to be restricted to one meaning only, and their possible interpretations are never mutually exclusive. Baptism, for example, is an extraordinarily complex rite with expansive theological signification. Therefore, artistic references to this sacrament ought to be as layered or multi-faceted as baptism itself which, at its absolute core, points to the essential hope of the Christian believer – the promise of eternal life. Baptism, after all, is the beginning of the hope of eternal life and the sign of that promise. Without doubt, especially in a funeral context, the symbolism of baptism points directly to the expectation of resurrection from death.

## Biblical themes before and after Constantine

Although Paul cites it as a baptismal typology (1 Corinthians 10:2), no known appearances of the Israelites' passage through the Red Sea in Christian art occur in the pre-Constantinian period. In the mid- to late fourth century, however, this image suddenly became popular, appearing in the reliefs of more than twenty sarcophagi and three known tomb frescoes: two in the Via Latina catacomb, and one at El-Bagawat in Egypt.[54]

When this new subject appears, certain older extremely popular motifs begin to disappear, starting around the year 325: the figures of Noah and Jonah in particular, along with the Good Shepherd and the praying figure (orant).[55] Such changes in the dominant themes of Christian art might have been the result of changes in the cultural or theological climate, or may be explained more simply by a change in what was appropriate for the new venues of Christian art that emerged along with the patronage of the emperor. Beginning in the second quarter of the fourth century, Christian iconography was no longer primarily oriented to a sepulchral context – that is, to a setting particularly suitable for themes related to death and resurrection, e.g. the Jonah cycle. However, new images that were created for tombs and sarcophagi, such as the crossing of the Red Sea, may have replaced earlier sacramental types.

Thus the expansion of possible settings for Christian art works after 325 coincided with the gradual disappearance of some extremely popular motifs and the arrival of entirely new ones. As we have already seen, the shift was not simply a one-for-one swap; the mid-fourth century saw a significant enrichment of the Christian iconographic repertoire. New subjects and themes that appeared throughout the fourth and fifth centuries included the above-mentioned Moses narratives (the giving of the law was also added), and new representations of Jesus: Jesus' nativity, Jesus as giver of the law, his entrance into Jerusalem, his arrest and trial, his resurrection and enthronement, and finally, in the early fifth century, Jesus' crucifixion. Equally significant were new, non-narrative images including the emergence of saints' portraits along with portraits of Christ and his mother.[56]

Perhaps far more than the catacomb frescoes, the mosaics and sarcophagus carvings of the fourth and fifth centuries reflected the changing artistic repertoires. Added to this development was the noticeable change to a more polished or refined style and technique of the work. To some extent this transformation can be credited to the changing fortunes and culture of the church. New upper-class patrons along with the imperial family subsidized a transformation in both artistic style and quality beginning in the reign of the pagan Diocletian and lasting until the end of the century under Theodosius. Thus Christian art works aimed to express the triumph and majesty of the newly arrived church, as well as its emerging central place in the dominant culture. Both secular (lay) and ecclesiastical treasuries funded the decoration of church buildings, purchased richly decorated liturgical as well as elegant private devotional objects, and paid for the adornment of family tombs. These commissions were new kinds of status symbols, lending honor to the donor as much as they glorified God.

Along with the general refinement of Christian art came a gradually increased formalism and frontality, as if in anticipation of the Byzantine style. A well-known example of both an aristocratic patron and the new opulence in art is the marble sarcophagus of the prefect Junius Bassus, dated

359 – his name, title, and the year of his consulship all known from the inscription on his coffin. In addition to a stylistic evolution in sarcophagus reliefs and wall painting, artists began to decorate the walls and floors of churches with mosaics, and the covers of gospel books (or ecclesiastical diptychs) with intricately carved ivory, and produced a variety of smaller vessels, furnishings, and textiles. The practice of illuminating manuscripts began in the mid-fourth century, although the earliest known illustrated Christian books date to the early fifth century.

Accounting for the fourth-century transition in iconographic themes is more difficult than explaining the revolution in style, variety, and quality of the works. As noted above, certain themes disappeared while others appeared in this era. In addition to the new Moses and Jesus representations, other previously unknown images include some healing scenes (the man born blind, and – perhaps – the leper), and some miracles (the transformation of water to wine at Cana, the raising of the son of the widow of Nain or Jairus' daughter from the dead). New themes taken from the Hebrew scriptures included the ascension of Elijah and the trials of Job. However, not all the "old images" disappeared when the new arrived. Adam and Eve, Daniel, the raising of Lazarus, Abraham's offering of Isaac, the woman at the well, the woman with the hemorrhage, the healing of the paralytic, and the miracle of the loaves and fishes were all carried over into the next era. Moses in the rock-striking scene was transformed into Peter (Figure 29), possibly inspired by a legend that told of Peter's baptizing his Roman jailers with water that sprung forth when he struck the walls of his cell.[57] These familiar subjects also make the transition to new media (e.g. mosaics, glass, and terracotta) and contexts (e.g. churches, and devotional objects) as well.

Many of these images appeared for the first (and often the only) time in the so-called Via Latina catacomb, whose frescoes all date to the post-Constantinian era. This burial place of approximately 400 persons demonstrates not only that Christians continued to use catacombs for burials into the mid-fourth century but also that, judging from the superior quality of the workmanship, some of them could afford highly skilled artisans. In addition, given the number of pagan subjects juxtaposed to Christian compositions, it appears likely that the wealthy Roman families who buried their dead in this catacomb were of mixed faiths, some (probably the menfolk) still honoring the traditional Roman gods, and some (their wives and daughters?) having converted to Christianity.[58]

Here were found unique representations of the offerings of Cain and Abel, Noah lying drunk, Joseph's dreams, Joseph meeting his brothers, a baby Moses being lifted out of the rushes, Absalom hanging from the tree, Samson waving the jawbone of an ass at the Philistines, Moses and the Israelites crossing the Red Sea (previously known in sculpture), Jacob's ladder, and Abraham entertaining his three visitors. These scenes are juxta-

*Figure 29* Peter striking the rock, Catacomb of Commodilla.
©The International Catacomb Society. Photo: Estelle Brettman.

posed to images of the Roman gods Demeter and, especially, Hercules performing his labors and, significantly, guiding Alcestis out of the underworld back to her husband Admetus. In addition to these unparalleled subjects, the Via Latina catacomb also reproduces some standard motifs – Jesus and the Samaritan woman at the well, Abraham offering Isaac, and Adam and Eve.

The most significant additions to the catalog of Christian images in the post-Constantinian period, however, were new representations of Jesus. Many of these new subjects are less narrative-based, and are more dogmatic in nature – reflecting on the nature, divine status, and work of Christ more generally. Whereas before Jesus had appeared primarily as a teacher or healer, during the fourth century Jesus began to be represented in a formal pose, standing on a rock from which flow the four rivers of paradise, or seated on a throne, sometimes resting his feet on the mantle of the god Caelus. These stately compositions show Jesus making a gesture of speech (or blessing) with one hand and holding a scroll or gospel book in the other (Figure 33). Two or more disciples are usually shown with Jesus, receiving the scroll, offering homage, or simply being instructed by their teacher.[59]

In addition, the post-Constantinian age contributed innovative representations of particular episodes in Jesus' life which had no previous place in the iconography. Although not entirely unique (there is one third-century image of the magi), scenes of the three wise men offering their gifts to the

Christ child seated on his mother's lap become quite common. Implicit references to Jesus' passion begin to show up in the art – his entrance to Jerusalem riding on a donkey, washing the disciples' feet, his arrest and trial, Pontius Pilate washing his hands, and references to Peter's denial. Although representations of the crucifixion *per se* are essentially unknown before the sixth century, the empty cross as a symbol of victory is one of the fourth century's characteristic images (Figure 43).[60]

The shift in Christianity's status and patronage alone is not sufficient to interpret the meaning of the new arrivals, the disappearance of other figures, or even to explain why some images survived the transition. New theological emphases are clearly evident when the iconographic themes are viewed programmatically. A definite movement away from the centrality of the sacraments, miracles, and healing stories clearly exists. Familiar types borrowed from the pagan catalog as well as other allegorical or typological figures are less frequent. These themes are not entirely displaced, but rather placed in relationship to powerful artistic representations of the risen and triumphant Christ, or alluding to his incarnation and passion. The content of the iconography may be less "scriptural" or less traditionally symbolic, but no less meaningful – a meaning that will be considered in the following chapters.

## Conclusion

Expanding our interpretative methods leads us away from seeing the pre- and post-Constantinian eras as being radically discontinuous. Instead, we are allowed to see the developments of the fourth century, both thematic and stylistic, as positive growth and change, organic to the faith itself as it spreads and gains converts among all classes of society. Moving out of the almost purely sepulchral realm, Christian art has a broader message, a larger audience, and may now accommodate itself to a grander "playing field." No doubt part of that grand field includes some imperial allusions, but our interpretation cannot be limited to seeing those allusions alone.

To reiterate, visual art was an important medium for theological reflection. Moreover, both broad iconographic themes and the particular subjects within these themes paralleled and reflected the presentation of the faith in other media, including dogmatic writings, homiletical or exegetical works, catechesis, and liturgies. In the early period, one of the main foci was the hope of resurrection from death, initially promised through the sacrament of baptism and reinforced through life in the worshiping Christian community. Those themes would thus naturally appear as the central motifs of early Christian art, not least in funerary contexts. As the circumstances of the church changed, so did the focus of this theological reflection (e.g. from individual death and resurrection to the triumph of the Christian faith and Christ's divine realm), a change of focus that was manifest as much in the visual art as in the literature produced in a particular era.

The previous chapter showed that Christian art of the early period both adapted and transformed elements already present in the religious and artistic environment, making them sensible to a new context. Such a program was not altogether different from the work of prominent theologians writing at the time. This chapter argued that Christian art also served the function of scriptural interpretation, again, along a parallel to Christian writings of the era. The key to understanding why particular emphases appeared in the art may lie, at least in part, in study of those texts.

A second, perhaps equally important, key is the social and cultural situation of the church and individual Christians at the time. Each of these keys points to the centrality of the community, both its formation and survival. Values represented in the imagery first reinforce this community in the face of present political opposition (leading to martyrdom) and against the lure of idolatry and cultural assimilation, and second in the reinforcement of its hope for the future – the eschatological home (promised in baptism).

Although primarily influenced by textual sources and the art of the surrounding culture, at some point along the way they developed an independent or substantial significance. Particular representations began to have a life of their own in the tradition and to an extent became detached from their earlier artistic/literary roots. Symbols may be weighted with enough meaning to stand on their own and cease to need their old connections by way of explanation. The image of Jonah in early Christian art may be one of these types. The whole story of the prophet Jonah is almost entirely superfluous to the significance of standard Jonah scenes on funerary monuments. A figure of Noah needs few textual props, since its meaning is almost entirely in its shorthand symbolism – symbolism which only distantly refers to the original story of Noah in the book of Genesis.

But whether text-based iconography gradually detaches from, or tenaciously clings to, its narrative sources, as tools for interpretation images open up texts in ways that writing or speaking alone cannot do. Pictures that previously were envisioned only in the individual imagination now become more concretely visible and even confrontational. Readers or listeners become witnesses – even participants; inhabiting the scene as audience in a different way than they did before. Moreover, since the art work is public and seen by others, the representation becomes a social, rather than personal, experience. Viewers hold the representation in common.

# 4

# PORTRAITS OF THE INCARNATE GOD

## Introduction

During the fourth century when Christianity made the transition from an oppressed minority religion with a fairly introverted and circumscribed system of visual symbols to an active and public religion patronized by the Roman emperor himself, a corresponding new set of images as well as contexts for those images emerged. The grand, newly constructed churches in Constantinople, Rome, and the Holy Land lent themselves to – and even demanded – a new program of iconographic themes and, in particular, new ways of presenting the figure of Jesus Christ along with the Virgin and the saints.

At the end of the fourth century, Paulinus, a monk and later bishop of Nola, built a church in order to house relics of St Felix. He commissioned artists to decorate this building with a program of painted images of Christ and the saints along with scenes from particular biblical narratives. Paulinus admits to a visitor that the practice was an unusual custom, but defends such adornment both as a way of counteracting the continuing popularity of pagan idols, and as a device for enticing pilgrims to come inside the church instead of focusing their attention on the graves just outside, thus adapting elements of "popular" religion for the purpose of conversion and edification of the masses. The colorful paintings not only brought these simple folk inside, but "nurtured their believing minds with representations by no means empty."[1]

Paulinus probably had intended nothing more than edification and moral training, providing examples of holy men and women to be admired by the faithful flock. Even so, this text suggests that the relative proximity of a graveyard filled with relics of buried saints was compelling enough to cause Paulinus to offer competing attractions of the portrait variety. For this to serve his purpose, these portraits would need to have some of the same drawing points, that is they would need to possess an intrinsic quality of sanctity and be able to mediate that holiness to the pilgrims who came in to look. No doubt people began to grant the images inside a parallel power to the relics outside.

But such a development took time and portraits were relatively late arrivals in a catalog of early Christian artistic productions. The figures who appeared in narrative scenes were not in any sense portraits or even intended to be likenesses. Of the two types of Jesus images that dominated third- and early fourth-century art the first included what were arguably metaphorical or symbolic references to the character, teaching, or divine position of the Christian Messiah, either in the guise of Good Shepherd or philosopher, or through iconography borrowed from the visual presentations of Orpheus or Sol.

The second type of Jesus portrayal was drawn directly from specific scriptural passages and, as such, was more literal and specific and less symbolic and general. Examples from this second type, painted in the catacombs or carved on sarcophagi, rarely represent Jesus alone, and instead show Jesus in a kind of narrative tableau. Usually a beardless youth, in a long tunic, Jesus is most often the central figure in a scene that included other figures and added props or story details. With the exception of the representation of his baptism by John (where he is often shown as child-sized and naked), Jesus is portrayed as healing, working miracles, or teaching. The other figures in the scene – the recipients or witnesses of these acts – normally have equal physical stature with Jesus and are similar in dress (although not in facial characteristics). For the most part, the other figures do not evidence extreme reverence or awe toward the figure of Jesus. Thus, these representations of Jesus would not be called portraits in the strict sense, but rather illuminations of scriptural narratives that seem to omit obvious manifestation of Jesus as unique Son of God or Divine Ruler (cf. Figure 31).

At the end of the third century and through the first decades of the fourth, new miracle or healing scenes were added to the Christian iconographical repertoire, including the healing of the man born blind, the changing of the water to wine at Cana, and the raising of Jairus' daughter (or of the son of the widow of Nain – Figure 30). Around the turn of the fourth century the adoration of the magi was included with the paintings in the Catacomb of Priscilla's Capella Graeca. In this early composition the three are shown approaching the mother and child, although without any other elements of the birth narrative – elements that would be added later in the fourth century (cf. Figure 25). The familiar iconic portrait of the Madonna and child had yet to appear.

From this one may conclude that early Christian representations of Jesus either presented general aspects of his character or teaching, or concentrated on his specific roles of wonderworker, healer, and teacher. His human nature or origin is apparent in his fairly ordinary stature, physical appearance, and relationship to other figures. His godly nature or identity may be portrayed through representations of his miracles and healings, but these compositions lack overt emphasis on divine majesty or power. Props, such as the wand he holds to change the water to wine, or the baskets of bread in the feeding

*Figure 30* Jesus raising Jairus' daughter (far right) with shepherds looking upon the Christ child and Jesus being baptized on a fourth-century sarcophagus, now in the Vatican Museo Pio Cristiano.

Photo: Author.

*Figure 31* Late fourth-century sarcophagus now in the Musée de l'Arles Antique (Arles).

Photo: Author.

96

miracle, serve a narrative function; they are not attributes specifically belonging to a god.

Although representations of Jesus speaking with the woman at the well or raising Lazarus continued through and past the Constantinian era, these scenes belonged more to the older cemetery context and gradually were replaced by the new iconographic themes of the mid-fourth and early fifth centuries, including Christ as enthroned, presenting the new law to the assembled apostles, nativity images showing the adoration of the magi, Jesus entering into Jerusalem, washing the feet of the apostles, or episodes from the passion narrative including representations of Jesus' arrest, his trial, Pilate's washing his hands, and the carrying of the cross (cf. Figures 32, 33 and 43, for example).

These new themes, which had little direct association with specific scriptural narratives, slowly replaced the older iconography, particularly on sarcophagus reliefs. By contrast, judging from the frescoes of the Via Latina Catacomb (generally dated to the mid-fourth century), catacomb frescoes conservatively continued to include scenes drawn from biblical stories, but now included some previously unknown scripture stories among their subjects. However, by the late fourth century underground burial in catacombs apparently ceased, and along with it this type of funereal decoration and many of its subjects.

Even so, the end of catacomb painting did not mark the end of narrative iconography altogether. Christian art maintained its scripture-based programs but in new contexts and different media. The early fifth-century mosaic panels along the naves of the basilicas of Sta. Maria Maggiore in Rome and a century later in S. Apollinare Nuovo in Ravenna continue to represent older biblical themes known from catacomb frescoes, along with many new ones. Fifth-century ivory plaques and book covers also were designed with small narrative scenes, many of which had been common in third- and early fourth-century catacomb or sarcophagus iconography. Later in the fifth century and through the sixth and seventh, liturgical objects made of precious metals or ivory also continued to show such scenes as Abraham offering Isaac, Moses striking the rock, Daniel among the lions, the raising of Lazarus, and the healings of the man born blind and the paralytic.

From the late fourth century on, illuminated manuscripts appeared that directly juxtaposed images with texts, making the artwork more clearly illustrative, although with no less potential to convey allegorical or typological meanings. Scholars who have theorized that lost, earlier illuminated manuscripts served as prototypes for such narrative cycles as the mosaic panels in Sta. Maria Maggiore or Ravenna's S. Apollinare Nuovo were undoubtedly influenced by the clearly illustrative aspects of these new narrative compositions. The proximity of text to the art work does not necessarily limit the function of the image to mere illustration, however. As is even more true in later medieval manuscripts, illuminations often played an

*Figure 32* Sarcophagus of Junius Bassus, *c.*359. Treasury of St Peter's Basilica, Rome.

Photo: Graydon Snyder.

exegetical function – if only in the matter of choosing which episodes they portrayed, and in what narrative sequence.

Thus narrative art based on biblical themes appears to have become somewhat more didactic, while the newer (less scripturally based) themes perhaps had a different purpose, despite the fact that the decoration of sarcophagi or ivories sometimes showed a combination of both types (Figure 32). In any event, it is clear from the gradual but certain shift of iconography that began in the late fourth century, that a new message was emerging in the visual vocabulary – one that spoke about the developing character of Christian faith in the post-Constantinian era. This new iconography was designed to emphasize the glory, power, and majesty of this triumphant religion, perhaps subtly associating it with the power and triumph of the Roman Imperium, or (alternatively) directly contrasting it with dying aspects of Roman traditional paganism and the old gods, and maybe even the imperial cult itself.

## The imperial Christ versus the human Jesus

A widely held hypothesis, here referred to as the "imperial style theory" explains some of these changes in artistic themes during the post-Constantinian era as Christian appropriation of imperial cult imagery: those artistic motifs or themes that glorified the Roman emperor and associated his rule with the divine will. For example, the visual presentation of a regnant Christ (Figure 35, for example) is thought to have been modeled on the figure of the enthroned emperor known from examples of imperial portraits, including those on early Byzantine coins and medallions. This explanation implies a further supposition that such transference of imagery was a less than subtle form of imperial propaganda – making the Christian savior the prototype of the secular ruler (or vice versa). These new compositions, evoking the majesty and power of the Byzantine court and its ceremonies became as much a glorification of the emperor as of the incarnate Son of God.

This "imperial style theory," hardly questioned in recent years and almost universally accepted by students of Christian art history, was primarily identified with the work of Ernst Kantorowicz in the 1940s and subsequently developed by such luminaries as Andreas Alföldi, and André Grabar.[2] Grabar thoroughly contrasted the pre- and post-Constantinian eras in his vastly popular handbook on Christian iconography in this way:

> [T]he earliest Christian iconography frequently employed motifs and formulas in more or less common use in all branches of contemporary art; what happened in the fourth century is similar, but distinct. All the "vocabulary" of a triumphal or imperial iconographic language was poured into the "dictionary" which served Christian iconography, until then limited and poorly adapted to treat abstract ideas ... . It is to the theme of the supreme power of God that Imperial art contributed the most, and naturally so, since it was the key theme of all the imagery of the government of the Empire.[3]

Although, at the beginning, art historians cautiously speculated that many of the sources of fourth-century Christian iconography might be found in imperial prototypes, recent literature has taken the hypothesis for granted and nearly every post-Constantinian art monument has been interpreted or explained in light of the theory, assumed to be valid.[4] For example, Robert Milburn's handbook on early Christian art and architecture states that "preoccupation with the authority of the emperor naturally led to emphasis on the majesty of Christ," and cites the portrait of Christ in the Catacomb of Comodilla as a clear expression of this "idea of Christ as Ruler of the Universe."[5]

This assumption has recently been challenged, however. In his monograph *The Clash of Gods*, Thomas Mathews critiques the scholarly presumption of an "emperor mystique" and suggests instead that Christians who had only recently gained cultural ascendancy translated the iconography of the pagan gods (rather than the imperial cult), in part as a way to signal or confirm the triumph and validity of the Christian religion. Thus, rather than ratifying the parallels between Christian God and Roman emperor, Christian art monuments actually challenged the ascendancy of both the traditional pagan gods and the enthroned secular rulers. According

99

*Figure 33* Jesus passing the law to Peter and Paul, late fourth-century sarcophagus now in the Musée de l'Arles Antique (Arles).

Photo: Author.

to Mathews, Christian art neither represented Christ as an emperor nor the emperor as Christ. Instead, the iconography promoted the changing of the gods, from the old to the new. As such the art of the fourth and fifth centuries had a more sacred than secular propagandistic purpose – it was a visual apology for the Christian God, not an elevation of the Christian emperor.[6]

This changed perspective offers a new interpretation of the figure of Christ handing the scroll to Peter or Paul (Figure 33), an image at least as full of theological as imperial implications. Jesus either sits with his feet upon the mantle of the god, Caelus, to indicate his place in heaven, or he stands on a rocky mound intended to represent Golgotha, the site of the crucifixion. The place of sacrifice is also the New Eden, however, since from it flow the four rivers of paradise. Here is neither the Jesus of the gospel stories, nor the antitype of the ruling emperor. Rather these new "dogmatic" images portray the post-resurrection Christ shown now above the mortal world and passing on the New Law to his apostles. Behind him are palms of victory, symbolizing his triumph.

Although Mathews' thesis offers an important moderating corrective to an overly simplistic explanation of fourth-century art that views post-Constantinian art as a radical departure from the earlier phase, the changing political situation of the fourth-century church undoubtedly contributed to the change in contemporary iconography. The Christian church underwent a transformation that changed it from persecuted cult into publicly supported religion, and along with that came the patronage of the ruler and his court – patronage that included building churches and adorning them in a manner befitting an emperor.[7]

Meanwhile, somewhat obscured by the debate about the reputed influence of imperial iconography on the character of Christian art of the fourth and fifth centuries, is the question of whether and to what degree doctrinal debates and constructive theology influenced the character and content of that era's imagery.[8] The first ecumenical council, called by Constantine and held at Nicaea in 325, tried to resolve the question of the full divinity of the Son. Subsequently the issues of the human and divine natures of Christ came to the forefront of theological debate. The degree to which these issues found expression in the visual art of the period has been an unresolved question.

A different analysis of the thematic changes in post-Constantinian iconography, however, might view this iconographic shift as evidence of a trend that moved away from an earlier, dominant, and even popular human, biblical, or "historical" Jesus and toward a self-sacrificing savior or, alternatively, a transcendent and mighty Lord and judge.[9] Such a conclusion brings in the issues of doctrinal debate, but only indirectly. Proponents of the argument support their thesis by noting that third- and early fourth-century representations of Jesus primarily as teacher, healer, and miracle worker contrast with theological, apologetic, or liturgical texts that emphasize Christ's self-sacrifice and his role as divine and resurrected savior, as well as apocalyptic judge. The distance between theological proposition and visual representation grows smaller in the fourth century, but not primarily because of ongoing debates about the nature of the Christ. Instead, the distinction between popular religion and official theology emerges as the explanation of the difference. Put simply, the art of the earlier period represents the life of Christ in a way not found emphasized by the doctrinal arguments of theologians or creeds promulgated by the churches. Such discontinuity between visual and literary data would support an argument that art and text in the earlier period served different audiences, social groups, or even ideologies, while later on art became conformed to the interests of the hierarchy of the church as well as the secular power.

By contrast, the proposition that representations of Jesus deliberately made visual comparisons with or allusions to the pagan gods and heroes who in a real sense were Jesus' competition offers a useful perspective. This theory presumes no necessary divergence between theological text and visual imagery, nor does it suggest that visual art emerged in and for a separate community from the one that included intellectuals, church officials, and theologians engaged with questions of Christian doctrine. Further adding to its appeal, this theory presumes that Christian iconography not only reflected aspects of Christian faith, but was directed outwardly, that it functioned both apologetically and as a tool of proselytizing. The imagery reflected more than a simple, naive faith. It actually played a role in presenting or explaining Jesus to those both inside and outside the believing community. This apologetic purpose was also the essence of Christian theology and rhetoric as seen in the literary evidence. Finally, such a theory explains the variety of presentations of Jesus in both art and literature, a variety that belies a simple dichotomy between the two modes of communication.

Moreover, neither an internal theological nor an external apologetic purpose limits Christian iconography to simple didactic or illustrative functions. Both usages presume that visual images could convey important aspects of Jesus' character or even larger matters of faith, typologically expressed through the use of scripture narrative. Perhaps the more interesting question is not whether the new images supported an imperial ideology, but whether (or how much) contemporary iconography can be seen to parallel or challenge the doctrinal formulations of the fourth- and fifth-century church and visually conveyed essential tenets of orthodox faith. That is, whether the two modes of communication (texts and images) are inherently different and diverge in their purpose (each having a unique theological function), or whether scholars can synoptically examine literature and visual art, looking for theological continuity or discontinuity without slighting what is special about each.

Both text and image emerge in a distinctly Christian and (considering the extant evidence) predominantly Roman context. Two divergent groups with clashing views of the savior seems improbable in what appears to have been a closely bonded community. Power struggles certainly existed, especially during and after stressful times of persecution, but prior to the Constantinian era recorded conflicts took place within the hierarchy, not between "simple believers" and their bishops and especially not between image users and text readers. Moreover, for the most part the art monuments were not inexpensive, nor entirely private. As such they were most likely commissioned by the wealthier members of the community – a group least inclined to dissent from the teachings of a literate hierarchy.

In fact, evaluation of the images and texts shows that they have similar, if not common, messages – especially if the narrative subjects are viewed as both broadly typological as well as more narrowly illustrative. Rather than widely divergent messages, the two modes (image and text) hold a fairly compatible kind of discourse. Furthermore, the fact that narrative compositions carried over from an earlier era continue to appear with "dogmatic" images from the next, both on the same monument, indicates a slow merging and then transition from one period to the next.

In any case, visual representations of Jesus, together with theological treatises, homilies, and apologies, helped establish and declare publicly what Christians believed about him, not solely for the purpose of formulating and expressing relatively subtle points of Christian doctrine, but also to narrate the stories of his life, to contrast the Christian divine man with the other gods and heroes of late antiquity, and to express some particular aspects of his character. If we examine early Christian imagery in terms of its apologetic function, then visual representations of Jesus' healing or working miracles can be seen as representing his divine attributes, not merely emphasizing his human ministry. This is why we see Jesus portrayed as Helios or Orpheus, or even the Good Shepherd or the philosopher in the third and early fourth centuries. According to Christian theology, Jesus is the sum of all those divine roles (e.g. light of the world, tamer of passions, caretaker of souls, teacher of wisdom) and perhaps much more than all the others in that he is all those things in one.

The conclusion one may draw from viewing Christian iconography in this way is that it neither directly serves the purposes of dogmatic treatises, nor contradicts them. Rather than positing diametrically opposed perspectives, audiences, or theological agendas, interpreters can examine art's active function as both an externally and an internally directed communication tool, rather than its more passive and limited role of merely reflecting official teachings, even popular views, about the person and work of Jesus. Both visual and literary imagery are complex and multivalent. No single Christological representation could ever serve the needs of the church and its people in the early centuries.

## Portraits of Jesus and the saints

In addition to those new iconographic programs described above, a new category (one perhaps deliberately avoided in the earlier period) appeared in fourth-century Christian art – the portrait. A bust of Christ found in the Catacomb of Comodilla is one of the first known "portrait" images of Jesus and in this case, against previous custom in the "narrative" scenes, Jesus is presented not full-figured but only to mid-torso, with halo and beard. No elements of scriptural narrative appear in this image – it is a simple portrait. On either side of Christ's head are the letters Alpha and Omega. Clearly this is a distinctive departure from earlier presentations and is an early version of what will come to be the standard presentation of the Christ Pantocrator (judge of all) of Byzantine tradition.[10]

Christians living in the fourth and fifth centuries were party to complex theological debate about the relationship of the Son to the Father, and the character of the two natures of Christ, truly divine and truly human. Throughout the debate theologians recognized that Christ must have had a human appearance (*persona* in Latin, *prosopon* in Greek), but before the mid-fourth century a formal portrait as such of Christ is unknown. After the mid-fourth century however, representations of Jesus begin to take on the qualities of portraiture. In addition to the portrait found in the Comodilla Catacomb, other fourth-century portrait images include those that show his disciples to his left and right. An example of this – a late fourth-century mosaic in the Catacomb of Domitilla – emphasizes the dogmatic expression of both Christ's divinity and his equality with the Father, the Domitilla mosaic in its legend: *Qui filius diceris et pater inveneris* ("The one said to be the

*Figure 34* Portrait medallion of Jesus with Peter and Paul, archepiscopal chapel, Ravenna (late fifth or early sixth century).

Photo: Author.

Son and found to be the Father"). This legend is arguably modalistic, even Sabellian, in its almost complete identification of the first two persons of the Trinity.[11] Other portraits are dated to around this time and soon after, and include portrait-style representations of Mary and the saints and apostles (Peter and Paul in particular) as well as of Jesus.[12]

One possible reason for the late appearance of such portraits is simple – no known portraits of Jesus or the saints were painted from life, and the gospels contain no written descriptions of Jesus' physical appearance. Traditions emerged regarding Jesus' facial features, expression, height, bearing, and so on, but these traditions developed gradually over many centuries. Legend also records miraculous portraits, such as the image of Jesus that was transferred to Veronica's veil when she wiped his face while he was carrying his cross to Golgotha.[13] Another such miracle is recounted in one version of the story of the first-century king of Edessa, Abgar, who, according to his request, received a portrait of Christ that was miraculously produced by direct impression of Jesus' face on a linen cloth (the *mandilion*).[14] These images "made without hands" (*acheiropoietos*) hold a special place in the history of icons, particularly as they are held to be the basis for subsequent portrait representations of Christ.

Even so, the lateness of a portrait tradition, especially given the Greco-Roman tradition of portraiture, suggests deliberate avoidance of this kind of iconography. Although art works in general were unaffected by a Judeo-Christian fear of idolatry, such fears may have impeded the development of portrait-painting because devotional images from other cults primarily took this form. In particular, images of the emperor, often used to test Christian loyalty to the state in times of persecution, may have hardened Christian antipathy toward this kind of pictorial art. In the imperial cult, as in the traditional cults of the pagan gods of Rome, statues or other portraits of emperor or gods were effective substitutions for the presence of the original. These depictions were offered a veneration that early Christian converts felt compelled to reject, even at the cost of martyrdom.[15] As stated above, representation of God's saving acts by means of narrative art was not equated with idolatry, and apart from some possible representations of the three persons of the Godhead on sarcophagi, no images of God, the first person of the Trinity, have come down to us from this early period.[16] Portraits of Jesus, that could become devotional objects in themselves, came much closer to being potentially idolatrous.

Nevertheless, several documentary sources suggest that there may have been anomalous early portraits of Jesus. One of these, an early third-century portrait of Christ placed in Alexander Severus' syncretistic pantheon, took its place along with other cultic images of Apollonius of Tyana, Abraham, and Orpheus.[17] In a slightly different version of the Abgar legend, the king of Edessa sent a messenger with a letter to Jesus, asking Jesus to come and cure him of an illness. The messenger returned with a portrait that he had painted of Jesus – a portrait that served as protection of the city of Edessa from enemy incursions.[18]

Another source, however, addresses the problem of idolatry directly. The second- or third-century apocryphal *Acts of John* relates an anecdote in which John's disciple, Lycomedes, surreptitiously obtained a portrait of John. Treating it as a devotional object, he brought it to his private chamber, crowned it with garlands, and set lamps and an altar before it. According to the story, when John learned that Lycomedes was venerating a portrait (without realizing it was a representation of John himself), he rebuked his disciple: "Lycomedes, what is it that you (have done) with this portrait? Is it one of your gods that is painted here? Why, I see you are still living as a pagan!"[19]

Although in the case of Lycomedes' icon, the disciple was venerating a portrait of an apostle who made no claim to divinity, the problem of divine representations emerges in a similar case recounted in a letter attributed to Eusebius of Caesarea. This document contains Eusbius' response to a request from the Empress Constantia (half-sister of Constantine and wife of Licinius) for a portrait of Christ that she had heard existed somewhere in Palestine.[20] Eusebius rejects the empress's request, not only by deriding such a practice as idolatrous, but also by arguing that because of his divine nature Christ could not be depicted pictorially. He asserts that no portrait could capture the "true unalterable image that bears Christ's essential characteristics" but rather only "his image as a servant in the flesh he put on for our sakes." However, because it cites arguments particular to the eighth-century controversy over icons (and unknown in fourth-century debate), scholars have rightly decided that the document is likely to be a forgery concocted by the later iconoclasts for the purpose of giving them ancient witnesses and authority.[21]

Because of the letter's doubtful date and authorship, we cannot regard it as evidence that fourth-century theologians, or even ordinary Christian consumers, were concerned about the practical problem of visually representing both of Christ's two natures in a portrait image. Jesus' divinity lay very much in the forefront of fourth- and fifth-century doctrinal debates, and councils concluded at least provisionally that both a truly celestial and a truly human nature were united permanently and "hypostatically" in Christ. However, no clearly established fourth-century document discusses the difficulty of artistically portraying Christ's conjoined human physical reality and divine glory.

In fact, in contradiction to this dubious letter, we find a different, more assuredly authentic Eusebian writing, in which the fourth-century bishop and church historian cited examples of Jesus portraits matter-of-factly and without severe criticism. In his *Ecclesiastical History*, Eusebius described certain bronze statues representing Jesus and the woman with the hemorrhage that were erected in Caesarea Philippi. He also mentioned having seen images of Christ preserved in painting.[22] In his treatise, *The Life of Constantine*, Eusebius also described sculptural figures of the Good Shepherd and Daniel commissioned by Constantine and erected to adorn public fountains in Constantinople.[23] The *Liber Pontificalis* similarly lists sculptural figures that were gifts of Constantine for the decoration of the Lateran Baptistery, including nearly life-sized figures of John the Baptist and Christ in cast silver along with a golden lamb and seven silver stags. The Lateran Basilica (to which the baptistery was attached) was also supplied with silver statues of Jesus and the apostles, as well as with an image of Jesus enthroned and surrounded by angels after his resurrection.[24]

Thus, despite ancient fears of idolatry and possible reticence about representing a savior whom the church asserted possessed both human and divine essences, portraits of Christ began appearing in the fourth century. With them emerged a new phase of Christian art. In this new phase, the image began to evolve as a form of revelation in its own right. In earlier generations themes of Christian art formed a continuum from the abbreviated, symbolic, and allusive on the one end, to the more literal and narrative on the other. Iconography, however, generally referred directly or indirectly to scripture. The emergence of the portrait changes the relationship of icon to source text. The image now transcends specific literary allusion, and has fewer obvious, external restrictions (Figure 34).

Once detached (partially or entirely) from familiar scriptural narratives, images arise out of new contexts, or relate to other needs or issues within the Christian tradition. These first portrait types fall somewhere along the trajectory that begins with visual images as a means of interpreting scripture, and ends with icons deemed worthy of veneration. While loss of direct biblical reference may seem to imply a gain of autonomy, these new compositions simply shift their point of reference to another place within the tradition. This new source appears to be the doctrinal developments of the fourth and fifth centuries. Thus Christian art of the mid-fourth century undergoes a shift in both form and content, while it both draws from and visually interprets the contemporary theological debates about Jesus' person, both human and divine.

## Dogmatic images and apse themes

Like the theological discussions which, while they draw upon scripture are not precisely biblical, portraits reinforce aspects of scriptural narrative they do not directly portray. Almost all theological arguments and constructions dealing with Christology and divinity operate from a scriptural base. Nevertheless, when the simplicity and familiarity of the older, narrative-based images are replaced with new representations of Jesus, these replacements appear to focus upon the transcendent and reigning savior of the church's creeds and away from the human miracle worker described in the gospels.

The first of these types, that of Jesus as giver of the new law, often referred to as the *traditio legis* (Figure 33), has already been discussed in brief. This image may be linked with the earlier philosopher figures (Figures 5, 6, and 10), since it presents Jesus as Moses' successor and begins to appear in the fourth century about the time the older image of the seated reader had begun to disappear. While early and mid-fourth-century iconography presented Christ seated and surrounded by his disciples, later fourth-, fifth-, and sixth-century compositions most often show Jesus seated or standing, and holding out an unrolled scroll (*rotulus*) to his apostles. An especially popular image for columnar sarcophagi during the Theodosian period, the type presents Jesus seated (sometimes on an orb but often with his feet upon the mantle of Caelus, the god of the heavens) or standing on an orb or rocky mount out of which flow four streams of paradise. Scholars have speculated that the type first appeared on the apse of St Peter's basilica and subsequently was copied elsewhere. In addition to the sarcophagi, extant fourth- and fifth-century apse mosaics also show these two variations on the theme of Jesus giving the law.[25]

This imagery might indicate the de-emphasis of pagan philosophical tradition or, more probably, Christianity's appropriation of it. The art presents Christ as divine mediator, and law- (or gospel-)giver – more suitable roles in an era when Christianity had triumphed, and no longer needed to claim intellectual legitimacy or equality with pagan religions or philosophy. Moreover, the crisis of Arianism challenged Christian theologians to expound a more uniquely Christian doctrine, at least superficially purged of Greek philosophical speculation and its semi-divine demiurge. Thus a discomfort with or suspicion of non-Christian philosophy in the fourth and fifth centuries may have precipitated the replacement of a generic philosopher figure with a specifically Christocentric model.[26]

Among the earlier fourth-century apse mosaics of the *traditio legis* are those in the mausoleum of Sta. Constanza in Rome (Figures 37–8), and the Chapel of S. Aquilino, adjacent to the Church of S. Lorenzo Maggiore in Milan. With these we should include the representation found on the domed ceiling of the baptistery of S. Giovanni in Fonte in Naples. While the two Sta. Constanza and the Naples mosaics present Jesus among the palm trees of victory, with one or two apostles (Peter and Paul), the Milan apse shows Jesus surrounded by all twelve apostles. The latter image, which presents Christ as a beardless youth, seated among his disciples and making the gesture of speech, seems to hearken back to the earlier, philosophical models and has striking similarities to the mosaic in the Domitilla Catacomb. The Milan Jesus holds a scroll taken from a *capsa* (a leather bag of scrolls) at his feet. However, the halo (with Christogram) and the unearthly gold background suggest that Christ is no ordinary teacher, nor is this a commonplace gathering of students.

The apse mosaic in the church of Sta. Pudenziana in Rome represents a different kind of transitional image (Figure 35). Here worshippers looked up from the nave of a large basilica and saw a majestic figure of Jesus enthroned in a high-backed, jeweled chair. Robed in purple and gold, the bearded and haloed Christ is larger than life-size and dominates the rest of the composition. Jesus holds an open book inscribed with the words, *"Dominus conservator ecclesiae Pudentianae"* ("I am the Lord, protector of the church of Pudenziana"). At either side of Jesus are seated the twelve apostles. Standing behind them are female figures, probably personifications of the churches of the Jews and Gentiles, offering crowns to Peter and Paul. The human figures are all seated in front of a tile-roofed portico behind which is a cityscape of Jerusalem, perhaps meant to represent the heavenly city. Above and behind Jesus' head rises a rocky mount and a gem-studded cross against a sky filled with clouds from which emerge the four beasts, symbols of the evangelists.

The original mosaic (which was radically trimmed in the 16th century) also had a lower register in the center of which (beneath Jesus' feet) stood a small *agnus Dei* (Lamb of God) on a hill out of which flowed the four rivers of paradise. Thus one majestic composition conveys almost the whole Christian theological program – vicarious sacrifice, victorious resurrection,

*Figure 35* Jesus enthroned with the apostles in the heavenly Jerusalem. Apse of the
Basilica of Sta. Pudenziana, Rome (*c.*400).

Photo: Author.

establishment of the universal church, judgment at the end time, and the
second coming Christ with the New Jerusalem. The lamb echoes the
message of the jeweled cross, and the four rivers of paradise the heavenly city.

Other existing fourth- through sixth-century apse compositions similarly
show Jesus in contexts that can only be described as unworldly, and drawing
upon theological or dogmatic themes rather than specific scriptural narratives. The apse of the basilica of SS. Cosmas and Damian in Rome presents
the now-familiar scene of Christ giving the scroll of the law to his apostles,
particularly Peter and Paul. In this early sixth-century composition
(*c.*526–30), however, Christ is shown ascending into a cloudy night sky.
Beneath him, still standing on the earth, are the church's two patron saints,
holding out their martyrs' crowns, and guided toward Christ by Peter and
Paul. Two other figures enter from the left and the right, behind the two
saints – St Theodore on the right, carrying his crown, and Pope Felix IV on
the left, holding a model of the church he founded. These six earth-bound
witnesses to Christ's ascension appear to be standing on the bank of the
Jordan River. In the lower register twelve sheep, probably representing the
twelve apostles, approach a central *agnus Dei* that stands on a rocky hill out
of which flow the four rivers of Eden. Above and to the left is a representation of the phoenix, symbol of resurrection, perched in a palm tree
symbolizing victory.

An earlier, fifth-century apse composition also portraying a transcendent Jesus is located in the church of Hosios David in Thessalonica (c. 425–50). This apse mosaic visually depicts John's vision of the Lord seated on a throne like a rainbow and surrounded by the four living creatures (Revelation 4). Christ, youthful and without beard, is shown enthroned on his rainbow, surrounded by a translucent aureole. Radiating beams of colored light emanate from the figure of Christ. Behind the bubble of light emerge the four winged creatures (ox, lion, eagle, and man). A jeweled cross is superimposed on Christ's halo and with his right hand he makes the gesture of speech or greeting, while with his left he holds a scroll that (translated) reads: "Behold our God in whom we hope and here rejoice in our salvation, for he will give us rest and hospitality in this house" (cf. Isaiah 25:9–10). At the lower right and left are human witnesses to this vision, the prophets Habakkuk (probably) and Ezekiel (certainly). The identification of Ezekiel is based on the fact that this prophet's vision was similar to the one described by John (cf. Ezekiel 10).[27] Beneath Christ's feet is a rocky mount out of which flow the four rivers, making a stream in which the submerged river god may be seen.

The glowing aureole, halo, and radiating beams of light were artistic representations of Christ's divine nature. The story of the Transfiguration particularly called for artists to portray Jesus' "transfigured" human persona. Gregory of Nazianzus, speaking of the illumination granted in baptism, says that "God is light … .That light, I mean, which is contemplated in the Father and the Son and the Holy Spirit, whose wealth is their union of natures, and the one extension of their brightness."[28] Gregory goes on to enumerate all the times light was manifest in the scriptures, including the light of the Transfiguration, too strong for the eyes of the three disciples who were present.

Images of the Transfiguration were composed for apses as well. Two well-known examples, one in the basilica of S. Apollinare in Classe, another at St Catherine's monastery on Mt Sinai, are quite different in appearance. In Classe the figure of Christ is reduced to a jeweled cross with a portrait bust, while at St Catherine's the figure of Christ is enclosed in a mandorla with several shimmering bands and radiating beams. His garments are pure white banded with shining gold (Figure 36). This depiction has parallels with Jerome's earlier written description:

> Yet our Lord was not so transfigured on the mountain that he lost his hands, feet, and other limbs, and suddenly began to roll around like a glowing sun or ball, but his hands and feet glowed with the brightness of the sun and blinded the eyes of the apostles. Likewise his clothes became white and glistening, but not ethereal … .[29]

*Figure 36* Transfiguration with Apollinaris, S. Apollinare in Classe, Ravenna.
Photo: Alinari/Art Resource, New York.

Haloes, aureoles, or mandorlas to indicate divinity first began to appear as attributes for Jesus around the middle of the fourth century – a signal that these motifs may reflect aspects of the debate about the nature and person of Christ. The radiate halo might also be associated with the figure of Christ-Helios as found in the third-century mosaic beneath the Vatican (Figure 9). The halo, borrowed from Hellenistic art as a symbol of divinity and occasionally seen on images of the Roman emperor, at first was applied in Christian art only to Jesus and the *agnus Dei*.[30] Eventually, the figures of the apostles, saints, Mary, angels, and the four evangelists' creature-symbols were also given haloes. Not necessarily gold, haloes were often blue, green, or white, and banded with contrasting colors. From the fifth century on, Christ's halo was often distinguished by its ornamentation with the Greek cross, a *chi-rho* monogram, or the letters Alpha and Omega.[31] The mandorla, a translucent round or lozenge-shaped disk bordered with concentric bands of color, differs from the halo in that it entirely surrounds the body of a divine being. Probably imported from Buddhist iconography originating in central India, the mandorla may have first appeared in Christian iconography mosaic in the Catacomb of Domitilla, and subsequently been applied in other apse compositions like those described above (Hosios David and St Catherine's).

All these iconographic devices – mandorlas or aureoles of light, enthroned and ascending figures of Jesus – communicated dogmas about the nature of the Christ and his judgment and salvation of the cosmos. These glorious and awe-inspiring visual compilations of Christian doctrine were significantly different from the didactic or exegetical images of previous generations, and yet viewers still learned much from them. Rather than emphasizing Christ's earthly ministry, this new iconography represents Christ's divine essence and his work of salvation, and such visual dynamics demand a visceral response of veneration or worship rather than an intellectual one of analysis or edification. Worshippers gazing at this kind of art while in prayer or participating in the liturgy could believe Christ was in some sense present in or through his image.

To a very real extent, the role of the image in this new context parallels the pagan traditions, including that of the emperor cult, although without making direct claims that the object itself was worthy of veneration. The art work brings the viewer into the presence of the prototype and acts as an intermediary between worshipper and object of worship. In Christ the invisible and eternal One became visible, present, and accessible (cf. Col. 1:15). But since direct engagement with the divine is impossible for ordinary humans, the image also protects both viewer and mystery. An invisible mystery is given a perceptible form.[32]

## Variations on a theme

One immediately apparent problem to viewers of Jesus' images in the fourth through sixth centuries is the wide variety of ways Jesus' appearance is depicted. Some images show him bearded and dark; some show him youthful and beardless, often with light hair and eyes. Rarer examples show an elderly Jesus, as on a sixth-century diptych from Constantinople. For example, consider the contrast between the two contemporaneous apses in Sta. Constanza (Figures 37 and 38) or between Jesus depicted in the Sta. Pudenziana mosaic and the Christ of the Hosios David apse. These latter two examples are also not so very far apart chronologically; the Sta. Pudenziana image is probably only twenty-five to thirty years older than its Greek counterpart.

Despite assertions in art-historical manuals, geographical distinctions alone do not sufficiently explain these divergent portrait traditions. The bearded Christ with dark hair, often referred to as an "eastern" or "Syrian" type, had been found in the west in fourth-century presentations in the Catacomb of Comodilla, a version in *opus sectile* from Ostia, and in the Sta. Pudenziana apse (Figure 35). Fifth- and sixth-century examples come from the Naples baptistery of S. Giovanni in Fonte, and the apse of SS. Cosmas and Damian. In contrast, we see the youthful, non-bearded type of portrait well-represented in Thessalonica at Hosios David.[33]

The two fourth-century examples of Jesus portraits in the relatively small mausoleum of Sta. Constanza present an interesting case in point. As we have seen, one apse shows Jesus blond, youthful, and mild-mannered; the other shows him heavily bearded, dark-haired and somber-faced. Something besides geographical traditions must account for these two distinct types –

*Figure 37* Jesus giving the law to Paul. Apse of Sta. Constanza Mausoleum, Rome (c. 325).
© The International Catacomb Society. Photo: Estelle Brettman.

*Figure 38* Jesus giving the keys to Peter. Apse of Sta. Constanza Mausoleum, Rome (*c.*325).

Photo: Author.

especially occurring at the same time in the same place. One possibility, that two different artists produced these works, is insufficient to justify the direct juxtaposition of contrasting images in a small building. Another explanation, that neither artists nor patrons would have noticed or cared cannot be countenanced.

A third possibility, that the two distinct images are simply perceptible forms given to particular intellectual or theological construct, must be considered. That the two types differentiate the pre-incarnate logos from the incarnate Jesus, one eternal and the other rooted in human history, is a tantalizing thesis, but very difficult to sustain when one studies the actual evidence. For example, both Christ figures in the mausoleum of Sta. Constanza are post-resurrectional images and to some extent have the same theme: Jesus' passing down of the law to the apostles Paul and Peter. In the mosaics that line the upper walls of the nave in S. Apollinare Nuovo, most of the New Testament images show Jesus without a beard, healing, teaching, and performing miracles (Figure 39). The bearded types appear in scenes associated with Jesus' passion (Figure 40).[34]

By the same token, the possibility that the bearded types are reserved exclusively for presentations of passion or of ruling majesty is contradicted by figures of a beardless Jesus in some of these same representations. Note

114

*Figure 39* Christ curing the man born blind, S. Apollinare Nuovo, Ravenna.
Photo: Alinari/Art Resource, New York.

*Figure 40* Christ before Pilate, S. Apollinare Nuovo, Ravenna.
Photo: Alinari/Art Resource, New York.

the images of Christ enthroned, entering Jerusalem (Figure 41), or standing before Pilate (Figures 42 and 43) from various late fourth- and fifth-century sarcophagi that maintain the youthful type. Moreover, many monuments show two distinct types of Jesus figures, both bearded and smooth-faced. No clear theological or narrative consistency dictates how or where these different Jesus images appear.[35]

Theoretically, the hypothesis that different theological stances produced the distinct images would explain the very different presentations of Jesus being baptized in the two famous baptistery medallions in Ravenna – one

*Figure 41* Jesus entering Jerusalem, sarcophagus from the last quarter of the fourth century, now in the Vatican Museo Pio Cristiano.

Photo: Author.

*Figure 42* Jesus before Pilate (on far right) on Traditio Legis sarcophagus (Abraham binding Isaac on far left); now in the Vatican Museo Pio Cristiano – *c.*360.

Photo: Author.

*Figure 43* Passion sarcophagus with empty cross, surmounted by Chi-Rho, now in the Vatican Museo Pio Cristiano (late fourth century).

Photo: Author.

built by the Arian king Theodoric, and modeled on the other, slightly earlier "orthodox" baptistery built by the catholic bishop Neon (Figures 44 and 45). The representation of Jesus' baptism in the Arian baptistery has clearly borrowed compositional elements from its earlier counterpart across town, and yet the face and body types of Jesus, as well as the Jordan River god, are entirely different in appearance.

*Figure 44* Mosaic dome medallion from the so-called Arian Baptistery (St Mary in Cosmedin), Ravenna, early sixth century.

Photo: Author.

*Figure 45* Mosaic dome medallion, Orthodox (Neonian) Baptistery in Ravenna, mid-sixth century.

Photo: Author.

As tempting as this hypothesis would be, however, no one has been able adequately to explain how these different portrayals relate to the doctrinal controversies over the full divinity of the second person of the Trinity. We cannot say that the Arian baptistery composition clearly emphasizes Jesus' humanity more than the comparable composition in the Neonian baptistery. Moreover, if such a theological program were overt and visible, it likely would have been erased or transformed when the Byzantine government reconquered Ravenna and turned the Arian baptistery into the "orthodox" church of Sta. Maria in Cosmedin.

A simpler and even more plausible solution might propose that the differences between these images correspond to traditional iconographic markers of youthfulness versus maturity. A full-bearded face suggests authority, majesty, and power and may be seen in the portraits of the senior male deities of the Roman pantheon – Jupiter and Neptune (Figure 46), or even the Egyptian import, Serapis. The clean-shaven visage more resembles the representations of Apollo or the youthful Dionysus (Figure 47), Mithras, and such semi-divines or human heroes as Orpheus, Meleager, and even Hercules.[36] A youthful appearance recalls the divine attributes most associated with personal savior gods.

119

*Figure 46* Busts of Apollo, Jupiter, and Serapis now in the British Museum, London.

Photo: Author.

Thus the diverse Jesus iconography may again point to the use Christians continued to make of the pagan prototypes. Christian iconography liberally borrowed from the classical repertoire in order to emphasize distinct divine activities or characteristics. The youthful Jesus type most commonly occurs in scenes of his "heroic" acts of healing or working wonders, images that may associate him with the suffering and tested heroes of pagan mythology who achieved immortality, sometimes by descending into the underworld (like Orpheus, Dionysus, and Hercules). The mature and bearded figure perhaps emphasizes Jesus' sovereignty over the cosmos. Here Christ takes Jupiter's place in the pagan pantheon, and the iconography makes that displacement explicit. Jesus' representation as a version of Apollo/Helios in the Vatican necropolis (Figure 9) demonstrates the way the Roman gods were directly challenged; Jesus usurps their place, often with iconographic attributes that make him quite similar in appearance to various pagan deities.[37] Christ is both judge and savior, and the iconography spells that out even if the direct parallels to other gods are indirect or unintentional.

## Jesus as wonderworker

Jesus often carries a wand (*virga*) in certain narrative scenes, both before and after the Constantinian era, especially when he is shown raising Lazarus from the dead or performing such wonders as changing the water to wine at Cana or multiplying the loaves and fishes. The wand, a prop not given to Jesus in

*Figure 47* Second-century figure of Dionysus-Bacchus, now in the British Museum, London.

Photo: Author.

scripture, belongs to Moses in scenes where he is shown parting the Red Sea or striking the rock that gushes water for the Israelites in the desert (Figure 17). This latter composition changes in the fourth century to show Peter striking the rock with a wand and baptizing his Roman jailers (Figure 29).[38] In an extraordinarily large number of sarcophagus reliefs, this scene of Peter is placed near, or next to, one of Peter being arrested. The implications for the association of Peter and Moses, especially on art monuments that originate in the vicinity of Rome, are obvious.

While Jesus commonly holds a wand in scenes of raising people from the dead or working certain wonders, he rarely holds the wand in contemporaneous images of healing. Rather, Jesus accomplishes these miracles by laying on his hand, making a gesture of speech or pointing to the sufferer. These images accord with the gospel accounts of Jesus' healings, in which touching or imposition of hands was the way healing was accomplished (for example Mark 5:23; 8.22; and Luke 22:51). The distinction between healing touch and working wonders by the aid of a wand sometimes appears in the same composition (Figure 48).

This iconographic distinction raises the possibility that Jesus' miracles divide into two distinct types, some that revealed his thaumaturgical abilities, others that distinguished him as healer, a role somehow different in significance from his function as wonderworker and revivifier. Although

*Figure 48* Fifth-century ivory diptych with miracles of Christ, now in the Victoria and Albert Museum, London (the Andrews Diptych).

Photo: Victoria & Albert Museum, London/Art Resource, New York.

both healing and wonders belong with the various "signs" of Jesus' power, third- and fourth-century Christians might have seen his healings as less "magical" in their performance. After all, they had seen magicians who worked amazing tricks and transformed inanimate objects or natural phenomena. Magicians usually were not healers. Moreover, despite the fact that the wand often turns into a cross in later compositions, its clearly restricted use in early Christian iconography demonstrates that that object cannot be explained simply as a staff of authority or royal scepter.[39]

The healing miracles are performed with gestures paralleled in Roman iconography, in particular the gesture of speech or blessing. The laying on of hands also appears in iconography that shows initiation to the Mithraic mysteries thus seeming to parallel the Christian images of Jesus' baptism. In addition to representation of baptism, the imposition of hands occurs in early Christian representations of Jacob's and Isaac's benedictions.[40] However, non-Christian healing iconography is virtually unknown, and none has been found associated with the pagan god of healing, Aesclepius, or the wandering hero-healer Apollonius of Tyana. Similarly, late-antique pagan parallels to Jesus' magic wand are also absent from extant compositions.[41] Thus both kinds of images are unique to Christianity, although the wand is more limited in its appearances and significance.

Even without iconographic evidence, however, historians of Christianity recognize the place and potency of magic in late antiquity. In the Acts of the Apostles (8:9–24), Simon the Magician tried to purchase the gift of the Holy Spirit from Peter and started up a competition between magical powers and the powers given by God to the followers of Jesus. Justin Martyr struggled to distinguish Jesus' miracles from the signs or wonders attributed to the pagan deities.[42] Origen was required to refute Celsus' comparison of Jesus with juggling tricksters and those "taught by the Egyptians" who practiced exorcism and healing, and who could make magnificent banquets appear out of thin air.[43]

When Celsus further argued that Jesus was an ordinary sorcerer whose wonders and miracles must be credited to satanic powers, Origen replied that supernatural acts can be credited either to divine or diabolical powers, and that Jesus' were the signs of his divine nature.[44] Here Origen recognizes Jesus' own purpose behind his extraordinary deeds. Such feats were (sometimes grudgingly) intended to proselytize. As Jesus said to the Roman official whose son was deathly ill, "Unless you see signs and wonders you will not believe" (John 5:48).

Like Justin Martyr and Origen, the gospel writers themselves acknowledged that witnesses perceived Jesus' acts as magical (cf. Mark 3:22 and parallels), but the evangelists stressed that the goal of these magical acts was to bring people to follow Jesus, and to help them recognize who had sent him (cf. John 11:42). The acts weren't ends in themselves; they affirmed Jesus' power and gave witnesses and recipients a foretaste of what salvation meant. In his treatise on the Incarnation, Athanasius repudiates any real parallels between Jesus and ordinary magicians:

> But if they call him a magician, how can it be that by a magician all magic is destroyed, instead of confirmed? ... but if his cross has won the victory over absolutely all magic, and over the very name of it, it must be plain that the Savior is not a magician, seeing that even those demons who are invoked by the other magicians fly from him as their master.

Athanasius then went on to compare the healing powers of Christ and Aesclepius. The one only healed bodies, the other restored the body to its original nature.[45] Thus Jesus is not the equivalent of an everyday magician; his supernatural acts were only a by-product of his identity. Nevertheless, Jesus' miracles, especially his phenomenological wonders, clearly fit the ordinary categories of Hellenistic magical practices, even if they demonstrate his ultimate victory over magic and all magicians.[46]

Representations of Jesus holding a wand gradually disappear after the beginning of the fifth century, when the wand is sometimes transformed to a cross, or dropped altogether. Interestingly, in the later scriptural narrative scenes that appear especially in ivory carvings or mosaics, when Jesus is shown with a halo his wand often is omitted. Conversely, in cases where Jesus is shown with a wand his halo is then omitted. This is very clear on two fifth-century ivories that show both halo and wand, but not in the same scenes. The significance of an apparently deliberate choice to give Jesus one or the other attribute is difficult to explain unless the wand somehow makes the halo inappropriate, a theory that would be challenged by the image on a fifth-century silver relief that shows both a halo and a wand.[47] The simplest answer is that the wand was an attribute that was gradually phased out – perhaps because viewers were more and more removed from a time when competing with the other gods or wonderworking was necessary. By the end of the fifth century the contest was over.

## Jesus' feminine attributes

One of the most striking and, to modern eyes, curious aspects of the beardless, youthful image of Jesus is Christ's endowment with feminine physical characteristics, including small protruding breasts, sloping shoulders, wide hips, and long curling hair. Such representation obviously contrasts with the darker, bearded type of Jesus image, but it also often presents an image of Jesus that differs from congruent representations of the apostles, who usually are given quite masculine appearances, with clipped beards, short hair, broad shoulders, and square jaws. The contrast between Jesus and his apostles shows up very clearly on several fourth- and fifth-century sarcophagi (cf.

Figures 42, 48). Such feminine features led to the original misidentification of a famous statue of Christ as a seated woman poet.[48]

Thomas Mathews discussed several fifth- and sixth-century representations of Jesus in feminine guise, with long, curling hair and prominent breasts, paying particular attention to Jesus' hairstyle and remarking: "In the ancient world, as indeed in all periods of human history, there was a language of hairstyles."[49] Such abundant and effeminate locks might have offended earlier Christian observers, however. The apostle Paul claimed that long hair was degrading to men (1 Corinthians 11:14–16), and Clement of Alexandria was similarly disapproving:

> Let men's heads be shaved unless they have curly hair, and let the chin have hair. Do not let curls hang far down from the head, turning into women's ringlets. For an ample beard is appropriate for men. And yet if a man shave part of his beard, it must not become entirely bare, for this is a disgraceful sight.[50]

In fact, a curly hairstyle and beardless chin would have been against the prevailing fashion for Roman men in general, evidenced by the way the apostles and other male figures are portrayed in the images as well as contemporary portraits of emperors.

However, in contrast to mortal human males, long ringlets and beardless cheeks characterized the iconography of certain late antique gods – Apollo and Dionysus in particular.[51] Moreover, Apollo and Dionysus iconographic types also share other feminine attributes seen in the youthful Jesus images, including the round shoulders, small but obvious breasts, wide hips, and full cheeks of the nearly hermaphroditic figures described by Euripides, Ovid, Diodorus, and Seneca, or portrayed in the classical iconography.[52] Dionysus, especially, underwent a transition from a mature, bearded, Zeus-like figure on archaic Greek vases to a late-classical and Hellenistic appearance as a youthful, androgynous and "Apollonian" image. However, while the changes in Dionysiac types have been noted by art historians, the variants in Jesus' iconography (which parallel those of Dionysus) are rarely discussed in modern secondary literature.[53]

The parallels between Jesus images and Apollo or Dionysus in earlier Roman iconography raise certain fascinating theological issues, including whether some art objects were specifically commissioned by or for women, who envisioned or experienced Jesus as female, and whether they emerged in non-orthodox Christian communities that varied their gendered images of the Triune God and transferred particular attributes from the pagan deities to Jesus, including Dionysus' role as a god of fertility. Jesus' application of the metaphor "true vine" to himself (John 15:1) may have strengthened the parallel.[54]

The Montanists had women adherents who experienced Christ as feminine, although these groups were well outside the camp of mainstream Christianity by the fourth and fifth centuries.[55] Moreover, there is no evidence for arguing that upper-class Christian women would have been likely specifically to have commissioned feminized Jesus images or to have evolved a particular "women's style" in contrast to the works commissioned by men.

Tracing feminine attributes in Jesus imagery to heterodox forms of Christianity or gnosticism also seems far-fetched, especially considering the date of the monuments in question and their "mainstream" derivation. Although there is some textual evidence that gnostics made and venerated images, and also worshipped an androgynous savior who had characteristics of both mother and father, and sometimes son and daughter, there is very little evidence that this tradition could have carried on into the fifth century or later and have influenced official Christian iconography.[56] Known examples of gnostic art present a body of iconography, mostly small magical talismans, distinctly different from these well-known examples of Jesus as enthroned, or as law-giver.[57]

A more likely possibility is that representations of Jesus were simply consistent with the portraiture of the savior deities of the Hellenistic mystery cults, especially Apollo, Dionysus, and Orpheus. The iconography of Jesus merely borrowed from the traditional and familiar portrayals of those gods, perhaps in part because of their similar divine attributes. Serapis, too, was known to be represented with female breasts (although not beardless) and statues of that god are known to have been restored as the goddesses Roma or Minerva.[58] These classical types had come to be visually synonymous with the concept of deity; certain physical characteristics automatically signified divinity to the ordinary viewer. The power of association encouraged those characteristics to be transferred to Jesus iconography, as they had become a kind of artistic marker – or shorthand – for the appearance of a certain kind of god.[59] Jesus' transformation of water to wine at Cana and his statement, "I am the true vine," may account for the adoption of Dionysiac vintaging scenes for Christian monuments.[60] Perfectly orthodox Christians could image Jesus with feminine physical attributes because those attributes visually signalled characteristics that were deeply rooted in the visual language of the surrounding culture. However, not only were these borrowings intended to suggest that Jesus possessed certain godlike qualities, but in fact subsumed all divine attributes in one person.

Jupiter's portrayal and perception as majestic and powerful – both Lord and Judge – could be borrowed to transfer these same characteristics to Jesus in compositions like the enthroned Christ in the apse of Sta. Pudenziana. Certain aspects of Orpheus' or Dionysus' portrayal as idealized, youthful "savior" gods were likewise applied to images of Jesus.[61] The gods featured in the mystery cults of late antiquity were immanent and personal gods with whom devotees had intense encounters, not unlike Jesus. Moreover, they were gods of resurrection who survived descents into the underworld. Orpheus additionally was often depicted as a shepherd in a paradisical setting – a figure that parallels the Christian Good Shepherd. Clement of Alexandria had already pointed out certain parallels that formerly misguided pagans might find between the old gods and the divine Son in Christianity.[62] No wonder, then, that aspects of traditional representations of these gods would be transferred to visual imagery of Christ, including the almost feminine beauty associated with such gods in particular.

The Good Shepherd figures, with some exceptions, are also depicted as clean-shaven youths with curling hair, although lacking the feminine physical features of later Jesus iconography. Their type is probably best described as Apollonian, although their appearance is a convention that was used for other pagan figures, including heroes such as Meleager, personifications of the seasons, and Hermes as guide to the underworld.[63] Still, visual expressions of the Good Shepherd suggests mercy, compassion, and loving care, characteristics not inappropriate to representations of Jesus.

Idealized beauty appropriate to the savior-god type had parallels in the Hellenistic representations of Alexander the Great, who was often consciously depicted to look like Dionysus or Helios, and presented as a kind of god-man. One aspect of his portrait was a youthful mien and long, abundant, curling hair, characteristics that in turn showed up on the images of certain Roman emperors, including Nero and Caligula, who adopted the flowing hairstyle in particular.[64] These imperial portraits clearly suggested that the emperor was a type of savior, and associated him not only with particular gods, but with the great Alexander himself.[65]

Of course, one can only speculate about Jesus' physical appearance. However, the issue was not inconsequential to early Christians. Origen responded to the Platonist philosopher Celsus, who had claimed that if Jesus were truly divine, he would have looked different from other men. According to Celsus, while a god-man should possess unsurpassable beauty, Jesus was reported to be short of stature and ill-favored. Origen presumes that Celsus knew only the text from Isaiah, "He had no form nor comeliness that we should look at him, and no beauty that we should desire him" (Isaiah 53:2b). Origen countered that the Psalmist spoke of the "mighty one" as the fairest of the sons of men (Psalm 45:2). Moreover, Origen cites Jesus' altered appearance in the Transfiguration to conclude that it is a subject of wonder that Jesus' physical appearance has so many variations and is so capable of transformation, at one time possessing the qualities of beauty and loveliness, and at another time having an ignoble form and unprepossessing appearance.[66] Thus Christ is both free and able to appear in different guises, including that of judge and mother, as we are free to envision Christ in these different ways. Such variability reinforces Christ's divinity and offers a new way to understand Jesus' humanity. The logos is polymorphous and transpersonal both prior to and after the incarnation.

Finally, consideration of Jesus' feminine appearance should not be surprising to modern viewers familiar with popular, contemporary representations of Jesus with gentle expression, shoulder-length hair, and a delicate appearance. Images of Jesus that emphasize masculine features are nearly as difficult to find today as in late antiquity. Throughout history, artists apparently have aimed to portray Jesus' kindness, compassion, and even meekness by endowing him with a sweet or pained expression on a fine-boned and somewhat feminine face. Moreover, many different portraits of Jesus, some quite contrasting, often exist within a single house of worship.

The many variations of Jesus' appearance in the art described above may be, in the end, a recognition that in his divine nature, Christ cannot be represented fully in art and ultimately must subsume or even transcend all efforts to portray his appearance. Early Christian art then did reveal truths about Christ, but limited truths, and only some of his many aspects. Portraits, in this case, are much more than simple external likenesses. They attempt to capture the reality of the divine presence. Cyril of Jerusalem made this same case in his fourth-century lectures to catechumens preparing for their baptism:

> The Savior comes in various forms to each person according to need. To those who lack joy, he becomes a vine; to those who wish to enter in, he is a door; for those who must offer prayers, he is a mediating high priest. To those in sin, he becomes a sheep, to be sacrificed on their behalf. He becomes "all things to all people" remaining in his own nature what he is. For so remaining, and possessing the true and unchanging dignity of Sonship, as the best of physicians and caring teachers, he adapts himself to our infirmities.[67]

## Conclusion

The emergence of the portrait introduced a different function of art to and for the church of the fourth and fifth centuries. That function was mystically to allow the presence of the holy person through the medium of image or icon. Like the presence of Christ invoked in the consecration of the material elements of a sacrament, these likenesses were sometimes viewed to have the power to connect the earthly world with the heavenly realm and the community of the living faithful with the community of the saints. In this case, representation is more than mere memorial (a funerary portrait to aid recollection of the deceased's physical appearance in life), and its purpose is far more than instructional, inspirational, or even devotional.

Pre-Christian parallels to this function existed in the ways that cult statues were understood, or in the uses regional authorities might make of a portrait of the emperor to bring the power of a long-distant ruler to a particular locale. Some believers also understood the sanctity of a martyr or holy person to be concentrated in or even transferred to particular material remains (i.e. relics) that were both portable and efficacious. In Christian theological understanding, from the moment the divine entered the created world in the flesh of a particular human being, that the holy could be both visible and tangible was more than possible, it was essential.

But that tangible material need not be restricted to mere presentation or consistent appearance. As holy, it also transcended the limitations of ordinary created matter and might take on many different forms. Although in some sense this was a validation of its participation in the order of creation – animals do grow and change in appearance – in another sense this adaptability expressed the uniquely divine attributes of ubiquity and unity, to be everywhere at once and to encompass all truth. God not only has a physical face, God may have any and all faces. Christ incarnate is not a static reality, but a multi-faceted truth.

Thus, like Plato's doctrine of forms and the ways the parts of created order participated in the world of ideals through their imitation of the transcendently true or real, the theology of icons asserted that the portrait was not merely a thing of wood and paint, but an effective and essential intimation of the ultimate reality that it portrayed. At the same time as such images provided a path or method for apprehending the supernatural, they yet served also to strengthen faith, provide models of character, and emblematically represent the values and the composition of the community.

# 5

# IMAGES OF THE SUFFERING REDEEMER

## Introduction

As noted above, the fourth century witnessed a gradual shift in the content of early Christian iconography – away from narrative scenes that primarily depicted Jesus as healer, wonderworker, and teacher and toward more dogmatic images – ones that portrayed Jesus' divinity, transcendence, resurrection, judgment and heavenly reign. Decidedly missing among these newly emerging images are portrayals of Jesus' suffering or dying on the cross. Apart from very rare examples, Christ is represented as triumphant over death, but not undergoing it. Contrary to the dominance of the crucifix in both Byzantine and medieval iconography, early Christian art seems to have deliberately avoided any graphic presentation of the savior's death.

Although well known to, if not fully understood by art historians, the paucity of early crucifixion images often surprises theologians and historians of Christianity, who take it for granted that a story so central to the biblical narrative as well as subsequent liturgical and theological exposition could have been missing from the subjects presented in the early centuries of Christian iconography. Medieval and renaissance sculpture and painting was saturated with scenes of the Lord's passion, a theme probably second only to the depiction of the Virgin and child. In general, Christ on the cross is probably the most recognizable Christian image, one that traverses both geographical and chronological boundaries.

However, an inventory of other popular themes that appear to be missing from early Christian art reveals some interesting gaps, and a possible pattern. Nativity scenes also are relatively late, although they first appear in the mid-fourth century (with a possible and unique pre-Constantinian exception). Early artistic representations of the holy child sitting on his mother's lap and visited by three magi also may belong more appropriately to the category of narrative than dogmatic images (Figure 25). Similarly, fourth-century portrayals of the passion story that include scenes of Jesus' arrest, trial, and his carrying the cross (but no presentations of the crucifixion itself) are all tied to recognizable episodes from the gospels.

130

Apart from two intaglio gems, probably dating from the fourth century, and a controversial second-century graffito found in Rome, the earliest known representations of Jesus crucified date to the early fifth century, and are extremely rare until the seventh.[1] Moreover, the earliest certain examples of an image of Christ crucified seem almost incidental – not at all monumental, either in size or scope. One of them, a wood relief sculpture on the door of Rome's Basilica of Sta. Sabina, is dated to about 430 (Figure 49). Another, a panel of an ivory reliquary casket now in the British Museum, might be a decade earlier than the Sta. Sabina image.[2] The next known examples date to the sixth century, including one manuscript illumination from the Syriac Rabbula Gospels (c.586) and several small representations, on gems, liturgical objects, and lead ampullae that pilgrims carried back from the Holy Land (Figure 50).

Thus while the earliest images portray Jesus' ministry (including his baptism), the stories that frame this ministry – the circumstances of Jesus' miraculous birth, and especially his suffering and death on the cross – are absent from the repertoire of Christian iconography until surprisingly late (at least surprising to us). In fact, it seems almost ironic that the church's early creeds refer only to these beginnings and endings – skipping right from "born of the Virgin Mary" to "suffered under Pontius Pilate" with no

*Figure 49* Crucifixion from the wooden door of Sta. Sabina, Rome.
Photo: Graydon Snyder.

*Figure 50* Pilgrimage ampullae, Monza, Italy.
Photo: Foto Marburg/Art Resource, New York.

mention of Jesus' life and work, while the art appears to take an opposite tack.

Using the artistic evidence as data, some scholars have thus constructed an argument against the centrality of crucifixion in the faith of "ordinary" early Christians, in contrast to a different kind of theology imposed by the church authorities.[3] Theological emphasis on a dying and rising savior, especially characteristic of Pauline literature, recently has been argued to be the church's interpolation of the gospel narratives – overlaying a heavenly savior on the human Jesus of history.[4]

Certain gnostic or docetic Christians in antiquity did, in fact, demonstrate a tendency to de-emphasize Christ's suffering and death. However, these sects did not prefer a "human" Jesus, but rather recoiled at the idea that the divine savior might undergo physical passion, change, or death. Such a denial of bodily suffering denied the human incarnation of Jesus, a dogma that the earliest Christian writers and theologians asserted in the strongest terms – including the emphasis on the centrality of Jesus' death on the cross. This human suffering and death was presented as a unique offering, one that offered humans reconciliation with God as well as annulling any need for similar future sacrifices.[5]

## Theories regarding the absence of crucifixion images

Several different explanations account for the absence of presentations of Christ hanging on a cross in early Christian art. Some of these explanations assume that the crucifixion was central to the faith of early Christians, but suggest other reasons for the lack of such artistic representations. One widely held theory proposes that early Christians, still relatively close to the actual event, might have been averse to representing their divine savior suffering so shocking or gruesome a death.[6] Constantine's prohibition of crucifixion as a form of capital punishment may have been the result of such sentiments, and led to a rejection of the scandalous image of God suffering so painful a death.[7] The possibility that such representations would have been so graphic as to seem almost to profane a holy mystery appeals to the power of imagery and the deep emotions it can stir. A static portrayal of Jesus crucified would seem to "freeze" the episode in an untenable way, undercutting Christian emphasis on the resurrection by concentrating on the crucifixion.[8] Such a view would account for artistic presentations of the passion that skip from the carrying of the cross to the empty tomb (Figure 51).

A parallel version of this thesis proposes that artists may have felt reluctant to depict Christ on the cross because it was too profound a mystery, something to be veiled from the uninitiated – somehow taboo. Such a depiction, more than any other, would seem less simply (and safely) narrative and more like an object of adoration or a particularly holy subject that should not be presented for public view.[9] Just as Moses was afraid to look directly at the face of God (Exodus 3:6), the image was veiled from sight, or at least

*Figure 51* Jesus holding the cross (center) with Peter's arrest and Jesus' trial, fourth-century sarcophagus now in the Vatican Museo Pio Cristiano.
Photo: Author.

mediated through some other symbolic form. Artists knew there were limits and dared not venture beyond them.

A slightly different explanation focuses on the stigma of crucifixion as a punishment. Crucifixion was a barbaric mode of execution reserved for slaves, foreigners, or low-class criminals and traitors.[10] Ironically, among the rare extant examples of a crucifixion is the well-known graffito found on the Roman Palatine Hill that depicts an ass-headed figure affixed to a *tau*-cross and the inscription: "Alexamenos: worship god." If we conclude that the cartoon was drawn by pagans in order to mock the Christian religion, the lack of other, kerygmatic images of crucifixion may be understood by contrast.[11] Massey Shepherd makes a connection between the legal and social status of Christians and the lack of crucifixion imagery: "Perhaps it was too much to ask that Christians openly represent the instrument of shame in times of persecution and ridicule."[12]

In fact, the Egyptian theologian Origen needed to refute the pagan Celsus' sneering accusation that Christians primarily regarded Jesus as Son of God merely because he suffered this particular punishment: " 'What then? Have not many others also been punished, and that no less disgracefully?' Here Celsus behaves like the lowest class of the enemies of the faith, who even think that it follows from the story about the crucifixion of Jesus that we worship anyone who has been crucified."[13] In Latin-speaking Roman Africa, both Minucius Felix and Tertullian find they must refute charges that Christians worship the cross in the same way that pagans worship idols. Tertullian distinguishes between the worship of idols, which was permeated with cross-forms, and the Christian understanding of the "sign of the cross" as transcending material reality or pagan idolatry. Tertullian also takes the trouble to deny the rumor that Christians worshipped asses (a charge both supported and illustrated by the Palatine Hill graffito).[14]

These two scholarly hypotheses are related, but they arise from different motives. The first – that the realistic portrayal of Jesus hanging on the cross would have offended early Christian viewers – is fundamentally connected to the problem of idolatry. The issue is not only whether one can represent the incarnate deity visually, but also how one does it respectfully and truthfully, without profaning a sacred mystery in finite material. The second – that such a subject would have embarrassed early Christians – has to do with public relations, propriety, and even safety as much as with idolatry. Christians had reason to fear the scorn and misunderstanding of their neighbors, especially in the era before the peace of the church.

A third line of argument approaches the problem dogmatically, looking for answers by sifting the second- and third-century Christological controversies and heresies. Here two divergent options emerge. The first suggestion, that the omission of birth, infancy, or death imagery suggests a docetic or gnostic Christology that denied the true humanity of the savior, implies that art works were potentially heterodox expressions. The second possibility, that such an omission reflects a "lower" or "popular" adoptionist-type Christology that emphasized Jesus' anointing at baptism and his earthly ministry over his divinity, similarly assumes deviations of the artistic images from theological "orthodoxy."

An example of the first option, outlined by E. J. Tinsley, proposes a theological basis for the lateness, not merely of crucifixion images generally, but especially of representations of an already dead Christ upon the cross that appear regularly only in the early tenth century. Tinsley argued that early Christian teachers worried that the death of a divinely incarnate Christ would be misunderstood as an ordinary human death. This issue emerged during the Christological controversies of the fifth and sixth centuries when theologians argued that Christ's death was unnecessary (i.e. voluntary), temporary, and without physical (i.e. bodily) decomposition. Tinsley regarded the eighth-century eastern defense of icons, which cites the incarnation as justification for the veneration of holy images, as the theological turning point with respect to the representation of a dead, crucified Christ.[15]

An example of the second dogmatic option is the assertion already cited – that many early Christians were more enamored of a human wonderworker and teacher than the Christ of doctrinal and theological reflection. This view proposes that the absence of crucifixion imagery demonstrates disinterest among those who espoused the "popular" aspects of the Christian faith, in the atoning aspects of suffering and vicarious death. Instead (this theory suggests), early Christians were drawn more to the human Jesus of the gospels – a moral teacher, champion of the poor and oppressed, and healer of the sick and lame – than to an incarnate deity, crucified savior, and victorious ruler to come again at the end of time. This "adoptionist" perspective potentially explains why the earlier art featured Jesus' baptism but not his transfiguration, crucifixion, resurrection, or his role as teacher instead of judge. As Graydon Snyder maintains:

> There are no early Christian symbols that elevate paradigms of Christ suffering (the *teologia crucis*), or even motifs of death and resurrection. In early Christian art, when Jesus does appear, he overcomes illness, political and social difficulties, and death ... . In a social situation in which persecution, harassment, prejudice, class hatred, and illegal treatment were always possibilities, the early Christians stressed deliverance and victory rather than death and resurrection.[16]

Snyder's argument suggests a basic incompatibility between art and the theological treatises of contemporary writers, who showed no tendency to de-emphasize Christ's sacrifice on the cross. For instance, Ignatius of Antioch (c.35–107) said he was "dedicated to the cross, which is an offense to unbelievers, but to us salvation and eternal life." For Irenaeus, the obedience of Christ on the cross was the source of human salvation since Jesus reversed the sin of Adam – the cross becoming the antitype of the tree of paradise.[17]

Clement of Alexandria claimed that "Christ transformed the sunset into sunrise, and by his crucifixion turned death into life."[18] Melito of Sardis (d. c.190) wrote an entire treatise on the passion, comparing Jesus to the sacrificial lamb of Passover. Origen spoke of Christ's death on the cross as the overthrow of Satan's domination. Tertullian, who often is credited with introducing the doctrine of atonement to western theology, spoke of Christ's sacrifice in this way: "Who has redeemed another's death by his one, but the Son of God alone? ... for to this end he came, that being himself pure from sin, and in all respects holy, he might undergo death on behalf of sinners."[19]

Despite the early and widespread theological emphasis on the significance of the crucifixion, the date and form in which the symbol was incorporated into the worship life of early Christians is less clear. The candidate for baptism was "signed" with the cross, and many daily activities were accompanied by the *"signum crucis"* (sign of the cross), which may have been more an apotropaic gesture than a direct reference to Christ's death.[20]

Scholars disagree about how early and how clearly Christians understood the eucharist as a reenactment of Jesus' sacrifice. Nevertheless, the liturgical sources demonstrate generally that early Christian worship celebrated the salvific power of Christ's suffering and death. Both the Epistle to the Hebrews and the Epistle of Barnabas compare Jesus' passion to the Jewish liturgy of sacrifice. Barnabas, for example, paralleled Jesus to the heifer that was slain and burned on the altar, its ashes sprinkled on the people to purify them from their sins.[21]

By the early third century, Christ's sacrifice had become a well-established element of the eucharistic celebration. The liturgy according to Hippolytus' *Apostolic Tradition* (c.200) linked the words of institution with Christ's passion. In North Africa, Tertullian and Cyprian were unequivocal about the sacrificial nature of the eucharist. Cyprian, for example, argued against those who would use water rather than wine as a eucharistic element by pointing out that the eucharist is a reenactment of Jesus' offering himself as a living sacrifice and that his body and blood are symbolized only by bread and wine.[22]

Abundant examples of the importance of the crucifixion in early dogmatic or sacramental treatises could be added here. However, for this discussion a more pressing issue is why the texts speak so profusely about a subject on which art is seemingly silent. A demonstrated incompatibility between artistic creations and theological writings has been taken to indicate that art serves in some sense as a corrective mechanism that might give insight into – or serve as a vehicle for – popular faith as opposed to the elitist emphases of theological speculation.

The artistic evidence, however, is more subtle and complex than this variety of explanatory hypotheses has allowed. Scholars have sometimes taken narrative art works for granted and treated them as if they were simply illustrations of their source texts. On the other hand, if narrative subjects functioned symbolically or metaphorically in addition to broadly illustrating particular narratives, new possibilities emerge – some of which might be subtle or veiled references to the cross. Scholars will need to reconsider whether there is, in fact, a complete absence of crucifixion imagery in early Christianity. Possible indirect references to the passion include such signs and symbols as simple crosses, "crypto-crosses" (anchors, ships' masts, trees, plows, axes), and *tau*-crosses. More complex figures that may refer symbolically or typologically to the crucifixion include the image of the Lamb (*agnus Dei*) or a type taken from the Hebrew scriptures – Abraham offering his son Isaac as sacrifice.

## Cross markings and inscriptions

Even without their potential function as indirect references to crucifixion, plain crosses, *tau*-crosses, and so-called "crypto-crosses" are notoriously difficult to interpret. Because of earlier over-interpretation of such examples as the cross/wall-bracket at Herculaneum or simple placement markings on Jewish ossuaries, most scholars now err on the side of caution when analyzing certain cross-like markings and inscriptions mostly found on tombs or grave slabs.[23] Yet some definite cross-markings found among the pre-Constantinian graffiti at the Vatican or on more formal Christian epitaphs elsewhere in Rome or found in other parts of the empire can be dated to the third century.[24]

Not all these marks were direct references to the cross of crucifixion, however. Rather, the Hebrew letter *taw*, the last letter in the Hebrew alphabet, made as a simple cross, or "x" figure, may be the source of many of these Christian cross markings, and originally served as a mark that identified the righteous. In Ezekiel 9:4–6, God commands that the foreheads of the repentant be marked with a special sign that will protect them from the coming slaughter of the guilty.[25] The Hebrew *taw* is equivalent to the Greek *tau*, a simple cross or "T"- shaped sign, used when marking a cross in oil on the foreheads of the newly baptized, or the sign of the cross made as a blessing or protection. In time, this sign came to be identified with the cross of crucifixion, but the relationship is complex and only established in degrees and in distinct contexts.[26]

Tertullian's treatise against Marcion (*c.*205–10) provides some documentary evidence for the association of Ezekiel's sign with the symbol of crucifixion, as well as the shift from the *taw* to the *tau*, and finally to the Latin "T": "Now the Greek letter *tau* and our own letter 'T' are the very form of the cross, which he predicted would be the sign on our foreheads in the true catholic Jerusalem." As an apotropaic sign to ward away evil and to remind Christians daily of their allegiance, Tertullian recommends continuous retracing of the symbol upon the forehead, "in all the ordinary actions of daily life."[27]

Following Tertullian, Cyprian cited both the Ezekiel text and the Exodus story of the Passover, furthering their association with Christ's passion and the sign of the cross:

> And that this sign [the sign of Christ marked on the body] pertains to the passion and blood of Christ ... . What preceded before in a figure in the slaying of a lamb is fulfilled in Christ the truth that followed later. Just as then, when Egypt was smitten, no one could escape except by the blood and sign of the lamb, so too, when the world begins to be laid waste and smitten, [he] alone escapes who is found in the blood and the sign of Christ.[28]

Although scholars generally date most variants of the *chi-rho* symbol, some of which suggest the cross of crucifixion as much as an abbreviation of the title *Christos,* to the post-Constantinian period, there are some exceptions, including examples from Phrygia and among the graffiti found in the Vatican that might date from the late third, or very early fourth century.[29] Additionally, certain early third-century Egyptian papyri employed a symbol that combined the letters *tau* and *rho* in such words as *stauros* or *staurothanai* in such a way that they made a kind of pictogram, the image of a man's head upon a cross. This mark has been interpreted as a *staurogram*, rather than a Christogram, as it seems to be an actual reference to the cross of crucifixion rather than to the divine name.[30]

Parallel to the *tau*-crosses are other somewhat ambiguous or hidden cross figures found in epigraphic representations of anchors, axes, masons' tools, and ships' masts (Figure 52). Examples of boats and anchors (especially anchors combined with fish) found on inscribed gems are consistent with Clement of Alexandria's advice on the proper subjects for Christian signet rings: "Now our seals ought to be a dove, a fish, a ship running before the breeze, a musical lyre, or a ship's anchor." While Clement did associate the sign of the fisherman with the apostles and the "children drawn up from the water" (i.e. baptized), he made no elaboration on the parallels between the shape of an anchor or mast and cross (just as he did not suggest a cross as an appropriate symbol).[31] Other writers, however, made a more explicit connection between such objects and the cross of crucifixion.

Boats are widely seen in early Christian art, sometimes without a particular narrative reference (Figure 53). The ship, of course, symbolizes the church as a whole, but its mast often takes the form of a cross. Limiting the ship's meanings to the body of the church or an even more metaphorical reference to safe passage through rough waters is overly restrictive, however,

*Figure 52* Third- and fourth-century funerary inscriptions, S. Lorenzo fuori le Mura, Rome.

Photo: Author.

*Figure 53* Jesus and apostles in a boat (the stilling of the storm?). Sarcophagus fragment now in the Vatican Museo Pio Cristiano.

Photo: Author.

considering contemporary written sources that explain the symbol quite clearly:

> The sea is the world. The Church is like a ship, buffeted by the waves but not swamped, for she has with her experienced pilot, Christ. Amidships she has the trophy of victory over death, for she carries Christ's cross with her ... . For her double rudder she has the two Testaments ... . With her she carries stocks of living water, the regenerating bath ... . The ladder rising upwards to the sailyard is an image of the sign of Christ's passion leading the faithful to climb up unto Heaven.[32]

The anchor shown combined with the fish (Figure 3) seems to be uniquely Christian and its common use suggests that it held a significant meaning.[33] The Epistle to the Hebrews (6:19) speaks of the hope of salvation as the anchor of the soul. Ambrose later commented on this passage: "Just as an anchor thrown from a ship prevents the ship from being tossed about and holds it securely, thus we hold fast to faith strengthened by hope."[34]

Dozens of examples of pre-Constantinian anchor images have been found among the epitaphs in the catacombs accompanied by such legends as *pax tecum, pax tibi,* and *in pace.* Examples of the anchor also appear with different forms of the Latin or Greek words for hope: *spes* or *elpis,* making the image consistent with the text of Hebrews. The fish that appear with the anchor may represent the Christian souls, with their hope in salvation – a salvation represented by the cross. Yet, such a conclusion may border on over-interpretation and this particular symbol may signify merely the more obvious expression of simple steadfastness or safe passage through rough water.[35]

Fear of over-interpretation also has caused many scholars to be conservative about identifying various signs as "crypto-crosses." Textual evidence, however, tends to support the association of certain objects with the cross. A number of documents reveal that the cross as a symbol of Christ's passion was recognized in all sorts of guises. Christians found examples both in the Hebrew scriptures and in the external world. For early Christian writers, at least, the cross's very ubiquity demonstrated the predestined character of Christ's sacrifice and triumph.

Cross figures from the Hebrew Bible include the bronze serpent that Moses set up on a pole (Numbers 21:9) and the wood that Elisha threw into the water to recover the sunken ax of his servant (2 Kings 6:1–7). According to the scripture, gazing at the serpent on the pole was life-giving to anyone who was bitten by a snake, and Justin Martyr moreover concluded that the object resembled the figure of Jesus Crucified.[36] According to Tertullian, Elisha's weighty ax symbolized the obduracy of the world, sunk deep in the waters of error, while the wood symbolized the cross that rescues sinners.[37]

Christians also saw figures of the cross in the external world. According to Justin Martyr, "The sea cannot be traversed unless the sign of victory, which is called a sail, remain fast in the ship; the land is not plowed without it; similarly diggers and mechanics do not do their work except with tools of this form."[38] And although the martyrs' deaths were always thought to be a kind of participation in the suffering of Christ, when Blandina of Lyons hung on a post in the arena, she also appeared to onlookers as the very image of the crucified Christ. Thus by "putting on Christ," in the most graphic sense, Blandina earned the crown of immortality.[39]

Minucius Felix contradicted the pagan slander that Christians worshiped crosses, but still saw the sign of crucifixion all around:

> And, surely, your military ensigns, standards, and banners, what are they but gilded and decorated crosses? Your trophies of victory copy not merely the appearance of a simple cross but that of a man fastened to it as well. And as for the sign of the cross, there is no doubt that we see it in the world of nature around us: when you see a ship sailing with canvas swelling or gliding with oars extended; or when you set a yoke in place you form the sign of the cross; or when a man pays homage to God with purity of heart, stretching out his hands.[40]

Thus the cross as symbol was clearly present in the visual imagination of early Christian writers, who saw it not only as an apotropaic sign, but also as a sign of Christ's victory over sin and death. No basis exists for asserting that visually presented cross-symbols lacked the same symbolic value. Tertullian especially emphasizes Christian veneration of simple, "adorned" crosses in contrast to the pagan veneration of idols: " The one who affirms that we are 'a priesthood of a cross,' we shall claim our co-religionist. A cross is mere wood in its material just as your object of worship is made of wood. Only, while with you the object is a human figure, with us the wood is its own symbol."[41]

## The lamb of God

The lamb as a visual metaphor for Christ and his passion certainly derives from frequent scriptural references to Jesus as the sacrificial lamb, the *agnus Dei*. Moreover, the two symbols of the *taw* sign and the lamb often occurred together, as demonstrated by the above quotations from Tertullian and Cyprian. However, before the mid-fourth century, artistic representations of the lamb usually appear with the Good Shepherd, and almost never alone. The difficulty of reconciling the ordinary pastoral signification of the image with a sacrificial symbol cautions against an overemphasis on passion symbolism in these earlier examples. For example, Graydon Snyder, arguing against early sacrifice imagery, asserts these lambs are symbolic references to "a kinship community both present and past (sepulchral art) where such community did not exist in a blood sense."[42]

Nevertheless, even these early pastoral figures may have overtones of sacrifice. Jesus' statement that as the Good Shepherd, "I lay down my life for my sheep" (John 10:15), introduces the theme of self-offering, although in this case the sacrifice is the shepherd's rather than the lamb's.[43] Regarding the lamb itself, the written sources clearly understand the lamb as a symbol of Christ's passion, perhaps most significantly in John the Baptist's cry: "Behold the Lamb of God who takes away the sins of the world" (John 1:29). Paul, employing metaphors of the Passover (Exodus 12:3–13) says, "Christ, our paschal lamb, has been sacrificed" (1 Corinthians 5:7). Revelation 5:6–14 describes a lamb with seven horns and seven eyes, a lamb who was slain and found worthy to receive power, wealth, wisdom, might, honor, glory, and blessing forever.

Christian theologians developed the theme of Christ as lamb from the beginning and the theme continued right through the Christological controversies of the fourth and fifth centuries. Justin Martyr was one of the first post-biblical writers to expound on the lamb of the Passover as a type of Christ: "And that lamb, which was commanded to be wholly roasted, was a symbol of the suffering of the cross which Christ would undergo ... . For one spit is transfixed right through from the lower parts up to the head, and one across the back to which are attached the legs of the lamb."[44]

The eating of the lamb at Passover as a prefiguration of the passion was a common theme of early Christian writers. Tertullian asserts that the command to immolate a lamb at sunset as preparatory for the Passover was the nearly exact type of the passion of Christ who was crucified on the "first day of unleavened bread ... and so that the prophecies might be fulfilled, the day itself hastened to make an eventide, and caused a darkness at midday."[45] Lactantius, writing around the turn of the fourth century, spoke of the significance of the cross, the Passover, and the spotless white lamb itself as a figure of Christ: "innocent, just and holy; who, being slain by the same Jews, is the salvation of all who have written on their foreheads the sign of blood – that is, of the cross, on which he shed his blood." Later in the same work Lactantius, like Melito of Sardis a century earlier, pointed out a significance of the words "pascha" – the feast of the slain lamb, and "passion" – the Lamb's redemptive suffering.[46]

Despite the ancient and frequent literary allusions to the Lamb of God, however, the earliest lamb iconography cannot patently be identified with the passion of Jesus and the redemption of sin. Even when, in the post-Constantinian era, the Christ-Lamb appears flanked by rows of other sheep or lambs probably representing the twelve apostles – the "lamb's flock" – there are few unequivocal symbols of the passion. We assume the reference to the *agnus Dei*, but without knowing the literary allusions, we might not realize the significance of that particular animal apart from its associations with the Good Shepherd.

The Lamb by itself began to appear as an allegory for Christ by the mid-fourth century. One composition showing the Lamb performing the miracle of the multiplication of the loaves was painted on the walls of a Roman catacomb. Paulinus of Nola speaks of the Lamb which appeared in the vault mosaics of his basilica and according to the *Liber pontificalis*, Constantine donated a golden lamb to furnish the Lateran baptistery.[47] By the fifth and sixth centuries the Lamb took the place of Jesus standing on the rock from which flowed the four streams. This motif appears in the vault of the baptistery of St John Lateran, on ivory covers made for gospel books, in the apex of the presbytery vault of Ravenna's S. Vitale (in a medallion supported by four angels) and on numerous sarcophagi (Figure 56). Although devoid of explicit references to the crucifixion, these Lamb figures (particularly those placed near or above altars) are finally detached from any pastoral context and can only signify the victory of the redemption, won by the sacrificed *agnus Dei*.

In 692, the Council of Trullo, also known as the Quinisext Council, forbade the symbolic representation of Christ as Lamb. The theological reason for this iconographic restriction was that such depictions tended to undermine the reality of Christ's human incarnation and redeeming sacrifice:

In order therefore that "that which is perfect" may be delineated to the eyes of all, at least in coloured expression, we decree that the figure in human form of the Lamb who taketh away the sin of the world, Christ our God, be henceforth exhibited in images, instead of the ancient lamb, so that all may understand by means of it the depths of humiliation of the Word of God, and that we may recall to our memory his conversation in the flesh, his suffering and salutary death, and his redemption which was wrought for the whole world.[48]

## Abraham's offering of Isaac

A different kind of indirect representation of Christ's passion was its type – the image of Abraham offering Isaac, a very common scene in early Christian sculpture and painting (Figures 19, 55). At least two and possibly three pre-Constantinian catacomb paintings of this theme are known along with several representations from sarcophagus reliefs of the same period. The fourth and fifth centuries produced at least twenty more catacomb frescoes and as many as ninety sarcophagus reliefs, as well as ivories, glass etchings, lamps, and ceramic bowls. Important Jewish artistic representations of the scene also occur in synagogues at Dura Europos and Beth Alpha (Figure 54).[49]

To understand representations of Abraham's sacrifice as referring to Jesus' passion requires moving from fairly simple referential symbols (*tau*-cross, anchor), to more complex allegories of the passion with sophisticated

*Figure 54* The binding of Isaac, Synagogue of Beth Alpha.
© The International Catacomb Society. Photo: Estelle Brettman.

*Figure 55* Abraham binding Isaac (far left) along with Jesus healing the blind man, the paralytic, the woman with the issue of blood, the multiplication of the loaves, Adam and Eve, and Jesus raising the dead. Now in the Vatican Museo Pio Cristiano.
Photo: Author.

144

theological implications. Parallel images of Abraham offering Isaac and of Christ crucified are well known in medieval Bible illumination, and clearly present Isaac's offering on Moriah as a prefiguration of Christ's sacrifice on Calvary. Similarly, at one time art historians simply assumed that earlier Abraham and Isaac scenes should also be understood as artistic typologies of Christ's sacrifice.[50] Some recent scholarship, however, has rejected the potential passion symbolism in these representations of Abraham's obedient offering of his son (Genesis 22:1–19).

Scholars who reject such a Christological interpretation, particularly for pre-Constantinian art, opt instead to view the early representations of Isaac's offering as a simple message of deliverance in the time of persecution. Although partially the result of a general tendency to avoid reading more than the most simple meanings into early images, this interpretation also sometimes accompanies an assertion that sacrifice or suffering was a theme absent from early Christian visual symbolism until after the peace of the church or even the early Middle Ages. Isabel Speyart van Woerden summarized her conclusions about the representation of Abraham offering Isaac: "[D]uring the age of persecutions it has been a symbol of deliverance; from 313 onwards it appears transformed into a dramatic scene with allegorical bynotes; from the early Middle Ages onwards, it becomes the principal prototype of Christ's death on the cross."[51] Similarly, J. Stevenson asserts that Isaac's offering was a particularly appropriate scene for a funereal context because it symbolized deliverance from danger, which might imply resurrection from death. Such signification, Stevenson argues, "surely prevails over a symbolic representation of the Passion."[52]

Graydon Snyder points out that Isaac is never shown actually bound upon the altar until the mid-fourth century, a fact he uses to argue for the relative lateness of the sacrifice–crucifixion analogy. In addition, Snyder calls attention to the earliest extant image in the Catacomb of Callistus that merely shows Abraham and Isaac as orants. Thus his conclusion regarding passion imagery stands: "[No early symbols] signify suffering, death, or self-immolation … . There is no place in the third century for a crucified Christ, or a symbol of divine death. Only when Christ was all powerful, as in the iconography of the Emperor, could that strength be used for redemption and salvation as well as deliverance."[53]

However, rejecting this image's function as a symbolic reference to Christ's passion requires that scholars discount the mass of textual evidence that makes this precise typological connection. Early Christian writers use the story of Abraham's offering of Isaac as an explicit paradigm for Jesus' sacrifice, beginning with the Epistle of Barnabas, usually dated to the early second century.[54] Later in that century, Melito of Sardis also noted the parallels between Isaac and Christ, although he added that while Isaac was released from his bindings, Christ actually suffered and died. Here he similarly employs the imagery of the Lamb of God:

For as a ram he was bound (he says concerning our Lord Jesus Christ),
and as a lamb he was shorn, and as a sheep he was led to slaughter,
and as a lamb he was crucified;
and he carried the wood upon his shoulders
and he was led up to be slain like Isaac by his Father.
But Christ suffered, whereas Isaac did not suffer;
for he was a model of the Christ who was going to suffer.
But by being merely the model of Christ
he caused astonishment and fear among men.
For it was a strange mystery to behold,
a son led by his father to a mountain for slaughter,
whose feet he bound and whom he put on the wood of the offering,
preparing with zeal the things for his slaughter ...
... That ram, slain, ransomed Isaac; so also the Lord, slain, saved us,
and bound, released us, and sacrificed, ransomed us ...
... For the Lord was a lamb like the ram
which Abraham saw caught in a Sabek-tree.
But the tree displayed the cross, and that place, Jerusalem,
and the lamb, the Lord fettered for slaughter.[55]

Irenaeus, Tertullian, Clement, and Origen also elaborated the Christ–Isaac parallels. As Tertullian explained it, the wood that Isaac carried was a figure of the wooden cross: "Isaac, being led by his father to be a victim, and carrying himself the firewood, at that moment was a figure of Christ's death, submitting himself to his father as a victim and lugging the wood of his own passion."[56]

This interpretive motif continued through the fourth and fifth centuries, cited by such writers as Ambrose, Ephrem, John Chrysostom, Paulinus of Nola, Gregory of Nyssa, Theodoret, and Augustine.[57] Yet, possibly the most significant use of the Isaac–Christ typology was liturgical. Documentary evidence indicates that the story of Isaac's offering was read during the Easter vigil in Jerusalem and possibly in Milan also by the late fourth century. Even more significant, perhaps, Isaac's offering joined those of Abel and Melchizedek as eucharistic typologies in the fourth-century Milanese Canon of the Mass, as well as in the Christmas Preface from the *Sacramentarium Veronese*, possibly composed by Leo the Great.[58]

A group of sixth-century mosaics in Ravenna, in the basilicas of S. Apollinare in Classe and S. Vitale, show the offerings of Melchizedek, Abraham, and Abel as types of the eucharistic offering that would take place at the high altar just beneath the images. Directly above the lunette mosaics which portray these offerings in S. Vitale are figures of angels bearing a medallion with a cross. Above, in the apex of the S. Vitale vault is the Lamb of God (Figure 56). Without having to depict the crucifixion literally, the connections among Old Testament sacrifices, Jesus' passion, and the church's

*Figure 56* Lamb of God on sarcophagus, S. Apollinare in Classe, Ravenna.
Photo: Author.

eucharistic offering show up very clearly through the medium of the rich visual imagery that surrounds the celebrant at the altar.

Added to the textual and liturgical evidence of a strong and early tradition of perceiving Abraham's offering as a prefiguration of Christ's crucifixion is the powerful mystique of overlapping sacred space. Christian pilgrims to the Holy Land reinforced the parallels between Isaac's offering and Christ's crucifixion and conflated the sites of both sacrifices (Moriah and Calvary). While the Bordeaux Pilgrim found the site of Abraham's offering at the traditional Samaritan site (Mt Gerizim), and southern Jews had identified the rock in the Jerusalem temple with the site of Isaac's binding, the Piacenza Pilgrim placed the altar of Abraham right next to the rock of Golgotha. In time a chapel dedicated to Abraham was erected there.[59] Thus the literary device of typology became a historical reality and Christian pilgrims could actually experience the coincidence of type and antitype for themselves.

## The first passion images and the symbol of victory

As noted above, the Christian iconographical repertoire of the mid- to late fourth century was significantly expanded by the emergence of images related to the gospel narratives of Christ's arrest and trial. Sometimes paralleling these narrative compositions were portrayals of the arrests of Peter and Paul. Primarily appearing on fourth-century sarcophagus reliefs, these new scenes included scenes of Jesus' arrest, his crowning with a wreath (usually of laurel rather than thorns), Simon of Cyrene carrying the cross, and Pilate washing his hands. None of these compositions included the actual crucifixion. Sometimes the programs included a dominantly placed figure of Jesus enthroned and handing the law to his apostles, or a symbolic representation of Christ's victory in the form of an empty cross surmounted by the *chi-rho* monogram. This monogram was enclosed in a wreath of victory and the cross itself was augmented by doves and the Greek letters *Alpha* and *Omega*. Two sleepy Roman soldiers sit at the foot of the cross (Figure 43). Many of these so-called "passion sarcophagi" also included representations of Abraham offering Isaac, probably a way to incorporate the crucifixion symbolically.[60]

This empty cross surmounted by a wreathed Christogram clearly expresses the idea that Jesus' passion leads to triumph. However, the imagery also has a secondary message. The composition was adapted from a familiar Roman military symbol – the *vexillum*, or Roman cavalry standard – a simple cross-shaped armature supporting the legionary insignia and banners. These standards were commonly seen on reverse types of fourth-century Roman coinage with such legends as *virtus exercitus* ("virtue or bravery of the army"), *spes publ* ("hope of the people"), or *fel temp reparatio* ("happy days are here again"). Even the captive and bound enemies shown on the coin reverses are uncannily like the Roman soldiers shown at the foot of the cross-bearing wreath on the passion sarcophagi.

As cited above, long before the iconographic type came into existence, Minucius Felix had already seen the cross-figure in the legionary standards and in the *tropaion* (or victory trophy) that soldiers erected on the field of battle: "What else are your military standards and banners and ensigns but gilded and decorated crosses? Your trophies of victory represent not only the shape of a simple cross, be even that of a man fastened to it."[61] Tertullian also notes this parallel: "You celebrate your victories with religious ceremony … the frames on which you hang up your trophies must be crosses … Thus in your victories, the religion of your camp makes crosses objects of worship … the banners and ensigns which your soldiers guard with sacred care."[62]

These victory-crosses with their dominant Christograms were initially associated with Constantine's heavenly vision of a divine symbol, his conversion to Christianity, and consequently his military conquests. According to Lactantius, whose record of the event pre-dates 318, Constantine dreamt that Jesus directed him to mark the shields of his soldiers with a divine symbol – the Latin letter X rounded at the top. Lactantius apparently wasn't aware of the *chi-rho* monogram, for that was not what he described, even though Constantine himself used the *chi*, bisected by the letter *rho*.[63]

Approximately twenty years later Eusebius recounted a waking vision of Constantine, rather than a dream, in which the emperor along with his whole army saw the "trophy of a cross of light" above the sun in the noonday sky, with the written message "by this conquer" (*touto nika*). On the next night, Jesus appeared to Constantine in a dream and commanded that he make the symbol his ensign, to safeguard him in all military engagements. According to Eusebius, Constantine then ordered a new war standard for his troops – a transverse bar attached to a spear, surmounted by a wreath of gold studded with gems. The monogram of the savior (the *chi-rho*) took up the center of the wreath, while below hung portraits of Constantine and his sons, and from the cross-bar a banner. This new standard came to be known as the *labarum*.[64]

Constantine apparently credited his subsequent victory over Maxentius at Rome's Milvian Bridge to the Christian deity's personal patronage and his obedient response to the command that he signify his allegiance with a new military symbol. The divine patronage was also repaid by Constantine's becoming, in turn, the first imperial patron of the Christian church.

Throughout the fourth century the *chi-rho* monogram continued to appear on coin reverses, but almost always in a military context (on helmets, shields, and military standards).[65] Sometimes the *chi* turned forty-five degrees to form an upright cross of which one arm was rounded to make a *rho*, perhaps merely a confused version of the sign, or possibly a deliberate transformation that made the mark appear more like the cross of Christ (a *staurogram*). Originally these symbols may have served as insignia primarily associated with the imperial dynasty and its military victories. However, apart from coin types and the passion sarcophagi described above, the monogram of Christ also began to be nearly ubiquitous on more simply decorated tombs, in basilica and baptistery mosaics, and on a wide variety of other objects (lamps, glass cups, patens, reliquaries, etc.). Detached from the narrative images of the passion, the Christogram referred to triumph over death in a general sense, whether Christ's on the cross or the neophyte's appropriation of that triumph in the baptismal font.

In the fourth century the simple cross also appeared, either carried by Simon of Cyrene, or held by Jesus as a sign of triumph. In many of these scenes Jesus is flanked by his apostles, who often carry crowns or greet Jesus with gestures of acclamation (Figure 51). In the fourth and fifth centuries, somewhat later than the first regular appearances of the *chi-rho* monogram, the simple cross began to occur frequently. The vaults of small chapels or mausolea had such crosses in gold mosaic against starry night skies. Crosses appeared mounted on empty thrones; held by the Good Shepherd, the Lamb, Peter and other saints and martyrs; studded with jewels and planted on the rocky mount from which the four rivers flowed; or surmounted with a bust of Christ. The cross also replaced the wand in some of the iconography of the raising of Lazarus or the miracles of Cana or the multiplication of the loaves.[66] In these compositions, however, the cross refers not simply to Jesus' crucifixion, but his transfiguration, his victory, his heavenly reign, and his second coming.

The emergence of the cross as a symbol both of Christ's death and of his victory over death probably should be credited partially to Constantine's mother Helena, who identified the actual cross of Jesus' crucifixion on Calvary in 326. Helena's discovery led to the building of a great pilgrimage shrine at Golgotha, and further to the tradition of venerating fragments of the cross (first in the Holy Sepulchre in Jerusalem and eventually in the spread of cross-relics across Europe), the addition of new liturgical feasts honoring the cross itself, and the spread of stories and legends about the crucifixion and the site of Calvary.[67]

## From cross to crucifix

The first crucifixion images probably were a by-product of the sensation caused by Helena's discovery of the True Cross and the subsequent pilgrimage traffic to the Holy Land. The earliest examples show Jesus on the cross, eyes open and physically robust, more than suffering and dying (cf. Figure 49). His outstretched arms do not droop, but in fact almost appear to make a gesture of speech, or embrace. The ivory plaque from the British Museum shows Judas hanging just to the left of Christ on the cross and the contrast between the hanging Judas and the very alive Christ is dramatic. The version that illuminates the Syriac Rabbula Gospels shows Jesus in purple and gold robe (rather than a loincloth) and adds a halo. Appearing in subsequent representations, whether painted on wood or enameled on metal, these details continue an emphasis on Jesus' dignity and his transcendence over human suffering and death.

Sixth-century pilgrims' souvenirs, including lead ampullae containing holy oil, depicted scenes of Jesus' nativity, baptism, or crucifixion. The crucifixon scenes on some of these ampullae show Christ on the cross between the two crucified thieves and above the tomb (Figure 50). On others, however, Christ's bust merely hovers above an empty cross, yet still between the two thieves and above a representation of the empty tomb approached by the women and attended by an angel. The cross stands upon the rocky mount (Golgotha), from which flow the four rivers of paradise. A sixth-century gem shows a similar composition – Jesus' bust, bearded and nimbed, hovers over an empty cross. At the foot of this cross, instead of Roman soldiers stand Peter (holding a cross) and Paul (holding a book). Above the heads of these apostles is the title "Emmanuel."

The two different presentations of this theme may reflect two distinct artistic prototypes, or perhaps a transition from narrative to dogmatic imagery. The second image with bust and empty cross avoids the graphic realism of the suffering redeemer, and instead emphasizes the triumph of the cross and anticipates the resurrection and ascension. The cross itself might have been modeled on the actual cross memorial erected in the mid-fourth century by Constantine at the site of Golgotha, and the soldiers positioned at the foot of the cross in the iconography could also be seen as pilgrims venerating a shrine.[68]

Their owners probably purchased these ampullae at sites they had visited in the same way that today's tourists pick up small keepsakes with pictures of Mount Rushmore or the Tower of London.[69] In fact, the inscriptions on many of them bear some reference to their provenance at "the holy places" (*ton hagion topon*). Moreover, the distribution of relics from the site of the True Cross itself also had an impact on the development of Christian portrayals of the crucifixion. Reliquaries containing dust or even small wood fragments were adorned with crucifixion images. Pilgrims brought these boxes to distant parts of Christendom, and their iconography was borrowed for the decoration of Bible manuscripts, liturgical implements, wooden icons, pectoral crosses, and ivory diptychs, as well as more monumental images in apses and vaults like those in S. Maria Antiqua (8th cent.) or S. Clemente (12th cent.), both in Rome.

The impressive martyrium at the site of Calvary – the basilica built over the tomb of Jesus and the rotunda of the resurrection – was the ultimate tourist stop in the Holy Land. This great basilica, in addition to containing the Rock of Golgotha, possessed a piece of wood from the True Cross contained in a gold and silver reliquary box, and the plaque reading "King of the Jews" affixed to the cross by Roman soldiers. These two last items were exposed for the pilgrims' veneration on Good Friday and possibly also at other times during the year.[70] Although the original Constantinian structure was essentially lost in the early Middle Ages and no surviving written documents describe its apse decoration, some art historians have theorized that the Holy Sepulchre's apse contained a large monumental mosaic of the crucifixion – an image that could have been the prototype for subsequent crucifixion iconography.[71]

## Christological controversy and the suffering redeemer

That the appearance of passion iconography coincides with the deep divisions among Christians regarding the extent of Christ's human nature and his capacity for ordinary mortal suffering may not be coincidental. If Christ were truly part of the Trinity, how could he, particularly in his divine nature, undergo the kind of suffering and death that would subject the impassable and transcendent God to the indignity and mutability of human existence? To some fourth- and fifth-century theologians, such a death could only have been borne by the human nature of Jesus. The logos – or divine nature – separated from the human nature at the last moment. Any other view would constitute the heresy of patripassionism, associated with the second- and third-century heretics Sabellius, Noetus, and Praxeas.[72]

To other theologians of the period (including Cyril of Alexandria), too clear a distinction between Jesus' human nature that was capable of suffering and his divine nature that was incapable of human passion constituted a form of Nestorianism. Nestorius, a student of Diodore of Tarsus and one-time bishop of Constantinople stressed the distinct characteristics of divine and human natures and believed their separation protected the divinity from attribution of human weakness. Such a construct, however, tended to separate the two natures of Christ so completely that it risked making of Jesus a kind of bifurcated creature, a being unable to redeem all of human nature, since his divine nature never assumed all aspects of mortal existence.

Nestorius' detractors insisted upon a real and unbreakable union between human and divine natures, a union that, from the moment of incarnation, transformed the physical human body and made it incorruptible.[73] Thus Christ's death was not like an ordinary human death but, instead, the temporary death of flesh that suffered without actual pain and was restored again in the resurrection. Cyril of Alexandria explained, thus: "though being by his nature impassible, [Christ] suffered in the flesh for us, according to the Scriptures, and he was in the crucified flesh impassibly making his own the sufferings of his own flesh."[74] Following Cyril, the fourth-century western father Hilary of Poitiers claimed: "He had a body to suffer, and he suffered, but he had not a nature that could feel pain. For his body possessed a unique nature of its own."[75]

The Christological debate was theoretically resolved with the Chalcedonian compromise (451) that Jesus existed as "one person in two natures" and in such a way that "the distinction of the two natures was in no way abolished by their union but rather the characteristic property of each nature preserved." This formula asserted the union's permanency from the moment of incarnation but also allowed the protection of the divine nature from the possibility of human suffering. However, the phrase "in two natures," was particularly unsatisfactory to many Christians, some of whom broke from the majority who agreed to the Chalcedonian compromise. Monophysites, or "non-Chalcedonian Christians," in Egypt continued to insist on the phrase "one nature formed *out of* two natures," and on the divine nature's full capability for human suffering.

Thus, between the fourth-century passion images that showed some reluctance to represent the crucifixion realistically, either substituting the Lamb or the cross of victory, and the sixth- and seventh-century artistic representations of Christ's actual crucifixion, although only later on visually suggesting his pain and anguish, a theological debate had been waged about the significance and nature of Jesus' suffering and death. The controversy remained through the early Middle Ages and played a role in the Iconoclastic controversies in the East.[76] Use of allegorical images (e.g. the Lamb) that merely suggested the passion came too close to denying Jesus' full incarnate humanity even as early as the Council of Trullo in 692.

Perhaps acceding to the "orthodox" view that Jesus' passion was unlike ordinary mortal agonies, the earliest portrayals of the crucified Christ seem to reveal some ambivalence about portraying Jesus' suffering or death, since he is shown on the cross, but also alive and without obvious pain.[77] One of the Trinity dies, certainly, but the death is still that of a transcendent deity. However, a conclusion that the almost morbid realism and increasing emphasis on physical suffering that characterizes medieval western art indicates a shift towards a "monophysite" or Sabellian Christology cannot be sustained by the textual evidence. These later compositions probably are less affected by Christological debates than by popular piety, specifically the emergence of a type of medieval devotional practice that included meditation on Christ's passion in detail.[78]

According to tradition, Francis of Assisi wrote an Office of the passion and received stigmata (marks that looked like Christ's nail wounds in the palms of his hands) after seeing a vision of a six-winged seraph in the form of a man crucified. Francis' reception of the stigmata stimulated a whole tradition of devotion to Christ's passion, particularly strong among the Franciscans, and exemplified by Bonaventure. Fourteenth-century visionaries and mystics also described their experiences of Christ's passion in language that spares no graphic details. For example, Julian of Norwich described her experience of gazing upon the image of the crucifixion, a vision that sometimes included her personal experience of pain and suffering, and sometimes transcended it:

> I looked with bodily vision into the face of the crucifix which hung before me, in which I saw a part of Christ's Passion: contempt, foul spitting, buffeting, and many long-drawn pains, more than I can tell; and his colour often changed. At one time I saw how half his face, beginning at the ear, became covered with dried blood, until it was caked to the middle of his face, and then the other side was caked in the same fashion ... [79]

Thus, the reasons for emphasizing the suffering of Christ on the cross in medieval art may be related to the reasons the early church avoided it, and have to do with the graphic potency of such an image. Although they could use words to describe the passion, third-, fourth-, and fifth-century Christians may have considered a visual presentation of Christ's suffering too disturbing or too powerful once given concrete form. Thus they resorted to metaphors or symbols that referred to the passion but yet concealed it from the profane world. Later Christians found the figure no less powerful but had developed a devotional or mystical language that could encompass and direct its deep impact.

## Conclusion

The centrality of both the empty cross and the crucifix in the history of Christian art is evident to anyone who cares to look. At different times, and in different versions, both the cross and the crucifix have symbolized death and expiation or life and victory, sometimes simultaneously. As instrument of death, the cross serves as the locus of the sin offering, the altar on which the lamb is slain. Crucifixion images which emphasize the pain and suffering of such an offering are intended to evoke both pity and gratitude in the viewer. As tree of life, the cross replaces the tree of Eden and opens again the potential for eternal life and favor with God. As sign of victory, the cross, often augmented with wreath and Christogram, suggests God's bene-faction toward a particular human community.

Despite its centrality both in the literary testimonies and in later visual art, however, the figure of Christ on a cross came surprisingly late into the visual language of Christianity. The emergence of this image significantly coincides with the widespread practice of making pilgrimage to the Holy Land, and when there to visit the sacred places (*loca sancta*) that marked episodes in the life of Christ. In these places pilgrims no longer heard about sacred events in the past, but encountered an aspect of their historical reality. They not only heard a story, they experienced it in its actual geographical setting. Narratives were given a vivid physicality and a sensory-activated memory.

Tours of the most sacred of all shrines, the Holy Sepulchre, must have countered any reticence about representing the historical actuality of the crucifixion. If pilgrims could kneel to kiss a fragment of the cross in the very place of the crucifixion, the fear of confronting such an event, either as scandal or as awesome mystery, was somewhat abated. As the climax to a pilgrimage, such an occasion needed to be commemorated via the closest approximation of the trip itself – a concrete visual token containing a visual representation of the place and its significance. Thus the association between text and image, story and material reality was made in a way that both honored the power of the narrative and recognized its impact on the hearer or (now) viewer.

In time, the pilgrimage became an interior journey, in which the contemplation of the crucifix was the goal, and the image was more than simple memorial or souvenir. In this way the viewer's imagination would be engaged in a deeply personal way with the subject, making the event of the passion move in time – from a distant point in history to the present. This real presence also makes the image itself an instrument of personal transformation in a way very like the work of the sacraments of the church. The drama came to life by making the individual one among the eyewitnesses at the foot of the cross. From that vantage point, the death of Jesus on the cross both provoked and sustained faith, and its visual contemplation continued to convert and shape the life of the beholder.

# 6

## BORN AGAIN

The resurrection of the body and the restoration
of Eden

### Introduction

Belief in resurrection was an essential part of Christian faith in late antiquity
and a hope visually expressed in the catacomb paintings or sarcophagus
reliefs. Christians understood their time on earth as only the rehearsal for
eternal life, which was initially promised and symbolically acted out in the
sacrament of baptism. As a tenet of the faith, the affirmation of belief in the
resurrection of the dead may be found in the earliest creeds and baptismal
confessions, including the formula contained in the third-century *Apostolic
Tradition* of Hippolytus. At the third immersion the initiate asserted that he
or she believed in the Holy Spirit, the holy church, and the resurrection of
the flesh.[1]

This wording specifically and literally speaks of flesh – a skin, bones, and
blood reality – and not "body," a term that is more ambiguous and not as
carnal. The confession of belief in a fleshly resurrection (*carnis resurrectionis*)
characterizes western creeds in general, including the Old Roman Creed,
and is the wording of almost all versions of the Apostles' Creed. The eastern
tradition offers more variants, however. While Cyril reports the affirmation
of a fleshly resurrection in the baptismal creed in Jerusalem (*sarkos anastasin*), the later, more dominant eastern tradition tends to confess a belief in
the resurrection of the dead (*anastasin nekron*).[2]

New Testament writings basically support the wording "resurrection of
the dead" or "resurrection of the body" (Matthew 22:30–2; 1 Corinthians
15). But even in the first century, textual evidence shows that other
Christian writers spoke about the resurrection as being specifically of flesh.[3]
In any case, all such confessions should be understood as referring to the
Christian expectation of a general resurrection, shown first and modeled on
Christ's resurrection on Easter morning. Moreover, the terms "flesh," "body,"
or even "dead" used in these creeds emphasized a physical resurrection, as
opposed to a distinctly different belief in the immortality of the soul or of
some purely spiritual, bodiless entity, proposed by the philosophical schools
and shared by gnostics, Marcionites, and other docetic Christians.[4] However,

the affirmation of the resurrection that comes at the conclusion of the baptismal confessions, either presumes general understanding or leaves the question open as to when the resurrection would happen, and where the resurrected ones would go.

By the second century the sense of urgency about Jesus' second coming had worn off and the teachings became even more vague on the how and when of resurrection, and equally hazy on the matter of where. Several different themes were related in some way to one another – Christ's second coming, the resurrection of the dead (with their bodies), final judgment, the end of the age, and the "life everlasting" (the last line of many of the creeds). According to one commonly held view, the souls of the dead would wait in an intermediate place for the end of time, when they would be reunited with their bodies and face the final judgment (both punishment and reward would have a bodily dimension since both soul and body sinned or overcame sin together in life).[5] The worthy (bodies and souls together) would be admitted to paradise, where the saints and martyrs were already waiting – an exception to the general resurrection that was proleptically established when the graves of the righteous were opened at the crucifixion (Matthew 27:51–3).[6]

This perspective still overlooks the question of whether the resurrection is of actual, earthly flesh, or a reunion of souls with bodies that have been transformed into something glorious and spiritual. At stake in this question is the essential goodness of physical, material reality over against Hellenistic, gnostic, and Marcionite repudiation of the perishable body – indeed any type of matter – as capable of immortality or as a locus of divinity. Since matter changed, decayed, and perished, philosophy viewed it as inferior, certainly having no direct connection with the immortal, eternal world of the divine – a result of the disintegration of original unity to multiplicity. Most gnostic systems viewed human fleshly bodies as the tragic consequence of the fall of humanity from an original good to a shadowed evil. One primary understanding of redemption, therefore, assumes an escape from the prison of fleshly existence and a return to (or resurrection of) the pure, spiritual, incorruptible and unified "true self."[7]

Gnostic writers also de-emphasized the literal (bodily) nature of Christ's resurrection and posited Jesus' resurrected self to be something other than the physical reality he had on earth.[8] Such assertions challenged "orthodox" Christian writers to refine their arguments on the actuality of Christ's bodily resurrection, even to make their case by emphasizing the reality of the fleshly resurrection in contrast to more spiritualized views of resurrection adopted by gnostics who even cited Paul's writings in their favor.[9] After all, the evangelist went to some pains to assert that the tomb was empty on Easter morning, and that despite rumors spread by the chief priests, no one had stolen it (Matthew 28:6–14).

Thus, against widespread tendencies to devalue or even to deprecate human bodily existence, mainstream Christian writers took pains to affirm its essential goodness, an affirmation supported by contemporary iconography, and related to the centrality of the Christian hopes for a life after death, both in text and in art. The incarnation, after all, required a different view of creation and its potential as a vehicle for the divine presence. Since the term "body" was perhaps too vague to be useful in this polemic, some theologians began to speak in more concrete terms of a resurrection of the flesh itself, both Christ's flesh and that of all believing Christians. Tertullian, in particular, maintained that flesh, created by God, had great "dignity" and was the hinge of salvation.[10] God would not have created something if it were unfit, and intend to abandon it in the end; and God certainly could remake what he had made in the first place. Tertullian even extended the dignity of the body to the bowels and sexual organs.[11] Moreover, flesh has an important function in Tertullian's understanding of the sacraments; it is an outward, external receptor of an inward, invisible grace. In baptism the flesh is dipped and anointed so that the soul may be cleansed and consecrated; in eucharist the flesh receives body and blood so that the soul might be nourished.[12]

Tertullian's argument parallels or even develops what other earlier (second-century) theologians had affirmed regarding the resurrection of the body, including Justin Martyr, Minucius Felix, Irenaeus, Theophilus, Tatian, and (to an extent) Athenagoras.[13] Justin Martyr (c.165) specified that the bodies that return in the resurrection are the same bodies humans have in life, but that those bodies are healed and whole.[14] A different approach was taken by Theophilus and Athenagoras (c.180–200) who develop Paul's simile of the seed and the plant (1 Corinthians 15:35–7) and use organic metaphors to stress the substantial continuity of earthly and heavenly bodies.[15] Tertullian and Irenaeus both worked to establish the goodness of the flesh against various gnostic and docetic groups around the turn of the third century. However, by the mid-third century, other views were also evident, in particular Origen's reworking of the Pauline transformation of the physical and perishable body into a spiritual and imperishable body (1 Corinthians 15:35–54) based on the metaphor of the seed becoming a plant. Origen argued that the resurrection body would be recognizable even if transformed, and cited the various changes in the earthly body in its journey through life as illustrative.[16] Although Origen backed up his argument by analogy to the many changes of the body in its earthly existence, he was refuted by a renewed emphasis on the resurrection of the flesh itself by such writers as Peter of Alexandria, Jerome, and Methodius of Olympus.[17] By way of reinforcement, many of the artistic symbols referring to resurrection include those which speak specifically to the transformation or incorruptablity of flesh itself, including the phoenix and the peacock.

The development of the doctrine of the resurrection continued through the end of the fourth and into the fifth century and beyond. Among the most significant thinkers on the subject was Augustine, who argued that human bodies would be transformed yet still substantial; composed of material that was angelic, luminous, and ethereal. For him the Pauline "spiritual body" was a fully enfleshed body, but one that had been fully united with and was thus obedient to the spirit, rather than one substantially transformed. In *The City of God*, Augustine particularly asserts the created and natural connections of body and soul, spirit and matter. Here he consciously contradicted neo-Platonist philosophers who argued that the existence of the body was a sign of inferiority. Instead, Augustine argued, the separation of these two parts of human existence (body and spirit) in death resulted from the sin of Adam and Eve. The reunion of the two (body and soul) parallels the restoration of Adam and Eve at the end of time, and brings to fruition the promise made by Christ's inaugural resurrection.[18] In line with this, the significance of the figures of Adam and Eve in Christian iconography, thus may have as much or more to do with the idea of restoration and new creation than with sin and fall.

Despite the variants in emphasis between either a resurrection of flesh or of a transformed body, the general principle of a physical resurrection was well established in Christian tradition, both east and west. In tandem with the textual tradition, a variety of resurrection symbols and themes occur in Christian art, some of which particularly resonate with the assertion of a fleshly resurrection. Three common non-narrative symbols include the dolphin, the phoenix, and the peacock (Figure 57). Similar to many of the symbols discussed in Chapter 1, these three connect to no particular scripture passage and moreover were also frequent in non-Christian contexts. The dolphin was a symbol borrowed from Greco-Roman iconography and was commonly found in funereal contexts, as well as in purely decorative maritime schemes in both Christian and pagan art. As a symbol fitting for a tomb its meaning probably was derived from a variety of myths and gods (esp. Dionysus and Apollo) that portrayed dolphins as the carriers of persons to safety or immortality.[19] The phoenix and the peacock were also non-narrative symbols that had clear references to resurrection; the phoenix because of its legendary rise from its own flames and ashes, and the peacock possibly because of the belief that its flesh was incorruptible.[20] Peacocks, like dolphins, were especially popular as decorative motifs, and were nearly ubiquitous in the catacombs, on Christian sarcophagi, and in later church decoration.

However, since many of the writers cited above used biblical typologies to illustrate their arguments regarding the resurrection of the physical body, one would expect also to find narrative images performing the same function. Among the collection of proof-texting analogies for the resurrection we find the story of Jonah, Jesus' raising of Lazarus, the resurrection of the dry bones, Daniel, the three youths in the furnace, the translation (or ascension)

*Figure 57* Peacock, Catacomb of Praetextatus.
© The International Catacomb Society. Photo: Estelle Brettman.

of Elijah and Enoch, the transfiguration, and the creation of Adam and Eve. When these figures also appear in art, they may well serve as allegories of resurrection since textual typologies are frequently paralleled by iconography. But alongside metaphors or symbolic figures of resurrection exist more literal, or illustrative images of resurrection.

Actual presentations of paradise are rare in early Christian art. Scenes of the last judgment appear infrequently, on rare sarcophagus compositions and in the sixth-century mosaic decoration of S. Apollinare Nuovo (Figure 58). These illustrations of the Matthean gospel text (Matthew 25:31–46) show Jesus separating the sheep from the goats, and bear no resemblance to later and very complex medieval iconography of the final judgment. Paulinus of Nola described a version of the same theme that was installed in the apse of his church in Fundi.[21] The only other artistic references to life in paradise include the heavenly banquet scenes described in Chapter 3, or simple pastoral or bucolic motifs (*putti* picking flowers, for example). On the earthly side, by contrast, other kinds of images speak to the expectation of resurrection, beginning with representations of Christ's empty tomb.

*Figure 58* Good Shepherd separating the sheep from the goats, S. Apollinare Nuovo, Ravenna.

Photo: Alinari/Art Resource, New York City.

## Christ's empty tomb and ascension

According to Paul, Christ's resurrection was the "first fruits" of the rest of those who had "fallen asleep" (1 Corinthians 15:20). Thus the resurrection of Christ is both prototype and promise. Like portrayals of the crucifixion, however, explicit representations of Christ's resurrection, ascension, or even images of his empty tomb, are unknown before the late fourth century. The single exception may be a fresco in the Dura Europos baptistery, which may represent the three the women approaching Jesus' tomb on Easter morning.[22] Earlier, indirect, representations of the resurrection include the representation of an empty cross of "victory" on the "passion sarcophagi" (Figure 43). Also, the *traditio legis* compositions that show Christ transcendent and enthroned or seated on an orb certainly are representations of the resurrected Christ, and frequently include heavenly backgrounds (new Jerusalem, cloud-streaked skies) to emphasize the point (cf. Figure 35).[23]

Beginning in the fifth century, representations of the empty tomb, guarded by an angel and visited by two or three women, begin to appear with some regularity. One of the earliest, an ivory diptych from Rome (now in Milan), shows, instead of the stone-barricaded and rock-hewn tomb described in the New Testament, a stone building typical of mausolea in late antiquity. This small rectilinear building topped by a drum-shaped cupola with clerestory windows may have been meant to represent the Anastasis Rotunda in Jerusalem (part of the basilica complex now known as the Holy Sepulchre).[24] Women bow or kneel before a young man seated in front of the shrine. The young man has a halo, holds a scroll, and makes a gesture of greeting (or blessing). Above, on the roof, two Roman guards respond with gestures of fear or awe. In the sky over their heads are the symbols for Matthew (a winged man) and Luke (the ox). Small decorative scenes of Jesus raising Lazarus and speaking to Zacchaeus can be seen on the doors of the tomb (Figure 59).[25]

This particular composition has been thought either to represent the angel announcing the resurrection to the two Marys (Mary Magdalene and "the other" Mary, Matthew 28:1–8), or a visual conflation of that event with Jesus' subsequent appearance to the two women (Matthew 28:9–10). The confusion is due in part to the fact that the young man has a halo and holds a scroll, attributes more appropriate for Christ than for an angel.[26]

A slightly different composition, also on an ivory (now in Munich) and from nearly the same time period, has been commonly identified as a representation of Christ's ascension but might be best taken as another conflation, this time of the resurrection and the ascension. The iconography shows Christ climbing a rocky hill to heaven, reaching up to clasp God's right hand in his (*dextrarum junctio*). The two apostles (Peter and James, according to the tradition recounted in the *Apocryphon of James* 14) who witnessed Christ's ascension are shown crouching below, at the base of the

*Figure 59* Fifth-century ivory diptych (now in Milan) – detail of women at the empty tomb.

Photo: Author.

hill. On the left stands the empty tomb that has a design similar to the Milan ivory, again perhaps evoking the actual shrine in Jerusalem (a domed clerestory set on top of a small square building), rather than the borrowed tomb of Joseph of Arimathea (Matthew 27:57–61). Also similar to the Milan ivory is the appearance of the young man who sits on a rock to the left of the door. His right hand is raised in a gesture of greeting or blessing to three women, but this time he has neither halo nor scroll (his left hand is covered as sign of respect in the presence of the holy). Behind the small building stand two men, either the Roman soldiers mentioned in Matthew's narrative, or the apostles Peter and John, who Mary called to the scene in John's version (John 20:2). The three women probably represent Mary

163

Magdalene, Mary the mother of James, and Salome from Mark's gospel (Mark 16:1).[27]

The image of Jesus climbing the mountain grasping God's hand has an artistic parallel in representations of Moses receiving the law on Sinai. In addition, the clasping of the two right hands, one emerging from heaven in the upper right corner of the scene, may have been derived from the Roman iconography of apotheosis in which the ascending emperor (riding up in a quadriga) stretches up his right hand to grasp the extended right hand of a deity. This imagery, of the emperor riding in a chariot drawn by four horses, was also a prototype for iconography of the ascension of Elijah [Figure 60] or the ascent of Ezekiel, who both typified the resurrection of the body as well as the ascension of Jesus (Acts 1:9).[28] A representation of Jesus ascending in a horse-drawn chariot, in a guise very like that of Helios or Apollo (Figure 9), figures in this discussion as well – especially when that particular image is juxtaposed with representations of Lazarus or Jonah. Compositions that showed Jesus ascending to heaven clearly belong to the iconography of resurrection.

A slightly later ivory casket also from Rome (c.420–30 and now in the British Museum) has four extant plaques, each showing a scene from Christ's passion or resurrection: Pilate washing his hands and Christ carrying the cross, Judas hanging and Christ crucified, the women at the empty tomb, and Thomas touching Christ's side.[29] The empty tomb's architecture is much like the other two ivories, and probably also meant to represent the shrine at the Holy Sepulcher. However, this time only two women are shown and they sit on either side of the tomb (as if in mourning), behind two Roman soldiers. The composition includes no young male angel or Christ figure. Instead the sepulcher's decorated open doors (one now broken off), reveal a bare pallet, draped with grave cloths.

A different kind of resurrection motif was carved on the wooden doors of the basilica of Sta. Sabina in Rome (c.432–40). Here two women approach a winged angel who guards the arched and curtained entrance to a peak-roofed architectural structure instead of one with a drum-shaped cupola. The angel makes a gesture of greeting. No other details are included. The Sta. Sabina doors also include a representation of Christ's ascension directly across from a scene of his second coming. In the former Christ is shown being lifted up to heaven by three angels, while below four apostles watch in awe. The second coming of Christ is presented as an image of Christ in a mandorla (an almond-shaped halo around the body). Standing on earth, just below, is the personification of the church (Ecclesia) who stands in the orant position and is being crowned by the apostles Peter and Paul.

An early sixth-century mosaic program, in Ravenna's S. Apollinare Nuovo, shows a sequence of scenes from Christ's life and significantly skips directly from a representation of Jesus carrying his cross to one of the empty tomb. The tomb in this sequence is portrayed as a small circular open-air

*Figure 60* Ascension of Elijah, from the wooden door of Sta. Sabina, Rome.
Photo: Graydon Snyder.

temple inside of which we see what might be an empty pallet, leaning against the columns. As in the Sta. Sabina image, only two women are shown, here greeting a seated angel who had both wings and a halo.

Similar abbreviated images (two women meeting an angel at a small tomb) also are found on sixth-century lead ampullae (cf. Figure 50). These "empty tomb" compositions ordinarily appear just below the representation of an empty cross that is surmounted by a portrait of Christ and flanked by the two crucified thieves. The ampullae present a standard architectural

165

design for the tomb, however, probably intended to be a representation of the Jerusalem shrine, or more specifically an architectural reference to the aedicula that covered an actual rock-cut tomb at the presumed site of Christ's tomb, inside the Rotunda of the Anastasis. Other ampullae portray Jesus' ascension, which in this case looks more like the illustration of Jesus' second coming found on the Sta. Sabina door panels. Here we see Jesus in a mandorla floating above a grouping of apostles with Mary as an orant in the center. The mandorla is being borne up by winged figures.

These ampullae were pilgrims' tokens, meant as souvenirs of sites visited in the Holy Land and, as such, would have been likely to include details from the sites themselves. Also in the general category of pilgrimage art is the wooden reliquary box now in the Museo Sacro in the Vatican. This box is covered with painted scenes from the life of Christ; the center panel contains an early crucifixion scene. Below are scenes of the nativity and the baptism of Christ and above are images of the empty tomb and the ascension. The sites of these five events had been located and were on pilgrims' itineraries. The owner of this particular box had collected pebbles and earth along the way and deposited them into this reliquary.[30]

Like the small images on the ampullae, the representation of the tomb on this box was probably intended to recall the interior shrine within the Anastasis Rotunda. Overhead the artist attempted to represent the rotunda's dome, with its arched clerestory windows. The scene shows Mary Magdalene and the beloved disciple arriving at the door of the shrine (John 20:2–4) and being met by a winged angel, this time seated to the right. The portrayal of the ascension, just to the right of the empty-tomb scene, also parallels the imagery found on the lead ampullae.

The late sixth-century Rabbula gospel, which contained one of the earliest images of the crucifixion, additionally portrays the empty tomb in a horizontal panel directly under the crucifixion scene. Serving more as illustration than representational metaphor, the composition is comparatively complex. The angel, seated to the left of a small, ornate tomb in the center of the picture, greets two women. The tomb's doors emit rays of light that strike down three Roman soldiers in the foreground. On the right, Jesus greets the same two women, who kneel before him. One of the women (Mary Magdalene?) has a halo, along with Christ and the angel.

A different full-page illumination in this gospel book is a portrayal of Jesus' ascension. In this version, rather than walking up a rocky hill, Jesus is shown from the front, surrounded by a mandorla, and being carried aloft by four winged angels, their hands covered in reverence. Beneath the mandorla is a wheeled and winged seraph made up of the four beasts described in the vision of Ezekiel (Ezekiel 1:4–25). The tetramorphic seraph bearing Christ to heaven eventually came to typify iconography of the ascension in the east, in contrast to the earlier (western) images that were based on Roman apotheosis iconography. Similarly the tetramorph in this portrayal is distinct from the appearance of the four distinct "beasts" that symbolized the four evangelists in the west.[31] On the ground, and watching in amazement, are a crowd of apostles with Mary, as an orant, standing in the center.[32] Ascension compositions that show Jesus in a mandorla demonstrate the typical eastern presentation of the scene from the sixth century onwards.

## Resurrection typologies: the dry bones, Jairus' daughter, the widow's son, and Lazarus

In the tradition, Christ's resurrection is presented as the prototype of the final resurrection of all the faithful. In both the art and biblical interpretation of the early church additional prototypes of resurrection emerge, including several scriptural accounts of the dead being raised. These figures, especially the raising of Lazarus, were prefigurements of Christ's own death and resurrection as well as that of the members of the Christian community.

Based upon the documentary evidence discussed above, most Christians were taught that the resurrection would be universal, after judgment at the end of time, rather than an individual translation to a happy "heavenly home" immediately after death, and that this resurrection would include their bodies – bodies that had been stored in tombs until the day would arrive. But representations of judgment were not popular, and art of the early church rather emphasized the resurrection that followed, and in one instance that resurrection was represented as a universal – or corporate one. Such expectation of corporate bodily (or fleshly) resurrection is artistically presented through a type, specifically the resuscitation of the "dry bones" described in Ezekiel 37. Other compositions which refer to the raising of the dead present individual miracles from the New Testament, in particular Jesus raising the widow's son (Luke 7:11–17), Jesus raising Jairus' daughter (Mark 5:22–43), Jesus raising Lazarus (John 11: 1–44), and (possibly) Peter raising Tabitha (Acts 9:40–1).

The vision of the prophet Ezekiel (37:1–14) describes a valley full of dry bones that came to life after Ezekiel fulfilled God's command that he should prophesy to them, telling them they would receive breath and flesh again. In written commentaries on this text, Ezekiel is taken to be a prefiguration of Christ, raising the dead from their graves at the end of time, which is how the fourth- and fifth-century artistic representations should be interpreted as well.[33] The earliest known visual presentation of Ezekiel's vision was painted on the walls of the Dura Synagogue, a faithful illustration of the story as told in the biblical text. By contrast, Christian art shows a distinctly different and far more truncated version of the scene, most commonly found on sarcophagus reliefs. These scenes depict a young man touching a wand (*virga*) to a small naked figure lying on the ground surrounded by skulls. Standing (already resuscitated) are more small naked figures (Figure 61). That the miracle-worker is meant to be Christ (and not Ezekiel) is made

*Figure 61*  Jesus (Ezekiel?) raising the dead with the adoration of the magi on a fourth-century sarcophagus now in the Vatican Museo Pio Cristiano.
Photo: Author.

clear through his appearance: his facial features (unbearded and youthful), his Roman dress, and his wand. Jesus, looking approximately the same, also often appears in adjacent scenes of healing or working wonders.[34]

Early Christian textual sources not only take Ezekiel as a prefiguration of Jesus raising the dead, but point out the story's particular emphasis on the resurrection of long-buried bones. Some early writers found polemical value in the story. Justin Martyr asserts that Ezekiel's vision forecast a future resurrection that would exclude the Jews ("the whole house of Israel," in Ezekiel 37:11), who will lament the "error" that lost them their hope.[35] Irenaeus uses the story to denounce gnostics who believe the creator-demiurge is a lesser god. For Irenaeus, the story clearly proves that the One who orders Ezekiel to prophecy is both God of creation and God of resurrection; the same God also manifest in the one who healed the man born blind, Jesus Christ.[36]

Tertullian, like Justin Martyr before him, incorporates the dry bones text into his anti-Jewish debate, but also expounds at length upon the prophecy of Ezekiel as proof of the resurrection of the flesh.[37] Jerome wrote an entire commentary on Ezekiel in order to refute Origen's spiritual view of the resurrection, and on the day when the text of Ezekiel was read from the lectionary, Cyril of Jerusalem devoted one of his catechetical lectures to the subject of the resurrection of the flesh and all its figures in the scriptures.[38]

Gregory of Nyssa's treatise, "On the Soul and the Resurrection" recounts his conversation with his sister, Macrina, after the death of their brother Basil. Gregory, grieving his brother and seeking consolation, opened the subject of the immortality of the soul and the specific meaning of the resurrection of the dead. Macrina, the "teacher," assures Gregory that the soul survives the body in its grave, awaiting the future time it will be reunited to its body. This body, however, will be a body restored to its original state as the image of God – incapable of weakness, corruption, or suffering – suffused with honor, grace and glory.[39] As she elaborated, Macrina called upon "proofs" of her teaching, found in several passages of scripture including the resuscitation of the dry bones by Ezekiel, the healings of Jesus, Jesus' raising of Jairus' daughter, the widow's son, and Lazarus, as well as Jesus' own resurrection on Easter morning. Each of these stories is an intimation of the future resurrection promised by Jesus in his words to Martha, Lazarus' sister: "I am the resurrection and the life; the one who believes in me, though dead, yet shall live, and whoever lives and believes in me shall never die" (John 11:25–6).[40]

All the New Testament figures that Macrina cites appear in Christian iconography from the mid-third century onwards. Portrayals of Jesus healing are particularly common and include the healings of the paralytic, the leper, the man born blind, and the demoniac. The raising of Jairus' daughter or the widow's son are less common. In these Jesus uses his wand to perform the miracle (rather than laying on his hand as in the healing stories – Figure 30). The raising of Lazarus, by contrast, is a popular subject, found in catacomb paintings, sarcophagus reliefs, mosaics, and in ivory on diptychs, reliquaries, and pyxides. Most of these scenes share a basic composition: Jesus, holding a wand, points at or taps on a small mausoleum at the door of which stands a diminutive mummified figure that we recognize to be Lazarus. One or both of Lazarus' sisters fall at Jesus' feet in supplication (Figure 62). In some of the examples a small crowd of witnesses may be seen in the background. In one version, a small nude male stands, to Jesus' left.

*Figure 62* Jesus raising Lazarus and multiplying loaves on a fourth-century sarcophagus in the Vatican Museo Pio Cristiano.

Photo: Author.

169

The sepulchral location of most of these Lazarus compositions suggests that the scene conveys a message of reassurance of resurrection, or life beyond death. Lazarus, returned to this life, is a prototypical figure symbolizing the recently dead one's resurrection to the next life. Although Lazarus will one day die again, his first raising is the proof that God can bring the dead back to life, either here or in paradise. As Macrina points out, the text itself gives the promise to those who believe in Christ.

The special place of Lazarus' resurrection story in the Johannine narrative, however, suggests additional layers of meaning in this image. First, the Lazarus narrative functions as the literary connecting link between Jesus' public ministry and the beginning of the passion drama, primarily because this final miracle (or sign) of Jesus was the last straw for his enemies and the precipitating cause of his arrest. Thus Lazarus' death, entombment, and resurrection also foreshadow Jesus' three-day ordeal and triumph. Certain narrative elements contribute to the parallels, including the weeping women, the stone lying against the door of the tomb, and the linen wrappings that bound Lazarus' body. Consider the figure of Lazarus found on the doors of the empty-tomb scene discussed above (Figure 59).

Second, much early Christian commentary on this uniquely Johannine story cites it (like the raising of the dry bones) as proof of the bodily (fleshly) resurrection, particularly in order to refute gnostic or Marcionite assertions that flesh and blood, as corruptible substance, would necessarily be excluded from salvation. Irenaeus, being especially literal, calls upon the Lazarus story as evidence that although the body decays after death (the women in the story even feared the stench from Lazarus' tomb), at God's command even decomposing flesh can be restored in glory. Irenaeus further elaborates on some of the symbolism of the text, specifically referring to the wrappings that bound Lazarus' hands and feet. According to Irenaeus, Jesus' command to "loose him and let him depart" signifies the forgiving of Lazarus' sins as much as a renewing of his physical life.[41]

Gregory of Nyssa also cites the Lazarus story as confirmation of the resurrection of the flesh. Gregory further explains that Jesus' raising of Lazarus was for the purpose of initiating the apostles into the mysteries of the general resurrection. If even a body four days in the tomb, swollen and beginning to rot, could be brought out whole and sound (not even hindered by grave wrappings), God could surely revivify any body, no matter how long dead.[42]

Following a different line, Cyril of Jerusalem cites the raising of Lazarus in his fourth-century catechetical lectures given to candidates for baptism. Speaking in midst of the complex that housed the traditional sites of Jesus' death and resurrection, the bishop of Jerusalem compared baptized Christians to Lazarus, as they too have been raised from the dead. Since baptism is in fact a sacrament that incorporates the symbolism of dying and rising, Lazarus' resurrection also is a prototype of baptism, a rite in which Christians participate in the passion of Jesus (Romans 6:3–5).[43]

Western writers of the later fourth and early fifth centuries (Ambrose and Augustine) picked up the moral interpretation begun by Irenaeus and further explored the story's allegorical possibilities. In his commentary on John's gospel, Augustine argues that Lazarus' tomb signifies his alienation from God, and the stone over its entrance the weight of guilty habits. Lazarus' resurrection, then, represents the grace given by God to overcome sin, his bindings symbolizing the fallen nature of the present human condition.[44] This overcoming of such sin, of course, begins with baptism and then continues through participation in the community's rituals and sacraments.

Arguing that this type of more allegorical or abstract theological reflection on the Lazarus story could have directly influenced iconography seems strained. The function of Lazarus as metaphor is both contemporaneous and popular. The earliest known examples are third century and found in the Catacomb of Callistus and on the so-called Jonah sarcophagus in the Vatican Museum. The Lazarus scene continued to appear in the Roman catacombs and on other sarcophagi through the mid- to late fourth century, after which it began to appear in mosaics and ivories in particular. Often found adjacent to other scenes of healings or miracles, including the multiplication of the loaves and fishes, the wedding at Cana, the healing of the man born blind, or the healing of the paralytic, the Lazarus scenes appear to be part of an integrated image program referring to baptism, healing, death, and resurrection. And when a representation of Lazarus' raising is paired with a scene of Abraham offering Isaac (as on a fifth-century ivory pyx from Syria-Palestine) the entire iconographic program points figuratively to Jesus' saving death and resurrection.[45]

### Allegories of resurrection: Jonah, Daniel, and the baptism of Christ

As noted above, in at least one of the Lazarus scenes, a small nude male stands at Christ's feet in a way quite reminiscent of the figures that appear in representations of the raising of the dry bones (Figure 61). The small naked figure in this particular Lazarus image has no narrative parallel, and thus must be meant to symbolize Lazarus himself, now resurrected, but shown as naked and child-sized instead of an adult-sized male. Such figures appear so commonly in early Christian art that they draw our attention and raise the questions: Why nude? Why childlike?

Several commonly presented scenes in early Christian art show similar small nude figures. As well as in the two settings described above, small, childlike nudes appear in scenes of baptism, and in illustrations of the creation of Adam and Eve. Jonah, whether going into or out of the mouth of the big fish; Adam and Eve in the garden; and Daniel, standing between his lions, are also often shown nude, although usually equivalent in size to other adult figures in the surrounding iconography. Thus, showing particular characters in art as nude, and some as small and nude, must have had particular significance.[46] Jonah is a special case in point.

The figure of Jonah was by far one of the most reproduced in early Christian art. Visual representations of different episodes of the Jonah story are among the earliest generation of recognizable Christian images and they appear with consistent frequency through the middle of the fourth century. The oldest known Jonah scenes appear in the third-century Catacomb of Callistus, in the chamber of the sacraments and the area known as the Crypt of Lucina. In the pre-Constantinian era, whether in the extant catacomb frescoes or on sarcophagus reliefs, Jonah occurs more than seventy times, of which at least thirty are series of three or four episodes. Such cycle iconography is unique in early Christian art, although like other, more abbreviated subjects based on scriptural narrative, much of the story is still omitted, including God's command to Jonah to preach to the Ninevites and their ultimate conversion. This series concentrates on Jonah's being tossed overboard and swallowed by the fish and his subsequent re-emergence on dry land, reclining under either a withered gourd vine or one freshly come to life (Figure 20).[47] The cycle episodes, usually painted in individual scenes, often on the domes or arscolia, were reproduced in a more connected set of images on the sarcophagi (Figure 63). In addition to frescoes and reliefs, Jonah appeared in mosaic and in rare small pieces of sculpture.[48]

*Figure 63* Jonah being tossed overboard from the so-called Jonah Sarcophagus now in the Vatican Museo Pio Cristiano (late third century).

Photo: Author.

The final scene of the narrative series, in which Jonah reclines under the gourd vine, shows him nude and reclining with his right arm lifted above his head and his right leg crossed over his left. This posture was clearly modeled on classical prototypes, including that of Endymion in Roman art.[49] Endymion, a character from Roman mythology cursed with both perpetual youth and perpetual sleep, was visited nightly by the moon goddess, Selene, who had sexual intercourse with the sleeping youth and bore him forty children.[50] Endymion's nudity as well as his peculiar posture influenced the visual presentation of Jonah at rest on land. Given the sepulchral nature of both the Endymion and the Jonah motifs, both must refer to death as the restful sleep of the blessed. However, for Jonah, unlike Endymion, the rest is only an interim state, since the iconography also clearly points to the resurrection.

The connection between Jonah and the resurrection has its most direct link in the "sign of Jonah" (Matthew 12:39–40), when Jesus evokes the prophesy that like "Jonah who was three days and nights in the belly of the fish, so will the Son of Man be three days and three nights in the heart of the earth." Ignatius of Antioch's letter to the Trallians cites this "sign of Jonah," partly to explain why the Lord's day is on Sunday rather than on the Jewish Sabbath.[51] Justin Martyr elaborates on the sign of Jonah by retelling the Jonah story and uses it to exhort his hearers to repent of their wickedness just as the Ninevites did.[52] Irenaeus, instead, makes good use of the story of Jonah as a sign of bodily resurrection in his polemic against the gnostics. If Jonah could stay in the belly for three days and yet be regurgitated whole then God could certainly raise dead bodies from their graves, in the same way that God could preserve the bodies of the three young men in the flaming furnace.[53] Tertullian also cites the examples of the three youths and Jonah, whose bodies remained intact despite fires or devouring sea monsters. To these cases he adds the precedents of the Israelites in the desert (whose hair and nails remained miraculously trim, and whose clothing and shoes remained fresh and unworn through their forty-year sojourn in the wilderness); and the bodily ascents of Enoch and Elijah, who, although they couldn't experience an actual resurrection (because they never died), came to know what it would mean to be exempt from all bodily corruption or decay.[54]

Basil of Caeserea took the sign of Jonah a step further and interpreted Jonah's three days in the belly of the monster as a figure of the triple immersion in baptism.[55] Since Christian baptism is itself a symbol of Jesus' passion, death, and resurrection, the baptismal connection would be logical even without the added detail of the water – water into which Jonah is tossed and the initiate is immersed. Jonah's nudity thus symbolizes the nudity of the candidates for baptism as they are dipped and "reborn" from the womblike waters of the baptismal font.[56]

This collective symbolism of baptism and resurrection is masterfully presented in the artistic composition of the sarcophagus of Sta. Maria Antiqua, a tub-shaped rather than rectangular sarcophagus. In this three-sided frieze, water that pours out from the jug of the river god on the left end provides the sea for scenes from the Jonah cycle, the river for the figure of John baptizing Jesus, and the lake for the fishers on the right end (Figures 13a–c). Other such integrated iconographical programs combine scenes from the Jonah cycle with a variety of the following: the raising of Lazarus, Noah in the ark, Moses striking the rock, pastoral scenes of the shepherd with his flock, Adam and Eve, the adoration of the magi, or Daniel between his lions.

Adam, Eve, and Daniel also appear as nudes in early Christian art. Adam's and Eve's nudity make sense since they are presented in the scripture narrative as originally naked and not ashamed of their nakedness (Genesis 2:25). This particular line of the Bible is cited by certain church fathers to explain why candidates for baptism enter the font nude. Daniel's nudity, however, is not based on the textual narrative, and must be explained in another way. The Greco-Roman iconographic convention of portraying the hero as nude might account for Daniel's nakedness (in the same way that Endymion serves as a classical prototype for Jonah). However, such an explanation would also suggest that Daniel (or Jonah) should be distinguished from other "heroic" biblical figures who are less frequently portrayed, but nonetheless shown fully clothed (e.g. Samson and Joshua).

In addition to showing him nude, most representations of Daniel portray him as beardless, standing (facing out), with his arms raised in prayer like the orant. Two lions sit on his left and right, in a kind of heraldic composition. An extremely popular figure, Daniel appears in the catacomb frescoes, sarcophagus carvings, on lamps, ivories, pottery, bronzes and glass from the third century through the sixth (cf. Figure 21). Not always nude, Daniel occasionally appears clothed, e.g. on sarcophagi in Gaul, Ravenna, and Istanbul, as well as in the sixth-century baptistery of the Orthodox in Ravenna.[57] Other early representations of Daniel portray his part in different scriptural narratives, including his role in the judgment of Susannah, with the three young men refusing to adore Nebuchadnezzar's statue, being aided by Habakkuk and the angel, or killing the Babylonian dragon (Figure 24). According to Eusebius, Constantine commissioned a gold and brass statue of Daniel with his lions (along with a figure of the Good Shepherd) for a fountain in the main forum of Constantinople.[58] While all these Daniel images might be interpreted as allusions to martyrdom, or resistance to idolatry even in face of threat from secular authorities, such interpretations overlook the potential significance of Daniel's nakedness in the most popular extant compositions – the one in which he appears with the lions.[59]

Early Christian writers who commented on the Daniel narratives focused mainly on his dreams and prophecies recounted in chapters 7–12, seeing in their messianic images and predictions of the coming eschaton, the figure of Jesus and Christ's final judgment. For Justin Martyr, Irenaeus, and Origen,

Daniel was the prophet who predicted the coming of Christ.[60] Irenaeus and Hippolytus also read in the Book of Daniel a prophecy regarding the end of the Roman empire and the coming of the millennium – the thousand-year Sabbath of the saints before the final battle with the Antichrist, judgment, and resurrection of the blessed.[61] Tertullian and Cyprian both interpreted Daniel morally, seeing him as a model of the brave and righteous Christian who refuses to bow down to idols, even willing to undergo persecution and death as a martyr for the faith.[62] Later commentators, including Gregory of Nazianzus and Cyril of Jerusalem, continued to see Daniel as the prototype of the Christian martyr while others, including Eusebius, Jerome, and Theodoret, rejected a purely moral interpretation and revived an emphasis on the eschatological and messianic prophecies in the book.[63]

Thus one might logically conclude that Daniel's significance in art was as a figure either of the martyr, or of the prophet who predicted the advent of the Messiah (Jesus) and the end of the age. That interpretation still leaves Daniel's nudity unexplained, however. Daniel's nakedness might instead point to his prefiguration of the resurrection, making Daniel (like Jonah), a symbol or type of rebirth. Yet unlike Jonah, the baptismal connection is not made via the motif of water.

Daniel's being understood as a prefiguration of Jesus' resurrection may have been due to a textual detail. The hero is sealed in the den of lions by means of a great stone laid over the mouth of the cave. The next morning, at daybreak, the king returns to the den to find Daniel alive instead of dead – rescued by a mysterious savior figure. Hippolytus, in a commentary on Daniel, notes the supernatural strengthening of the prophet by the "one in human form" (Daniel 10:15–19) as a foreshadowing of the restoration of the physical body, and has the prophet proclaim:

> But while I was in this position, I was strengthened beyond my hope. For one unseen touched me and straightway my weakness was removed, and I was restored to my former strength. For whenever all the strength of our life and its glory pass from us, then are we strengthened by Christ, who stretches forth his hand and raises the living from among the dead, as it were from Hades itself, to the resurrection of life.[64]

In Christian practice, the ritual that grants supernatural healing, strengthening, and the promise of rescue from death is baptism, and (in the early church), the baptized were disrobed and immersed nude. Nudity at baptism had three symbolic values. First it symbolized the stripping off of the old "self," second it represented the original state of Adam and Eve in paradise (thus a return to the pre-lapsed state of humanity), and third it is the way children are born from their mothers' wombs.[65] Thus, if the iconography of Daniel was intended to suggest the resurrection begun in baptism, his nudity has symbolic logic. Moreover, nearly the only actual early Christian representation of baptism *per se* portrays John the Baptist baptizing Jesus, who usually is presented as a small nude, childlike figure (Figure 64).[66] John, often identifiable by his animal-skin tunic, places his right hand on top of Jesus' head, a gesture that may have been intended to suggest the anointing after immersion, or the laying of hands.

According to the gospel narratives, Jesus was an adult when he was baptized in the Jordan by John. The child-like size and appearance of Jesus in these scenes thus appears to contradict the literary source. Some interpreters have even taken these compositions as evidence of the practice of infant baptism in early Christianity.[67] On the contrary, the most logical explanation for the diminutive size or child-like appearance of Jesus is that the iconography reveals an aspect of the rite itself, an aspect also symbolized by the nudity shown in the image – it returns the candidates to the status of children. The figure of Jesus here symbolizes all neophytes. As newly born, just emerged from the waters of the font, they are like naked babes.

Textual evidence supports this interpretation. In the first week after baptism the newly initiated were referred to as "infants" (*infantes*) in the

*Figure 64* John baptizing Jesus on the right end of a fourth-century sarcophagus now in the Musée de l'Arles Antique (Arles).

Photo: Author.

west. Augustine, in a sermon for Easter Sunday, explains why the week following is called the "Octave of the Infants:"

> Of these days, the seven or eight which are now in progress are set aside for the sacraments of the newly baptized. Those persons, who not long ago were called *competentes*, are now called *infantes*. They were said to be *competentes* because they were beating against their mother's womb seeking to be born; they are now called *infantes* because they, who were first born to the world, are now born to Christ ... at first they are but little ones [*parvuli*].[68]

Portraying the newly baptized as children also has a ritual parallel in addition to being immersed nude and that is the taking of a mixture of milk and honey along with the bread and wine at the first eucharist, directly after baptism. This practice not only symbolized the initiates' entrance into the promised land ("of milk and honey") but also symbolized their first "food" as new-born Christians, based in part on a passage from the Epistle to the Hebrews (5:12). Both Hippolytus and Tertullian record the practice in the Roman and African churches and it was subsequently set out in the sacramentary attributed to Leo I.[69] Around the turn of the sixth century, John the Deacon, writing from Rome to the aristocrat Senarius, explained the significance of milk and honey:

> You ask why milk and honey are placed in a most sacred cup and offered with the sacrifice at the Paschal Sabbath ... . This kind of sacrament, then, is offered to the newly-baptized so that they may realize that no others but they, who partake of the Body and Blood of the Lord, shall receive the land of promise; and as they start upon the journey thither, they are nourished like little children with milk and honey ... so that they, who in their first birth were nourished with the milk of corruption and first shed tears of bitterness, in their second birth may taste the sweetness of milk and honey in the bowels of the Church.[70]

Thus, the symbolism of nudity might well refer to the ritual of baptism, and as such also to the death and resurrection enacted in that rite. As types one can interpret both Jonah and Daniel as figures who escape death and are "resurrected" to new life. The story of Jonah explicitly is a figure of resurrection (Matthew 12:39–40) and supplementary iconographic details of the Jonah scenes showing both water and nudity clearly extend the scope of the figuration to baptism. And while the compositional details of the baptism of Jesus scenes make sense in light of the tradition of both naked immersion and the return to child-like state, Daniel's symbolic nudity does not alone signal that the image must be baptismal. However, the direct association of

Daniel with resurrection strongly suggests that Daniel also might be a figure of the newly baptized Christian.

## Adam and Eve: creation and restoration

The newly baptized receive a cup of mixed milk and honey not only because they are like small children but also to symbolize their journey from death to life and from earth back to paradise. According to the writings they, like the Israelites, have crossed the Red Sea and the Jordan and now have entered the promised land. This promised land is not the land of Israel, but rather the newly restored Eden, architecturally symbolized by the baptistery.[71] Thus each is a second Adam or Eve and placed back again in the original Garden – a garden fed by the four streams running with the water of life.

Although regional distinctions characterize the various elements of the baptismal rite, certain aspects of the ceremony appear to enact the Adam and Eve typology. In addition to the nakedness of the candidates, the ritual sometimes included a renunciation of Satan while facing to the west and standing barefoot on a haircloth or animal skin, which may have symbolized the garments of skin donned by the original couple in Genesis 3:21.[72] After the renunciation candidates turned toward the east (the place of Eden) to affirm their faith. Cyril of Jerusalem spoke of the rites that took place outside the door to the baptistery: "When you renounce Satan, trampling underfoot every covenant with him, then you annul that ancient 'league with Hell,' and God's paradise opens before you, that Eden, planted in the east, from which for his transgression our first father was banished. Symbolic of this is your facing about from the west to the east, the place of light." Earlier in the treatise the bishop had referred to the baptistery itself as a "brighter and more fragrant second Eden."[73]

Therefore, the many representations of Adam and Eve in early Christian art may not be as they are so often identified – as references to the pair's disobedience, fall, and disgrace. The images may instead refer to Adam's and Eve's (thus all humanity's) potential for redemption, restoration, and resurrection. The inclusion of the figures of Adam and Eve over the font at Dura Europos may illustrate this idea. Even more significant may be those portrayals of Adam and Eve that are juxtaposed with representations that appear to show their original creation. In conjunction with motifs that signify baptism or resurrection, this iconography then points not only to creation but to new creation, a subject surely more suitable for a funerary context than visual references to sin and failure.

The creation of Adam and Eve is illustrated on two well-known sarcophagi dated to the early to mid-fourth century. The compositions, remarkably alike, show the couple as small and nude. In one case they are both standing (Figure 65), and in the other only Eve is standing (Adam is still asleep after giving up his rib). Most interpreters have identified the three men just to the left of the small nude couple as the Trinity, suggesting that creation was an act of the triune deity. One of the three (the Son or Second Person?) places his right hand on the woman's head (similar to John's gesture in the baptism scenes).[74] The appearance of the small man and woman is quite similar to that of the figures in the scenes of the resurrection of the dry bones (Figure 61) and the small nude in one of the versions of the raising of Lazarus.[75]

Both of these creation images are grouped with other baptismal/resurrection typologies including the healing of the paralytic and the man born blind, Daniel, Moses striking the rock, the raising of Lazarus, and the transformation of the water to wine in Cana.[76] Each of them is also near or next to a representation of Adam and Eve as fully grown adults in the garden. On other sarcophagi reliefs the larger figures of Adam and Eve are adjacent to the portrayals of the raising of the dry bones. Occasionally, in the place of the tree standing between the first couple, the composition substituted Jesus, perhaps to indicate the pair's judgment, but possibly as a reference to Jesus' role as the new Adam in effecting the restoration. The association of Adam and new Adam with baptism and resurrection, or with creation and new creation, echoes the theology of Paul, who also speaks of being "in Christ" as a new creation in which the old world has passed away and everything has become new (1 Corinthians 15; 2 Corinthians 5:1–17).

*Figure 65* The Trinity creating Adam and Eve (upper left) with other healing miracles and wonders on an early fourth-century sarcophagus, now in the Musée de l'Arles Antique (Arles).

Photo: Author.

The motif of old and new Adam was balanced in literature after Paul with the parallels of old and new Eve. Just as Christ both parallels and restores the original human male, Mary parallels and in some sense redeems the original female. The balancing of the first duo's disobedience against the second pair's obedience is symbolized by the tree in the garden and the tree at Calvary. Irenaeus was among the first fully to develop this parallelism:

> For doing away with [the effects of] that disobedience of man which had taken place at the beginning by occasion of a tree, "He became obedient unto death, even the death of the cross"; ... [also] that deception being done away with, by which that virgin Eve who was already espoused to a man, was unhappily misled, – was happily announced, through means of the truth [spoken] by the angel to the Virgin Mary, who was also espoused to a man. And if the former did disobey God, yet the latter was persuaded to be obedient to God, in order that the Virgin Mary might become the patroness of the Virgin Eve. And thus, as the human race fell into bondage to death by means of a virgin, so it is rescued by a virgin; virginal disobedience having been balanced in the opposite scale by virginal disobedience.[77]

This kind of typological parallelism may not be limited to the literature of the early church. Consider the two images of creation described above. In both, a central figure sits in a basket-weave chair as if enthroned to receive the two new creatures. Directly below, in the lower register of both sarcophagi, are representations of Mary, similarly seated in a basket-weave chair, with the baby Jesus in her lap, and receiving the three magi with their gifts. The first of the magi points upwards as if to a star, but perhaps also to the story of the original creation, recreated now in the figures before him (Figure 66). Given the compositional similarity of all four scenes we can conclude that they were meant to be understood as a visual presentation of first and second creation.[78]

## Conclusion

The inescapable fact of death may be the most profound source of spiritual anxiety or the basic religious instinct. Whereas others might remain skeptical, reserve judgment, or even resist the possibility of life after death, Christians clung (and still cling) to their hope of eternal life and, what is more, clung to the assertion that that life would be a bodily one and not simply amorphous or spiritual. Even angels have bodies.

That the future existence would be full-bodied is essentially derived from the dogmas of the incarnation and bodily resurrection of Christ, who was the prefigurement of all those to follow. These doctrines, confessed in the creeds

180

*Figure 66* Detail of Trinity sarcophagus, Arles, adoration of the magi.
Photo: Author.

and enacted in both the symbols and words of the sacraments of baptism and eucharist, permeate the art of the early church, particularly that art which was meant to decorate (or illuminate) the burial places of members of the community. The dearest hope of the dying, the assurance or comfort for the living, or even a claim made to the unbeliever, is expressed in these some-times rather simple images. These images, however, were not derived from myths, or even shored up by philosophical argument, they were drawn from the scripture stories that are asserted to be the testimony of eyewitnesses – events that really happened in the very concrete past. For this reason the expectation was firmly anchored to reality and not a mere fanciful hope.

And so art crystallizes, or perhaps materializes, certain points of doctrine which, while based on scripture, are sometimes more often encountered in theological arguments than in ordinary daily experience. Images can make the bridge between the material and the intellectual via an interesting kind of hypostatic union – logos and icon. Complex and sophisticated symbols that communicate on many levels and refer to different stories, ideas, and matters of faith, visual images also speak directly and clearly, even to the simplest believer. Thus "religious pictures" are not merely for the theologi-cally untrained, or for the illiterate, or for the practitioner of popular religion at all, even while they serve the needs of persons in those categories. By the same token, neither is the deepest value of art restricted to the elite, the intelligentsia, or to those trained in the lore or techniques of its interpretation.

But, in the end, interpretation cannot be done without reference to a community and to the many ways its central values are expressed, including texts, rituals, and artifacts. Most religious communities are diverse enough to allow a rather broad scope and range of interpretation, but yet narrow enough to cohere as a group, guiding researchers ultimately back to certain core beliefs. Unless it is about to go into schism, fundamental continuity among these different modes of expression should be presumed about any group. Thus both verbal and visual eventually come down to the same thing and reinforce one another.

# NOTES

## INTRODUCTION

1 L. Carroll, *Alice's Adventures in Wonderland* (New York: D. Appleton and Co., 1866).

2 I won't try to list these here and many would be obvious to readers, including such pioneers in Christian iconography as André Grabar, Ernst Kitzinger, and Kurt Weitzmann; or more currently Mary Charles Murray, Hans Belting, and Thomas Mathews. The following chapters give many such examples. I would refer readers to the succinct bibliography at the end of this book for a listing, however.

3 Gregory I, *Ep.* 13; Migne, *PL* 77, 1027–8; 1128–30; trans. J. Barmby, *NPNF*, ser. 2, vol. 13, 53–4.

4 See an excellent recent article by Mary Charles Murray, "The Image, the Ear, and the Eye in Early Christianity," ARTS 9.1 (1977), 17–24; or M. Miles, *Image as Insight* (Boston: Beacon Press, 1985), 41–8.

5 See the recent work of J. Elsner, *Art and the Roman Viewer* (Cambridge: Cambridge University Press, 1995) for a serious study of the relationship between viewer and object.

6 A prominent exception to this is Paulinus of Nola's *Ep.* 32, in which he describes the decoration of two churches, one at Nola and the other at Fundi.

## 1 THE CHARACTER OF EARLY CHRISTIAN ICONOGRAPHY: ISSUES AND PROBLEMS OF INTERPRETATION

1 Both Tertullian, *De pud.* 7.1–4; 10.12; and Clement of Alexandria, *Paed.* 3.11.59, give second-century testimonia to Christian use of etched eucharistic cups and engraved signet rings.

2 Both G. De Rossi (at the end of the nineteenth century) and J. Wilpert (in the early twentieth) dated the catacomb frescoes to the end of the first century. For a more modern discussion of the dating of catacomb paintings see H. Brandenburg, "Überlegungen zum Ursprung der frühchristlichen Bildkunst," *ACIAC* 9.1 (1978); also H. G. Thummel, "Die Anfänge der Katakombenmalerei," *ACIAC* 7 (1965), 745–52. F. Gerke is generally credited with establishing the dating of the catacombs, based on the archaeological data more than on stylistic considerations. There is pretty firm evidence that no communal cemeteries existed before the late second century and only ten or eleven catacombs can be dated prior to the Constantinian era. See F. Gerke,

"Ideengeschichte der ältesten christlichen Kunst," *Zeitschrift für Kirchengeschichte* 59 (1940), 1–102.

3 Henry Chadwick, *The Early Church* (*Pelican History of the Church*, vol. 1; London: Penguin, 1967), 277, sums it up: "The second of the Ten Commandments forbade the making of any graven images. Both Tertullian and Clement of Alexandria regarded this prohibition as absolute and binding on Christians. Images and cultic statues belonged to the demonic world of paganism. In fact, the only second-century Christians known to have images of Christ were radical Gnostics, the followers of the licentious Carpocrates." See also J. D. Breckenridge, "The Reception of Art into the Early Church," *ACIAC* 9.1 (1978); and R. Grigg's article "Aniconic Worship and the Apologetic Tradition," *CH* 45 (1976) 428–9. An opposing position was proposed by M. Charles Murray, "Art and the Early Church," *JThS* n.s. 28.2 (1977), 304–45; and *Rebirth and Afterlife: A Study of the Transmutation of Some Pagan Imagery in Early Christian Art* (Oxford: BAR International Series, 1981), 13–36. Sr. Mary Charles Murray points out both the presuppositions and the biases of much of this scholarship.

4 The problem of aniconism will be discussed below, while the question of the "imperial influence" on fourth-century art comprises a section of ch. 4.

5 T. Klauser's serially published essays which used archaeological evidence to argue that early Christians were aniconic appeared under the title "Studien zur Entstehungsgeschichte der christlichen Kunst," *JAC* 1 (1958), 20–51; 2 (1959), 115–45; 3 (1960), 112–33; 4 (1961), 128–45; 5 (1962), 113–24; 6 (1963), 71–100; 7 (1964), 67–76; 8–9 (1965–6), 126–70; 10 (1967), 82–120.

6 Texts to demonstrate that church authorities were adamantly opposed to art and perceived it as an essentially pagan practice are culled mainly from Clement of Alexandria, Tertullian, Eusebius, and Epiphanius. Scholars who amassed these texts include H. Koch, *Die altchristliche Bilderfrage nach den literarischen Quellen* (Forsch. zur Relig. und Lit. des A. and N. Testaments, Göttingen: Vandenhoeck and Ruprecht, 1917); and W. Ellinger, *Zur Entstehung und frühen Entwicklung der altchristlichen Bildkunst*," ibid. 23 (1934), 1–284.

7 The supposed aniconism of the early church is simply assumed by many standard church histories, including H. Chadwick's (see above, n. 3). This aniconism has also been suggested as a basis for the eighth-century iconoclastic controversy. See L. W. Barnard, "The Graeco-Roman and Oriental Background of the Iconoclastic Controversy," *DOP* 7 (1953), 3–34; and E. Kitzinger, "The Cult of Icons before Iconoclasm," *DOP* 8 (1954), 85–150, esp. 88–9. Klauser and others' representation of an anti-material and purely spiritual early Christianity that became gradually "Hellenized" may have been influenced by A. von Harnack's writings. See his *Lehrbuch der Dogmengeschichte*, vol. 2, 4th edn (Tübingen, 1909), 467–79.

8 Mary Charles Murray developed this argument in her excellent article, "Art and the Early Church." P. C. Finney's recent study of this matter is the basis of his book, *The Invisible God: The Earliest Christians on Art* (New York: Oxford University Press, 1994). In this work Finney concurs with Charles Murray that early Christians were far from aniconic, despite the ways they were cited during the iconoclastic period. Finney further asserts that the relative lateness of Christian art must be explained by social or economic factors rather than religious ones. That first- and second-century Christians had some art is demonstrated by both Tertullian and Clement of Alexandria, who refer to cups and signet rings, or seals, with figures of the Good Shepherd or other "acceptable" images. See Tertullian, *De Pud.* 7.1–4; and Clement, *Paed.* 3.59.2–3.60.1.

In addition see the discussion of second-century lamps with figures of the Good Shepherd in Finney, *Invisible God*, 116–32.

9  See Finney, *Invisible God*, 108–10, for a summary of his argument to this effect.

10  This conclusion is well supported by archaeological research, despite the efforts of New Testament scholars to find epigraphical evidence of other artifacts from the first and second centuries. See the discussion of this problem by P. C. Finney in his recent book, *Invisible God*, 99–103. Finney compares the earliest Christians with Pythagoreans or Gnostics in this respect.

11  Different ways of categorizing Christian iconography have been suggested in various handbooks. See for instance K. Weitzmann (ed.), *The Age of Spirituality* (New York: Metropolitan Museum of Art, 1979), which classifies its material into abbreviated, narrative, and iconic images, although sometimes these distinctions seem blurred. I have here adapted a suggestion of Paul Corby Finney's from his article "Art" in the *Encyclopedia of Early Christianity*, ed. Everett Ferguson (New York: Garland, 1990), 99.

12  J. Wilpert or E. Goodenough would have found meaning even in these figures, however. See Wilpert, *Roma sotteranea: le pitture delle catacombe romane* (Rome: Desclée, Lefebvre, 1903); and a relatively brief work of Goodenough, "Catacomb Art," *JBL* 81 (1962), 113–42, in which he argues: "the devices used again and again to fill the spaces in the catacomb create an atmosphere, express a hope, but atmosphere and hope are not the deepest meaning we know. In *Symbols I* I gave reasons for supposing that vines and baskets with animals or birds drinking and eating still expressed hope of life here and hereafter [and for eschatological?] eating and drinking, and that with Christians they had eucharistic implications" (117).

13  This is discussed at more length in ch. 3.

14  See discussion of these developments below in chs 3, 4, and 5.

15  See Hippolytus, *Haer.* 9.12.14.

16  These sarcophagi are well presented and discussed by F. Benoit, *Sarcophages paléochrétiens d'Arles et de Marseille, Gallia* Suppl. 5 (Paris: Centre Nationale de la Recherche Scientifique, 1954).

17  P. C. Finney summarizes the ideological aspects of scholarly assertions that Rome was the source and center for Christian artistic output. See *Invisible God*, 151 and footnotes 8 and 9, 264.

18  The Cleveland marbles may have also been created for a funereal context. See W. Wixom, "Early Christian Sculptures in Cleveland," *Bulletin of the Cleveland Museum of Art* 45 (1967), 65–88k.

19  I am indebted here to P. C. Finney's work. See *Invisible God*, 288f.

20  See the work of E. Testa, for example: *Il simbolismo dei Guideo-Cristiani* (Pubblicazioni dello Studium Biblicum Franciscanum, n. 14 , Jerusalem: Tip. dei PP. francescani, 1962).

21  Breckenridge, "The Reception of Art," 368. See also Chadwick *The Early Church*, 280: "With the conversion of Constantine, the Church no longer had to be reticent in expressing its faith ... and the tide became a flood in the course of the fourth century. Nevertheless, the older puritanism was not stifled or killed."

22  Graydon Snyder tends toward this viewpoint in his presentation of two competing parties of early Christians: rural, "cemetery" Christians versus an urban intellectual party. See *Ante Pacem: Archaeological Evidence of Church Life before Constantine* (Macon, GA: Mercer University Press, 1985), 164, 167–8. Also consider M. Mile's statement in *Image as Insight* (Boston: Beacon Press, 1985), 38: "Images can also reflect the discontinuity featured in women's physical existence; religious imagery delights in themes specific to the stages of women's life

experience … is different from the universality of the subjective consciousness, articulated by language … . The antagonism of a few theologians to visual images and their injunctions to "spiritual" – that is, verbal – worship of God reveal a fundamental disdain for the vast majority of human beings, women and men, whose perspective was based in the exigencies of physical existence."

23  A significant exception, this might prove the rule, actually. In the first decade of the fourth century, the Spanish Council of Elvira condemned the painting of religious images on the walls of churches in order to differentiate Christian practice from pagan (canon 36). See R. Grigg, "Aniconic Worship and the Apologetic Tradition: A Note on Canon 36 of the Council of Elvira," *CH* 45 (1976), 428–33.

24  The changes in iconography during the Constantinian and post-Constantinian era are discussed below, chs 3 and 5.

25  This is the general approach of Graydon Snyder, *Ante Pacem, passim.*

26  See I. S. van Woerden, "The Iconography of the Sacrifice of Isaac in Early Christian Art," *AJA* 2nd ser. 26 (1922), 159–73; and Snyder, *Ante Pacem,* 51–2, for example.

27  The "Roman School" is exemplified by the publications and excavations of Roman Catholic archaeologists associated with the Pontificio Istituto di Archeologia Cristiana.

28  Possibly the classic source for this style of interpretation is the indispensible *Dictionnaire d'archéologie chrétienne et de liturgie,* ed. F. Cabrol and H. Leclercq (Paris: Letourzey et Ané, 1924–53). See the helpful discussion of many of these problems in E. A. Judge, "'Antike und Christentum': Toward a Definition of the Field. A Bibliographical Essay," *ANRW* 2.23.1, 3–58.

29  A good example of this mode of interpretation can be seen in the writings of J. Wilpert, especially in his summary monograph, *Erlebnisse und Ergebnisse im Dienste der christlichen Archäologie* (Freiburg: Herder, 1930), and in *La fede della chiesa nascente: secondo i monumenti dell'arte funeraria antica* (Rome: Pontificio Istituto di Archeologia Cristiana, 1938), but also in many others, including O. Marucchi, *The Evidence of the Catacombs* (London: Sheed and Ward, 1929). See H. Lother, *Realismus und Symbolismus in der altchristlichen Kunst* (Tübingen: Mohr, 1931). G. Snyder also gives useful summary criticism of these approaches, *Ante Pacem,* 5–7.

30  See P. Styger, *Die römischen Katakomben* (Berlin, 1933) and E. Dinkler, *Signum Crucis. Aufsätz zum Neuen Testament und zur christlichen Archäologie* (Tübingen: Mohr, 1967). Also, Dinkler's work, "Die ersten Petrusdarstellung," *Marburger Jarbuch für Kunstwissenschaft* 11 (1939), 1–80, in which he challenges earlier arguments about the so-called Petrine evidence in early Christian art.

31  L. von Sybel, *Christliche Antike,* 2 vols (Marburg, 1906–9); T. Klauser, "Studien zur Entstehungsgeschichte der christlichen Kunst," *JAC* 1–10 (1958–67); and E. Kitzinger, *Byzantine Art in the Making* (Cambridge, MA: Harvard University Press, 1977).

32  This approach characterizes the work of G. Snyder, who refers to it as proceeding from "contextual methodology," *Ante Pacem,* 7–11. In laying out his method, he is very clear about the distinction between the "great tradition" and the faith of the "common folk" and he cites the "Chicago school" which has emphasized the tension between the educated upper classes and the unempowered or illiterate.

33  F. Dölger, **IXΘYE**: Das Fisch Symbol in frühchristlicher Zeit (*Münster in Westf.: Aschendorffschen, 1910) and E. Goodenough,* Jewish Symbols in the Greco-Roman

Period, *13 vols (New York: Pantheon, 1953–68). Dölger was actually T. Klauser's teacher.*

34 This approach essentially agrees with the thesis of Mary Charles Murray, which argues for a *theological* analysis of early Christian art – a strategy which sees the imagery as more than a set of symbols to be decoded by historians of religion, or formal types to be categorized by art historians. See her introduction to *Rebirth and Afterlife*, 5–12.

## 2 NON-NARRATIVE IMAGES: CHRISTIAN USE OF CLASSICAL SYMBOLS AND POPULAR MOTIFS

1 See the fine work of Mary Charles Murray, *Rebirth and Afterlife* for an extended discussion of many of the images presented below as well as useful bibliography.

2 See C. H. Dodd, "The Cognomen of the Emperor Antoninus Pius," *Numismatic Chronicle* 4th ser. 11 (1911), 6–41 and esp. 11f. For an exhaustive study of the figure see T. Klauser "Studien zur Entstehungsgeschichte der christlichen Kunst II. 6–10," *JAC* 2 (1959), 115–45; *JAC* 3 (1960), 112–33; and *JAC* 7 (1964), 67–76.

3 Justin Martyr, *1 Apol.* 3.2 and *Dial.* 4.7; Clement of Alexandria, *Strom.* 1.24; Eusebius, *Ecc. hist.* 4.24 and *Prap. ev.* 11.15; and Athanasius, *Contra Arian.* 2.45, for example.

4 For a survey of the possible political significance of the term in Roman times see T. Ulrich, *Pietas* (Pius) *als politischer Begriff im römischen Staate bis zum Tode des Kaisers Commodus* (Breslau: M. and H. Marcus, 1930).

5 See discussions by H. Leclercq, "Orant, Orante," in *DACL*, vol. 12.2 (1936), 2291–322; W. Neuss, "Die Oranten in der altchristlicher Kunst," in *Festschrift Paul Clemens* (Bonn: Schwann, 1926), 130–49; A. Mulhern, "L'Orante, vie et mort d'une image," *Les dossiers de l'archéologie* 18 (1976), 34–47; G. Seib, "Orans, Orant," in *Lexikon der Christliche Ikonographie*, vol. 3 (Freiburg im Breisgau, 1971), 352–4; and Graydon Snyder, *Ante Pacem*, 20.

6 K. Wessel, "Ecclesia orans," *Archäologischer Anzeiger* 70 (1955), 315–34.

7 The function of the orant figure as a portrait is one of T. Klauser's points in "Studien zur Entstehungsgeschichte," pt. 2, *JAC* 2 (1959), 115–45 and again in pt. 7, *JAC* 7 (1964), 67–76.

8 See L. de Bruyne, "Les lois de l'art paléochrétien comme instrument herméneutique," *RAC* 39 (1963), 12ff.

9 Tertullian, *De orat.* 14.

10 Minucius Felix, *Oct.* 29.6.

11 From L. Ouspensky and V. Lossky, *The Meaning of Icons* (Crestwood, NY: St Vladimir's Seminary Press, 1982), 77.

12 See W. N. Schumacher, "Hirt und Guter Hirt," *Römische Quartalschrift Supplementheft* 34 (Freiburg: Herder, 1977); and N. Himmelmann, *ber Hirtengenre in der antiken Kunst*, (Opladen: Westdeutscher, 1980).

13 H. Leclercq identified more than 300 examples in Christian art between the third and fifth centuries in his 1924 article, "Pasteur (Bon)," in *DACL*, vol. 13.2, 2272–390. Also see A. Legner, "Hirt, Guter Hirt," *LCI* 2 (1970), 289–99.

14 See P. C. Finney, "Good Shepherd," *Encyclopedia of Early Christianity* (New York: Garland, 1990), 845–6.

15 This line is most identified with T. Klauser, "Studien zur Entstehungsgeschichte," *JAC* 1 (1958), 20–51; *JAC* 3 (1960), 112–33; and *JAC* 8–9 (1965–6), 126–70. See also Snyder, *Ante Pacem*, 22–4.

16 Shepherd of Hermas, *Vis.* 5.1.

17 *De pud.* 7.1–4 and 10ff.
18 See *Paed.* 1.7 and 3.12. Clement's hymn has recently been translated and annotated by Annewies van den Hoek in an anthology *Prayer from Alexander to Constantine*, ed. M. Kiley (Routledge, 1997), 296–303. Also see Clement of Alexandria, *Protrep.* 11.116.1.
19 The Abercius inscription is recorded in Johannes Quasten (ed.), *Monumenta eucharistica liturgica vetustissima* = *Florilegium Patristicum VII* (Bonn: Hanstein, 1935–7) 1.22. For more bibliography see footnotes 57 and 63. The vision from the passion of Perpetua (*Passio* 4) was later cited by Augustine in a sermon (*De temp. barb.*) that claims that the provision of the milk specifically assisted Perpetua in her suffering.
20 Clement of Alexandria, *Paed.*, 3.12, lines 40–53. Cf. id., *Paed.* 1.6.
21 For another example of the symbolism of milk see the *Odes of Solomon* 4.10, 8.14, 35.5, 40.1, and especially *Ode* 19. The tradition of offering the newly baptized milk and honey was known in Milan, Rome, and Africa. See *Ep. Barnabas* 6.8–17; Ambrose, *De Sac.* 5.3.12; Zeno of Verona, *Inv. ad font.* 7; the Third Council of Carthage, *Can.* 4 (*PL* 56, 513); John the Deacon's *Ep. ad Senarius* 12; the *Leonine Sacramentary*; Tertullian, *De Bapt.* 12; *De Cor.* 3; and *Adv. Marc.* 3.22; and Hippolytus, *Ap. trad.* 3.
22 J. Quasten, "Das Bild des Guten Hirten in den altchristlichen Baptisterien und in den Taufliturgien des Ostens und Westens," *Pisciculi, Ergenzungsband zu "Antike und Christentum"*, ed. F. J. Dölger (Münster in Westf.: Aschendorff, 1939), 220–44.
23 See Cyril of Jerusalem, *De Myst.* 4; and Ambrose, *De Myst.* 8.43 and *De Sac.* 5.3.12 for evocations of Ps. 23 in the baptismal liturgy of the fourth-century church. Also Prudentius, *Perist.* 12.43; and Paulinus of Nola, *Ep.* 32.5. Some discussion in R. M. Jensen, "Living Water: Images, Settings and Symbols of Early Christian Baptism in the West," (Ph.D. dissertation, Columbia University, 1991), 348 and 401–3.
24 See J. Quasten, "Der Gute Hirt in frühchristlicher Totenliturgie und Grabeskunst," *Miscellanea Giovanni Mercati. Studi e testi 121* (Vatican City: Biblioteca Apostolica Vaticana, 1946), 1:373–406. This suggestion was also made by J. N. Carder in the *Age of Spirituality Catalogue*, ed. K. Weitzmann, entry 462, p. 518.
25 See discussion of this issue in ch. 5.
26 B. Ramsey, OP, "A Note on the Disappearance of the Good Shepherd from Early Christian Art," *HTR* 76 (1983), 375–8.
27 Ibid., 376.
28 For example, Basil of Caesarea, *De Spir.* 8.17.
29 This transition is made especially clear in Chrysostom's *Hom. in Joh.* 59 beginning at verse 11. The lamb image is discussed below, in ch. 4.
30 Augustine, *Tract. in Joh.* 46.3, trans. J. W. Rettig, Fathers of the Church series, 88 (Washington, DC: Catholic University Press, 1993).
31 Clement of Alexandria, *Protrep.* 1; and also in ch. 7, where he says that Orpheus really sings about the Word. See also Eusebius, *De Laud. Const.* 14.
32 An excellent, detailed discussion of this imagery and its literary parallels was produced by Mary Charles Murray, *Rebirth and Afterlife*, ch. 2, "The Christian Orpheus," 37–63. See also an earlier, interesting but overly-enthusiastic and somewhat unreliable analysis in R. Eisler, *Orpheus the Fisher: Comparative Studies in Orphic and Early Christian Cult Symbolism* (London: J. M. Watkins, 1921), 51–8.

33 In her seminal study, Mary Charles Murray disputes this identification of Orpheus in the Jewish iconography: "The Christian Orpheus," *Cahiers archéologiques* 26 (1977), 19–27; and subsequently in her longer work, *Rebirth and Afterlife*, ch. 2 (op. cit.), 37–63, in which she presents many of the issues discussed below. See also P. C. Finney, "Orpheus-David: A Connection in Iconography between Greco-Roman Judaism and Early Christianity?" *JJA* 5 (1978), 6–15.

34 See M.-T. and P. Canivet, "La mosaique d'Adam," *Cahiers archéologiques* 24 (1975), 46–9. Cf. the somewhat problematic "Orpheus Cross," in *DACL*, vol. 12 (1936), 2735–55, fig. 9249, briefly discussed by H. Rahner, "The Christian Mystery and the Pagan Mysteries," in *The Mysteries* (Papers from the Eranos Yearbooks, 2, 1955), 379.

35 The image was published in *DACL*, vol. 12 (1936), fig. 9249. Contained in article, "Orphée," cols. 2734–55.

36 Not all scholars agree that this image is really meant to be Jesus. Synagogue floor mosaics have also been found with images of Helios (or Sol Invictus) in the center of a zodiac – at Beth Alpha, Na'aran, and Husefa. For literature on the subject see O. Perler, *Die Mosaiken der Juliergruft im Vatikan* (Freiburg in der Schweiz: Universitatsverlag, 1953); and J. M. C. Toynbee and J. B. Ward-Perkins, *The Shrine of St. Peter and the Vatican Excavations* (London: Longmans, 1956).

37 For dated, but worthwhile study of these parallels see F. J. Dölger, *Sol Salutis. Gebet und Gesang im christlichen Altertum* (Münster in Westf.: Aschendorff, 1925), Liturgiegeschichtliche Forschungen, 4–5.

38 For examples see *Did.* 14.1; Justin Martyr, *1 Apol.* 67.3–5; Zeno of Verona, *Pasch. hom.*

39 Pliny *Epist.* 10.96.

40 Tertullian, *Ad nat.* 1.13.

41 Clement of Alexandria, *Protrep.* 9, possibly quoting Ps. 110:3. Ephesians 5:14 also seems a possible source for Clement's language here. *Odes of Sol.* 15: "Because He is my Sun, and His rays have lifted me up; and His light has dismissed all darkness from my face" provides another parallel. Trans. and notes see J. H. Charlesworth, *Odes of Solomon* (Missoula, MT: Scholars Press, 1977), 67.

42 *Protrep.* 11. For an excellent discussion of these texts see Murray, *Rebirth and Afterlife*, 94–6.

43 Text in F. C. Conybeare, *Rituale Armenorum* (Oxford: Clarendon, 1905), 427; trans. H. Rahner, "Christian Mystery and the Pagan Mysteries," 396. Rahner also quotes a passage from Ps.-Athanasius' *De passio Dom.* which compares and contrasts the illumination offered by Helios with the illumination of Christ's cross in baptism.

44 Justin in particular calls the candidates "illuminati," (in Greek, *photizomenoi*) *1 Apol.* 61: "This washing is called illumination, since those who learn these things are illumined from within." Epiphany, a baptismal day, was also called the "Feast of Lights" to signify the illumination of the neophytes, and symbolized by the candles they carried from the baptistery to the church. See Greg. of Nazianzus, *Orat.* 40.

45 This custom was recorded by Cyril of Jerusalem, *Myst. cat.* 1.2–2.2; and in an emended text of Ambrose's *De Myst.* 2.7.

46 G. Rodenwalt believed he identified the prototype for this image in a sarcophagus bearing an image of a philosopher dating from the 270s (Plotinus?). See "Zur Kunstgeschichte der Jahre 220 bis 270," *Jahrbuch des deutschen archäologischen Instituts* 51 (1936), 82–113.

47 Tertullian, *Ad nat.* 1.4. Also Justin Martyr, *1 Apol.* 5, 44, 46; *2 Apol.* 10 and 13; Clement of Alexandria, *Protrep.* 6, 11; and *Strom.* 1.28.3. See Celsus' rebuttal of the points found in Origen's, *Contra Cels.* 6 and 7, for more examples.

48 Justin speaks of Abraham, Elijah, the three youths, and Moses as pre-Christian philosophers. See *1 Apol.* 44, 46. Some biblical figures are shown wearing a short tunic and sandals, in particular Jonah and John the Baptist. E. Kitzinger has compared this representation with Hellenistic images of the wandering Cynic philosophers, "The Cleveland Marbles," *ACIAC* 9 (1978), 671–3. Also see W. Wixom, "Early Christian Sculptures at Cleveland," *Bulletin of the Cleveland Museum of Art* 45 (1967), 88e.

49 See *1 Clem.* 26, which cites the Septuagint translation of Job 19:25–6: "Job says: 'You will raise up this flesh of mine, which has suffered all these things.'"

50 Klauser identified five late third- or early fourth-century sarcophagi with this combination, as well as sixteen other sarcophagi which show the Good Shepherd and orant but which lack the reading philosopher. See "Studien zur Entstehungsgeschichte," pt. 3, *JAC* 3 (1960), 112–33.

51 See discussion of this image below, ch. 4.

52 Probably the most thorough work on this subject is by F. J. Dölger, **IXΘΥΣ**: *Das Fisch Symbol in frühchristlichen Zeit* (Münster in Westf.: Aschendorff, 1910); *Der Heilige Fisch in den antiken Religionen und im Christentum* (= **IXΘΥΣ**, vols 2 and 3 (Münster in Westf.: Aschendorff, 1922); *Die Fisch-Denkmäler in der frühchristlichen Plastik, Malerie, und Kleinkunst* (= **IXΘΥΣ**, vols. 4 and 5 (Münster in Westf., 1927–32). A good, earlier discussion by C. R. Morey, "The Origin of the Fish-Symbol," was published serially in *PTR* 8 (1910), 93–106; 231–46, 401–32; 9 (1911), 268–89; 10 (1912), 278–97. See also G. Stroumsa, "The Early Fish Symbol Reconsidered," in *Messiah and Christos: Studies in the Jewish Origins of Christianity,* ed. I. Gruenwald, S. Shaked, and G. Stroumsa (Tübingen: Mohr, 1992); and Hans Achelis, *Das Symbol des Fisches und die Fischdenkmäler der römischen Katakomben* (Marburg: Elwert, 1888). For a wildly speculative but extremely interesting treatment of the subject see Eisler, *Orpheus the Fisher,* which connects the imagery of Orpheus (as fisher god) with the images of fish and fishers in early Christian art. A recent dissertation on the subject merits consideration for its extensive and valuable analysis: L. H. Kant, "The Interpretation of Religious Symbols in the Graeco-Roman World: A Case Study of Early Christian Fish Symbolism, vols 1–3" (Yale University, 1993).

53 Origen discusses the significance of Peter and the fish with the coin in its mouth in his *Comm. in Mat.* 13.10. When Optatus of Mileve discusses the story of Tobit he claims the fish typifies Christ: *De schism Don.* 3.2. Eisler refers to this tradition in *Orpheus the Fisher,* 91–106.

54 See discussion below, ch. 6. H. Leclercq, "Dauphin," *DACL,* vol. 4.1 (1920), 285–95, was among those who suggested that the dolphin represents Christ.

55 See more discussion of sacramental symbolism, below, ch. 3.

56 See Tertullian, *De Bapt.* 9; Irenaeus, *Adv. haer.* 3.17.2; Jerome, *Ep.* 69.6; Optatus of Mileve, *Contra Parmen.* 5.4–5; also the *Gelasian Sacramentary* 91 and the *Bobbio Missal* 236, which provide these types during the liturgies for the exorcism or blessing of the font.

57 Tertullian, *De Bapt.* 1, trans. author's (Latin text, E. Evans, *Tertullian's Homily on Baptism,* London: SPCK, 1964, 20–1).

58 Origen, *In Matt.* 13.10. For translation, commentary, and discussion of this short passage see Morey, "Origin of the Fish-Symbol," pt. 3, 406–8.

59 Cyril of Jerusalem, *Procat.* 5, trans. A. Stephenson, *The Works of St. Cyril of Jerusalem* (Washington, DC: Catholic University Press, 1969), 74. Clement of

Alexandria (*Paed.* 3.11), discussing the symbols appropriate for rings, suggests the fisherman – a reminder of an apostle and children "drawn from the water." For other passages that use the metaphor of fish for baptism see Dölger, *Ichthys*, vol. 5. 308–20.

60 Clement of Alexandria, *Paed.* 3.12.23–8, trans. A. van den Hoek, in forthcoming anthology: *Prayer from Alexander to Constantine.*

61 See more discussion of these texts below. Abercius Inscription, trans. J. Quasten, *Patrology*, vol. 1 (Utrecht: Spectrum, 1966), 171–3; also E. Ferguson, *Early Christians Speak* (Abilene: ACU Press, 1981), 156; and recent article by W. Wischmeyer, "Die Aberkionsinschrift als Grabepigramm," *Studia Patristica* 17.2 (1987), 777–81.

62 See the discussion of this text and its symbolism by Morey, "Origin of the Fish-Symbol," pt. 4, 268–89.

63 Augustine, *De civ. Dei* 18.23; Maximus of Turin, *Contra pag.* trac. 4. Eusebius quotes the text in full in his account of Constantine's oration to the assembly of the saints: *Orat. ad coetum sanct.*, 18–19. See also Pseudo-Prosper of Aquitaine, *De prom. praed. Dei* 2.39. Fuller citations and translations of these texts are found in Morey, "Origin of the Fish-Symbol," pt. 3, 401–32.

64 *Sibylline Oracles* 8.217–50. The Greek text of the *Oracles* may be found in the edition of J. Geffcken, *Die Oracula Sibyllina* in Die Griechischen Christlichen Schriftsteller 8 (Leipzig: J. C. Hinrichs'sche, 1902), 153–7. See J. J. Collins, "Sibylline Oracles," *The Old Testament Pseudepigrapha*, vol. 1, ed. J. H. Charlesworth (Garden City, NJ: Doubleday, 1983), 423–4. The particular text in question is quite difficult to date and may have been later than Tertullian, thus reflecting an already existing acrostic tradition. F. Dölger argued that the acronym actually appeared around the end of the second century corresponding to a Christological title, see *Ichthys*, vol. 1, 51–68. Other scholars sought pre-Christian or Jewish sources for the fish-symbol. For examples see I. Scheftelowitz, "Das Fisch-Symbol in Judentum und Christentum," *Archiv für Religionswissenschaft* 14 (1911), 1–54, 321–92; and summary discussion in Stroumsa, "Early Christian Fish Symbol," 199–200.

65 See discussion of fish and the banquet image, below.

66 Optatus of Mileve, *De schism Don.* 3.2.1, my translation. Text ed. M. Labrousse, *Optat de Milève, Traité contre les Donatistes* (Paris: Éditions du Cerf: Sources Chrétiennes no. 413), 1996.

67 Trans. Morey, "Origin of the Fish-Symbol," pt. 4, 282–9. Cf. Quasten, *Patrology*, vol. 1, 173–5; and Dölger, *Icthys*, vol. 1, 12–15, 177–83; and vol. 2, 507–15. Also discussion by, G. Grabka, "Eucharistic Belief Manifest in the Epitaphs of Abercius and Pectorius," *American Ecclesiastical Review* 13 (1954), 254–5.

68 See R. Jensen, "Dining in Heaven," *BR* 14.5 (October 1998), for a short, illustrated article on this problem.

69 For the image as it appears in an earlier era see J.-M. Dentzer, *Le motif du banquet couché dans le Proche-Orient et le monde grec du VIIe au IVe siècle avant J-C* (Paris: Bibliothèque des Écoles français d'Athènes et Rome, 1982). Late antique Roman examples of this kind seem to have Greek prototypes. See examples in G. Koch, *Roman Funerary Sculpture: Catalogue of the Collections* (Malibu, CA: J. Paul Getty Museum, 1988), entries 9, 33, and 34. A full catalogue with analysis was produced by N. Himmelmann, *Typologische Untersuchungen an römischen Sarkophagreliefs des 3. und 4. Jahrhunderts nach Christus* (Mainz am Rhein: Zabern, 1973), 24–8 and 47–66. E. Jastrzebowska has written the most important recent article on the subject: "Les scènes de banquet dans les peintures et

sculptures chrétiennes des IIIe et Ive siècles," *Recherches Augustiennes* 14 (1979), 3–90, with catalog and full bibliography.

70 It seems that these images first appeared in Roman Imperial times. See examples in Tran Tam Tinh, *Catalogue des peintures romaines (Latium et Campanie) du musée du Louvre* (Paris: Editions des museés nationaux, 1974), 50–1, fig. 57; and D. Levi, *Antioch Mosaic Pavements*, vol. 1 (Princeton: Princeton University Press, 1947), pls 294–304, pl. 66b. For discussion of the Roman dining arrangement known as the *stibadium*, see K. Dunbabin, "Triclinium and Stibadium," in *Dining in a Classical Context*, ed. W. J. Slater (Ann Arbor: University of Michigan Press, 1991), 121–48

71 Dölger identified some Christian funeral images of the former (*kline*): *Ichthys*, vol. 4, pls 246 and 252, for example.

72 See Snyder's summary, including identifying the scene both as the multiplication of the loaves and fishes and as the funeral meal, *Ante Pacem*, 64–5.

73 See J. Wilpert, *La fede della chiesa*, 95–6; and A. Stuiber, *"Refrigerium Interim," die Vorstellungen vom Zwischenzustand und die frühchristliche Grabeskunst* (Bonn: P. Hanstein, 1957), 125. For more recent discussion see Finney, *Invisible God*, 214–15.

74 J. Wilpert, *"Fractio Panis": Die alteste Darstellung des eucharistischen Opfers in den "Capella greca"* (Freiburg im Breisgau: Herder, 1895); and id., *La fede della chiesa nascente*, 97–9. Other scholars who consider these images to be representations of agape meals or actual eucharists include Morey, "Origin of the Fish-Symbol," pt. 8, 432; R. Eisler, *Orpheus*, 217–19; W. Elliger, *Zur Entstehung und frühen Entwicklung der altchristlichen Bildkunst* (Leipzig: Dieterich, 1934); J. Finegan, *Light from the Ancient Past* (Princeton: Princeton University Press, 1946), 386; R. Hiers and C. Kennedy, "The Bread and Fish Eucharist," *Perspectives in Religious Studies* 3 (1976), 21–48; and more recently J. Dominic Crossan, *The Historical Jesus* (San Francisco: Harper, 1991), 398–9, who refers to the earliest of these images as evidence of an alternative bread and fish eucharist in the "early tradition." Also see V. Osteneck, "Mahl, Gastmahl," *LCI* 3 (1971), 128–35.

75 Some scholars have suggested this rather inconclusive image is evidence that women were permitted to act as celebrants at early Christian eucharists. See for instance D. Irvin, "The Ministry of Women in the Early Church," *Duke Divinity School Review* 45.2 (1980), 76–86, esp. 81–4. For a full discussion of the place of women in meals, both Christian and pagan, see K. Corley, *Private Women, Public Meals* (Peabody, MA: Hendrickson, 1993), esp. ch. 1, "Women in Early Christianity and Early Christian Communal Meals," 3–23.

76 Hippolytus, *Ap. trad.* 6 mentions a blessing of cheese and olives, following a blessing of oil, suggesting the gifts often included elements other than wine, bread, milk, and honey. A listing of such items is found in C. Vogel, "Le repas sacré au poisson chez les Chrétiens," *Revue des Sciences Religieuses* 40 (1966), 1–26.

77 *Adv. Marc.* 1.14.

78 Dölger analyzes the eucharistic imagery of the fish in the Abercius and Pectorius inscriptions, *Ichthys* vol. 2, 486–515.

79 Cited, translated, and analyzed by Morey, "Origin of the Fish-Symbol," 426–9.

80 Paulinus, *Ep.* 13.11 (Ancient Christian Writers series, trans.). Cf. Augustine, *Conf.* 13.21 and 23; the Abercius and Pectorius inscriptions cited above.

81 See the eucharistic services described in Justin Martyr, *1 Apol.* 65, 67; Hippolytus, *Ap. trad.* 4; Cyril of Jerusalem, *Catech.* 3; or *Apost. Const.* 8.6–15, for fairly detailed descriptions of the rite at different times and places.

82 See J. Kilmartin, *The Eucharist in the Primitive Church* (Englewood Cliffs: Prentice-Hall, 1965). Augustine, *Contra Faust.* 20.20 speaks of the love-feast as meals for the poor.

83 Whether the pagan images can be interpreted with reference to a particular expectation of the afterlife is a somewhat open question, although it appears more plausible that the Roman images (as distinct from the earlier Greek ones) *did* project a paradisical image rather than an earthly one. A Roman epitaph in Avignon presents one explanation of the meaning of such images: "But what good is it to the dead to be shown feasting: They would have done better to have lived that way" (cited in *A History of Private Life*, vol. 1, ed. P. Veyne (Cambridge, MA, 1987), 180). See further discussion in J. M. C. Toynbee, *Death and Burial in the Roman World*, (Ithaca, NY: Cornell University Press, 1971), 37, 50–1, 137.

84 Tertullian, *De Cor.* refers to the tradition of Christians making offerings for the dead as birthday honors.

85 There are very helpful illustrations of these items along with a fairly complete bibliography in Snyder, *Ante Pacem*, 82–92.

86 The literature on this subject is vast. See, however, R. Krautheimer, "Mensa-Coemeterium-Martyrium," in *Studies in Early Christian, Medieval and Renaissance Art* (New York: New York University Press, 1969), 35–58.

87 See J. M. C. Toynbee, *Death and Burial*, ch. 3, esp. pp. 50–64 for a very good introduction to the subject; also on the question of Roman and Christian understandings of the *refrigerium interim*, see A. Stuiber, *Refrigerium Interim*; and a helpful review of the above by J. M. C. Toynbee, *JThS* n.s. 9 (1958), 141–9. The term *refrigerium interim* seems to have been coined by Tertullian in his treatise, *De monog.* 100.10. The epitaphs containing these terms are mostly found in the *triclia* of S. Sebastiano. For a full listing of these see A. Silvagni and A. Ferrua (eds), *Inscriptiones Latinae Christianae Veteres*, 3 vols, 2nd edn, ed. J. Moreau (Berlin: Weidmann, 1961).

88 For instance, see Augustine, *Ser.* 252, 310, 311; and *Ep.* 22 and 29.9, in the latter of which he explains the origins of feasts dedicated to the martyrs as an antidote to other, less decorous feasts. Also see Augustine, *Conf.* 6.2, where he describes Monica's practice of bringing cakes, wine, and bread to oratories built in memory of the martyrs, as well as *Contra Faust.* 20.21, in which Augustine refutes Faustus' claim that Christians worshiped their saints like idols, offering them gifts of food and wine. Other sources include Tertullian, *De resurr. carn.* 1; Ambrose, *De Elia et Jejunio* 17; and Paulinus of Nola, *Ep.* 13.11–13; and *Poema* 27.

89 This was suggested to me by Dennis Smith in a conversation about the place of fish in the New Testament banquets. See Smith's forthcoming book, *The Banquet in the Early Christian World*.

90 See Dölger, *Ichthys*, vol. 3, pls 42 and 64; vol. 4, pl. 268; Goodenough, *Jewish Symbols* vol. 3, figs 973–4; I. Schüler, "A Note on Jewish Gold Glass," *Journal of Glass Studies* 8 (1966), 55–60; and D. Barag, "Glass," in the *Encyclopaedia Judaica*, vol. 7 (Jerusalem: Keter, 1971), cols. 604–12 and pls 7 and 11.

91 Persius, *Satire* 5.180–4.

92 Tertullian, *Ad nat.* 1.13; and *Adv. Marc.* 5.4; also Irenaeus, *Adv. Haer.* 1.14.6. See J. Engemann, "Fisch," *RAC* 8, 959–1097 (esp. 1019). For a long and detailed discussion of the fish at Jewish meals see W. Bacher, "*Cena Pura*," *ZNTW* 6 (1905), 200–2; Dölger, *Ichthys*, vol. 2, 536–55, and summary discussions by Hiers and Kennedy, "Bread and Fish Eucharist," 36–40; and Stroumsa, "Early Christian Fish Symbol Reconsidered," in *Messiah and Christos*, ed. I.

Gruenwald, S. Shaked, and G. Stroumsa (Tübingen: Mohr, 1994), 199–202. Goodenough proposes that the *cena pura* was a meal of fish, bread, and wine – like the meals portrayed in early Christian art: *Jewish Symbols*, vol. 5, 41–7. A. D. Nock, however, disagrees with Goodenough's interpretation, "Religious Symbols and Symbolism II," in *Essays on Religion and the Ancient World*, vol. 2 (Oxford: Clarendon, 1972), 905–6. The fact that Tertullian knew of the tradition gives credence to the possibility that Christians could have known and artistically referred to a rabbinical tradition. See, however, the image of a banquet from the fifth-century Vergilius Romanus manuscript, reproduced in color in K. Weitzmann, *Late Antique and Early Christian Book Illumination* (New York: George Braziller, 1977), pl. 13.

93   On eating Leviathan in rabbinic literature see Vogel, "Le repas sacré," 17–24; L. Ginzberg, *The Legends of the Jews* (Philadelphia: Jewish Publication Society, 1913–25), vol. 1, 27–8 and vol. 5, n. 127, 43–6; H. Strack and P. Billerbeck, *Kommentar zum Neuen Testament* IV.2 (Munich: Oskar Beck), 1157–9; Goodenough, *Jewish Symbols*, vol. 5, 35–8; and J. Gutmann, "Leviathan, Behemoth and Ziz: Jewish Messianic Symbols in Art," *Hebrew Union College Annual* 39 (1968), 219–30.

94   See Origen, *In Epist. Ad Rom.* 5.10; and Jerome, *In Ionam* 2.4. Also see Y.-M. Duval, *Le livre de Jonas dans la littérature chrétienne greque et latine: sources et influences du Commentaire sur Jonas de Saint Jerome* (Paris: Études Augustiennes, 1973), 201–3.

95   See Dunbabin, "Triclinium and Stibadium," 132–5. Note the exceptions to this, e.g. the scene of Virgil and Dido in the *Vergilius Romanus* (fig. 55). Dunbabin, cited above, points out that the sigma table eventually came indoors and may have taken the place of the older *triclinium* form of dining arrangement.

96   *Epigrams* 10.48; 14.87.

97   See Justin Martyr, *1 Apol.* 65 and 67.

98   Augustine, *Tract. in Joh.* 123.21.2, trans. and discussed in Morey, "Origin of the Fish-Symbol," pt. 3, 417–20. Morey follows with two parallels to this text, from Eucherius and Chrysologus, which refer to the roasted fish of the Lukan post-resurrectional meal, 420–3.

99   This interpretation of the imagery was also proposed by Vogel, "Le repas sacré," and agrees with H. Lietzmann's identification of two types of early Christian eucharists: an *anamnesis* and an eschatological meal: *Mass and Lord's Supper: An Essay in the History of the Liturgy*, trans. D. H. G. Reeve, intro. and discussion R. D. Richardson (Leiden: Brill, 1979).

100   See. A. Thomas, "Weintraube," *LCI* 4 (1972), 494–6.

101   See, for instance, the fifth-century ivory diptych of Helios and Selene which shows a classic Dionysiac vintaging scene, R. Brilliant, in the *Age of Spirituality Catalogue*, ed. K. Weitzmann, entry no. 134, p. 158.

102   See detailed discussion of the image of Adam and Eve below, ch. 6.

103   See Goodenough, *Jewish Symbols*, vol. 2, 26–37; and vol. 3, fig. 789. Particular examples have been found in the Jewish catacombs of Rome, especially the Vigna Randanini Catacomb and the Catacomb of the Villa Torlonia.

104   Regarding the seasonal symbolism of these images, see the discussion and detailed notes in E. Struthers Malbon, *The Iconography of the Sarcophagus of Junius Bassus* (Princeton: Princeton University Press, 1990), 95–103, in which the author critiques earlier attempts to decipher the harvesting scenes on the ends of some Christian sarcophagi as seasonal allegories. Malbon goes on to argue that although modeled on pagan seasonal cycles, these images in Christian contexts should be understood as eucharistic metaphors.

105 *Did.* 9.2.

106 Clement of Alexandria, *Paed.* 2.1ff. See also *Paed.* 1.6; and *Strom.* 1.9. Also see Irenaeus, *Adv. haer.* 5.2.3.

107 Including Origen, *In Gen. hom.* 17.7; and *Cant. Cant.* 2; Zeno 2.27; and Ephrem, *Ser. 3 in Nat. Dom.* Many of these are discussed in C. Leonardi, *Ampelos. Il simbolo della vita nell'arte pagana e paleocristiana* (Rome: Edizioni Liturgiche, 1947). Leonardi interprets the grapevines as symbolic of martyrdom, but also of eternal life. Also see O. Nussbaum, "Die grosse Traube Christus," *JAC* 6 (1963), 136–43.

108 Irenaeus, *Frag.* 55.

109 Origen, *Contra Cels.* 5.12.

110 Basil, *Hex.* 5.6. A different parable of the church as vine was offered earlier by the Shepherd of Hermas, *Sim.* 2.1ff.

111 Hippolytus, *De bene. Iacob* 25, cited also in *The Crucible of Christianity*, ed. A. Toynbee (London: Thames and Hudson, 1969), 274. The translation used here is from this source. Also see Hippolytus, *Frag. in Gen.* 49.11.

112 Such an interpretation was also offered by W. Oakeshott, in regard to the mosaics in Sta. Constanza: "the idea of harvest, the end of one life and the beginning of another, is central," in *The Mosaics of Rome: From the Third to the Fourteenth Centuries* (London: Thames and Hudson, 1967), 62.

## 3 PICTORIAL TYPOLOGIES AND VISUAL EXEGESIS

1 It should be noted that many of these other themes appear among the wall paintings of the Dura Synagogue – suggesting a significant difference of emphasis between Jewish and Christian art of the third and fourth centuries.

2 The lateness of these particular images is discussed more fully below, in ch. 5.

3 See discussion of the sacrifice of Isaac as a type of Jesus' passion, ch. 5.

4 Art historians have long presumed a funerary interpretation of catacomb or sarcophagus art. See, for instance, Wilpert, *Roma sotterranea: le pitture delle catacombe romane* (Rome: Desclée, Lefebvre, 1903), 141; or a dissenting view by P. Styger, *Die altchristliche Grabeskunst, ein Versuch der einheitlichen Ausslegung* (Munich: Josef Kösel, 1927), 75f. See also A. Fausone, *Die Taufe in der frühchristliche Sepulkralkunst* (Vatican City: Pontificio Istituto di archeologia cristiana, 1982), in which the author presumes a funereal significance present in catacomb painting. This conclusion has also been challenged by those who would see a more this-worldly significance in early Christian tomb decoration. See, for instance, Snyder, *Ante Pacem, passim.*

5 See further discussion of this below, and in ch. 4.

6 These counts are only estimates and are based on the identifications of J. Wilpert, *Die Malereien der Katakomben Roms* (Frieburg i. Beiesgau: Herdersch Verlag, 1903); F. Deichmann, G. Bovini, and H. Brandenburg, *Repertorium der christlich-antiken Sarkophage* (Wiesbaden: Steiner, 1967); and the tabulations of T. Klauser, "Studien zur Enstehungsgeschichte der christlichen Kunst," *JAC* 4 (1961), 128–45; P. Styger, *Die altchristliche Grabeskunst*, 6–8, and the most helpful enumeration by Snyder, *Ante Pacem*, 43.

7 See, for instance, O. Wulff, *Altchristliche und byzantinische Kunst*, vol. 1 (Berlin-Neubabelsberg: Akademische Verlagsgesellschaft, 1914), 36–72; J. Strzygowski, *Orient oder Rom; Beiträge zur Geschichte der spätantiken und frühchristlichen Kunst* (Leipzig: J.C. Hinrichs'sche Buchhandlung, 1901). H. Chadwick offers the Jewish model theory as nearly conclusive, *The Early Church* (*Pelican History of the Church*, vol. 1; London: Penguin, 1967), 279–80.

8 See E. Goodenough, "Catacomb Art," *JBL* 81 (1962), 113–42.

9 See K. Weitzmann, "The Illustration of the Septuagint," in *Studies in Classical and Byzantine Manuscript Illumination*, ed. H. Kessler (Chicago: University of Chicago Press, 1971), 45–75; and K. Weitzmann and H. Kessler, *The Frescoes of the Dura Synagogue and Christian Art* Dumbarton Oaks 28 (Washington, DC: Dumbarton Oaks, 1990) for discussion and elaboration of this hypothesis. For an example of the way this theory has been widely accepted see K. Schubert, *Jewish Influence on Earliest Christian Paintings*, pt. 3 of *Jewish Historiography and Iconography in Early and Medieval Christianity* (Minneapolis: Fortress Press, 1992).

10 Joseph Gutmann has consistently made this cautionary argument. See his article "The Illustrated Jewish Manuscript in Antiquity: The Present State of the Question," *Gesta* 5 (1966), 39–44; in his introduction to *Hebrew Manuscript Painting* (New York: George Braziller, 1978), 9–12; his article "Early Synagogue and Jewish Catacomb Art and its Relation to Christian Art," *ANRW* 21.2 (1984), 1313–42; and his review of Weitzmann's and Kessler's work in *Speculum* 67 (1992), 502–4.

11 A. Grabar pointed this out more than thirty years ago in his 1961 Mellon lectures when he suggested that Christian art emanated from a desire to demonstrate the unity of sacred history, and these Old Testament images were "references to some mysterious but all-important link established by providence between the two Testaments." See *Christian Iconography: A Study of Its Origins*, 141f.

12 On Isaac as prefiguration of Jesus see, for example, Tertullian, *Adv. Jud.* 10.6 and 13.20–2; Irenaeus, *Adv. haer,* 4.10.1; Clement of Alexandria, *Paed.* 1.23; and Origen, *Hom. in Gen.* 8. Paul himself makes the baptism–rock-striking typology in 1 Cor. 10.1–5. See J. Daniélou, *The Bible and the Liturgy* (South Bend, IN: University of Notre Dame Press, 1956), for countless other examples.

13 E. Le Blant, *Études sur les sarcophages chrétiens antiques de la ville d'Arles* (Paris: Imprimerie Nationale, 1878), may have been the first to suggest this origin for catacomb iconography. See also his later version, *Les sarcophages chrétiens de la Gaule* (Paris: Imprimerie Nationale, 1886). H. Leclercq, in his *Manuel d'archéologie chrétienne*, vol. 1 (Paris: Letouzey, 1907), 187–9 and 110–16; and "Défunts (commémoraison des)," an article in *DACL*, vol. 4.1, cols. 427–56 (esp. 434–7), identified prayers in the Gelasian sacramentary (the *commendatio animae*) and a prayer from Pseudo-Cyprian of Antioch which mentions Noah, Jonah, Enoch, Abraham, Lot, Rahab, Elisha, Elijah, Job, Moses, and Daniel. Those who follow Leclercq include A. Ferrua, "Parlipomeni di Giona," *RAC* 38 (1962), 7–69; A. Grabar, *Early Christian Art: From the Rise of Christianity to the Death of Theodosius*, trans. S. Gilbert (New York: Odyssey Press, 1968), 102–5; E. Dinkler, "Abbreviated Representations," in the *Age of Spirituality Catalogue*, ed. K. Weitzmann, 393–9; and most recently, Finney, *Invisible God*, 282–4. See also the important presentation in A. Stuiber, *Refrigerium Interim*,169ff.

14 V. Schultze, *Grundriss der christlichen Archäologie* (Munich: Beck, 1919). For the *Constitutions* themselves see M. Metzger's edited version in Sources Chrétiennes 320, 329, 336 (Paris: Éditions du Cerf, 1987). Alternatively, see David A. Fiensy, *Prayers Alleged to be Jewish: An Examination of the "Constitutiones Apostolorum"* (Chico, CA: Scholars Press, 1985).

15 *Ap. Const.* 5.7.

16 The most accessible article on this subject is by M. Lawrence, "Three Pagan Themes in Christian Art," in *De Artibus Opuscula*, vol. 40, ed. M. Meiss (New

York: New York University Press, 1961), 323–34. See more discussion of this below, ch. 6.

17 See the arguments for dependency of Christian art upon pagan, beginning in the nineteenth century, by D. R. Rochette in his *Discours sur l'origine, le développement et le caractère des types imitatifs qui constitutent l'art du Christianisme* (Paris: A.Leclere, 1834), cited by Finney, *Invisible God*, 270. n. 83. Regarding the significance of such borrowing, see, for example, the discussion of Daniel below, ch. 6.

18 For full exploration of this tradition of adaption, see the vast work by L. von Sybel, *Christliche Antike*, 2 vols. (Marburg: Elwert, 1909); and *Frühchristliche Kunst: Leitfaden ihrer Entwicklung* (Munich: Beck'sche, 1920); or the shorter Lawrence article, "Three Pagan Themes in Christian Art."

19 As may be true with Orpheus or Helios (see above, ch. 2). This is the basic thesis of T. Mathew's recent book, *Clash of Gods: A Reinterpretation of Early Christian Art* (Princeton: Princeton University Press, 1993).

20 For instance, Snyder, throughout *Ante Pacem*, interprets many Old Testament images as artistic expressions of peace in "moments of extreme threat." In particular he includes Noah, Jonah, Daniel, Susannah, the three youths in the fiery furnace, the praying figure (orant) and the Good Shepherd. Snyder's hypothesis may have been influenced by André Grabar or Theodore Klauser. For discussion of Isaac as a type of Christ see below, ch. 5. The Moses/Peter parallel is elaborated below (this chapter).

21 For example see Styger, *Die altchristliche Grabekunst*, 75f.; or id., *Die römischen Katakomben* (Berlin: Verlag für Kunstwissenschaft, 1933).

22 Graydon Snyder objects to a specific funereal context for these images, arguing that many of the same images appear in the Dura Baptistery, *Ante Pacem*, 47.

23 See Origen, *De princ.*, bk. 4.

24 These images are discussed again, in more detail: Lazarus in ch. 6 and Isaac in ch. 5.

25 For several examples of this kind of approach applied to classical art see J. Esler (ed.), *Art and Text in Roman Culture* (Cambridge: Cambridge University Press, 1996).

26 See B. Ott, "Junglinge, Babylonische," *LCI* 2 (1970), 464–6 and Snyder, *Ante Pacem*, 54–5.

27 See E. Dassmann, *Sündenvergebung durch Taufe, Buße und Martyrerfürbitte in den Zeugnissen frühchristlicher Frömmigkeit und Kunst* (Münster i. Westf.: Aschendorff, 1973), 258–70, 425–38. Also see discussion of this image below, ch. 6.

28 *1 Clement* 45.7.

29 Tertullian, *De idol.* 15; *De scorp.* 8; *Adv. Marc.* 4.41; also Origen, *Exhort. ad martyr.* 33. In *De jejun.* 9; and *De anima* 48.3, Tertullian makes the three youths models of abstinence. Cyprian, *De lapsis* 19; *De unitate* 12; and *Ep.* 6.3, 58.5, 57.8, and 61.2. Also see Irenaeus, *Adv. haer.* 5.5.2; and Hippolytus, *Schol. in Dan.* 3, which emphasize Nebuchadnezzar's vision of the three children as well as a fourth – "like the Son of God." J. Daniélou discusses several of these texts in *The Origins of Latin Christianity* (Philadelphia: Westminster, 1977), 321–3.

30 Cyprian, *Ep.* 6.3, trans. G. Clarke, *Letters of Cyprian*, vol. 1 (Ancient Christian Writers Series, 43, 1984), 65.

31 Cyprian, *Ep.* 61.2. See also Hippolytus, *Frag. of discourses* 9.

32 On the former – the flood/fire parallels – see J. Daniélou, *From Shadows to Reality*, trans. W. Hibberd (Westminster, MD: Newman Press, 1960), 85–90. This parallel also was suggested by one of my students, Gail-Lenora Staton, the first time she saw the images.

33 On the destruction of the world by water and fire see Justin *2 Apol.* 7.2; Origen, *Contra Cels.* 1.19; and Irenaeus *Adv. haer.* 5.29.2.

34 Tertullian, *De res. mort.* 58.6; and Irenaeus, *Adv. haer.* 5.5. More discussion of the symbolism of bodily resurrection follows, ch. 6. See also M. C. Murray, *Rebirth and Afterlife*, 98–111, in which she discusses possible pagan iconographic sources (specifically the rescue of the ark of Perseus and Danaë) for Noah as a symbolic reference to resurrection.

35 See *1 Clement* 9.4; Justin Martyr, *Dial.* 138.2–3; and Tertullian, *De bapt.* 8, among others. See discussion of sacramental symbolism below.

36 Irenaeus, *Adv. haer.* 4.36.4.

37 John Chrysostom, *Hom.* 15.12 (on Matthew); and cf. *Hom.* 18.6 (on 1 Cor.). See also Chrysostom, *De stat.*, hom. 5.14, which specifically treats the story as an escape from death.

38 This designation for six chambers in the Catacomb of Callistus is fairly traditional and seems to have been first used by G. Marchi in the mid-nineteenth century, *Monumenti delle arte cristiane primitive* (Rome, Tip. di. C. Puccinelli, 1844), 161–3. J. Wilpert, although he objected to the terminology, continued to use the designation in *Die Malereien der Katakomben Roms*, 152f.

39 The baptismal symbolism of fish and fishers was taken up above, ch. 2.

40 This scene is discussed in more detail above, ch. 2.

41 "The Day of Lazarus" (the Saturday before Palm Sunday) in the Orthodox calendar is a baptismal day, and the reading of John 11 is the third scrutiny in the Rite of Christian Initiation in Adulthood in the Roman Catholic tradition. See extended discussion of the Lazarus image in ch. 6.

42 Justin, *Dial.* 138.1–3. The relationship between Noah and the Three Youths, and Noah and Daniel are discussed below, and again in ch. 6.

43 Tertullian, *De bapt.* 3, 4, 5, 8, and 9.

44 Ambrose, *De myst.* 10–18. On Naaman as a type see also Irenaeus, *Adv. haer.* 5.34; and Cyprian *Ep.* 63.8, in which he asserts that every reference to water "proclaims baptism.".

45 The new Roman Catholic "Rite of Christian Initiation in Adulthood" continues the tradition of reading the four Johannine pericopes prior to baptism at Easter.

46 The wedding at Cana story is cited in both the *Gelasian Sacramentary* 44 and the *Bobbio Missal* during the liturgy of the blessing of the baptismal font. Both of these texts are reprinted in E. C. Whitaker, *Documents of the Baptismal Liturgy* (London: SPCK, 1960). Although these sources are significantly later than the art works under discussion, they may be based on ancient traditions. The miracle at Cana also comes up in the *Benedictio Fontis*, the blessing of the baptismal font still used in the Roman church and attributed to Peter Chrysologus, a fifth-century bishop of Ravenna. The wedding imagery in baptism is a well-attested eastern practice. See J. Daniélou, *Bible and Liturgy* (Ann Arbor, MI: University of Notre Dame Press, 1956), 215–22 for a helpful summary discussion.

47 See T. Talley, *The Origins of the Liturgical Year* (New York: Pueblo, 1986), 125–9 for a fuller discussion of this complex season and its various observances.

48 See R. P. J. Hooyman, "Die Noe-Darstellung in der frühchristlichen Kunst," *VChr* 12 (1958), 113–35 on Noah as a figure of baptism; and Dassmann, *Sündenvergebung*, 258–70 and 425–38 on Noah, and 222–32 and 385–97 on Jonah. Also see Ferrua, "Paralipomeni di Giona," 112–14.

49 A survey of these typologies in patristic literature was conducted by J. Daniélou, *Bible and Liturgy*, chs 4–6. Also see Dassmann, *Sündenvergebung*, 196–208.

50 *Ep.* 62.8.

51 The symbolism of the Good Shepherd was discussed above, ch. 2. The image of Adam and Eve will be discussed again in ch. 6 (below).

52 See discussion of Daniel with Noah and Adam and Eve, below, ch. 6.

53 With some detailed work, even these might find a place. See discussion of Lazarus below, ch. 5.

54 A to-date unique portrayal of the infant Moses being lifted out of the Nile by Pharaoh's daughter also occurs in the Via Latina catacomb and may have baptismal significance.

55 Jonah continues to appear in the Christian art of the post-Constantinian era, for example in the Via Latina catacomb, in El-Bagawat in Egypt, and in many of the fifth-century North African mosaics. This scene's appearance in Roman art, however, is rare after 325–50.

56 This is the subject of ch. 4, below.

57 For more discussion of the Peter/Moses parallel see C. O. Nordström, "The Water Miracles of Moses in Jewish Legend and Byzantine Art," *Orientalia Suecana* 7 (1958), 78–109, reprinted in *No Graven Images*, ed. J. Gutmann (New York, KTAV, 1971), 277–308; and R. Jensen, "Moses Imagery in Jewish and Christian Art," *SBL Seminar Papers* (1992), 395–8.

58 The Via Latina catacomb was first discovered in 1955 at a totally unexpected site, unconnected with any ancient martyr cult or church structure. Bibliography on the catacomb probably begins with A. Ferrua, "Una nuova catacomba cristiana sull Via Latina," *La Civiltà Cattolica* 107 (1956), 118–31, and id., *Le pitture della nuova catacomba di via Latina* (= Monumenti di Antichità Cristiana 8, Vatican City, 1960). See also W. Tronzo, *The Via Latina Catacomb* (University Park, PA: Penn State Press, 1986).

59 These images are discussed in more detail below, ch. 4.

60 See discussion below, ch. 5.

## 4   PORTRAITS OF THE INCARNATE GOD

1 Paulinus, *Poem* 27.511–83, trans. P. G. Walsh, *The Poems of St. Paulinus of Nola*, Ancient Christian Writers Series (New York: Newman Press, 1975), 289–92.

2 A fairly thorough, and rightly critical, review of this scholarly development was recently undertaken by Thomas Mathews and forms the substance of his ground-breaking work, *The Clash of Gods*, in which the first chapter is devoted to explaining and refuting "The Mistake of the Emperor Mystique."

3 A. Grabar, *Christian Iconography*, 41–2 (also cited by Mathews, *Clash of Gods*, 13–14).

4 For example, see B. Brenk's article, "The Imperial Heritage of Early Christian Art," in *The Age of Spirituality: A Symposium* ed. K. Weitzmann (New York: Metropolitan Museum of Art, 1980), 39–52, that claims to work out the subtle chronology of the imperial influence on Christian art.

5 R. Milburn, *Early Christian Art and Architecture* (Berkeley: University of California Press, 1988), 47.

6 Mathews, *Clash of Gods*, esp. pp. 23–4.

7 Several attempts to identify Arian vs. orthodox theology in Christian art of the fifth and sixth centuries have concentrated primarily on the art of the Ostragoths and Visigoths. See, for instance, E. Demougeot, "Y eut-il une forme Arienne de l'art paléochretien?" *ACIAC* 6 (Vatican City, 1965), 491–519; S. Kostof, *The Orthodox Baptistery of Ravenna* (Yale University Press, 1965), 55–6; and D. Groh, "The Arian Controversy," *BR* (February 1994), 21–32.

8 Interestingly, both A. Grabar's discussion of the dogmatic images in *Christian Iconography*, chs 5 and 6, and much of T. Mathews' work in *The Clash of Gods* take theological context seriously, but Grabar views "theological iconography" as "incomplete and accidental," and Mathews pays less attention to the formation of doctrine than to the "clash of gods."

9 Snyder, *Ante Pacem*, 165, dates the beginning of this perceived shift to the post-Constantinian era: "It was only after Constantine, about the time of Damasus, that the picture of Jesus was changed from the youthful wonder-worker to the royal or majestic Lord."

10 One of the most important treatments of the development of the portrait in recent years has been by Hans Belting, *Likeness and Presence*, trans. E. Jephcott (Chicago: University of Chicago Press, 1994). Also see R. Brilliant, *Portraiture* (Cambridge, MA: Harvard University Press, 1991).

11 See Mathews, *Clash of Gods*, 117–18. Regarding the Buddhist influence, Mathews refers his readers to A. C. Soper, "Aspects of Light Symbolism in Gandharan Sculpture," *Artibus Asiae* 12 (1949), 252–83, 314–30; 13 (1950), 63–85. Concerning the Domitilla mosaic as the possible product of a modalist theology see J. Stevenson, *The Catacombs* (London: Thames and Hudson, 1978), 116–17.

12 On the Roman portrait tradition in general, and the absence of a portrait tradition of Jesus in earliest Christian art, see Grabar, *Christian Iconography*, ch. 3, "The Portrait," esp. pp. 66–73; and Johannes Kollwitz, *Das Christusbild des dritten Jahrunderts* (Münster in Westf.: Aschendorffschebuch, 1953), 5–6.

13 For more information see E. Kuryluk, *Veronica and Her Cloth* (Oxford: Blackwell, 1991).

14 The literature on the Abgar legend includes S. Runciman, "Some Remarks on the Image of Edessa," *Cambridge Historical Journal* 3 (1929–31), 238–52; and S. Brock, "Eusebius and Syriac Christianity," in *Eusebius, Christianity, and Judaism*, ed. H. W. Attridge and G. Hata (Detroit: Wayne State University Press, 1992), 212–34. About the miraculous (unpainted) images in general see Belting, *Likeness and Presence*, ch. 4, 47–77.

15 See Finney, *Invisible God*, ch. 4: "The Emperor's Image," esp. p. 86. Also, see Belting, *Likeness and Presence*, ch. 6, 102–14.

16 The so-called Trinity sarcophagus in Arles is one example of a possible representation of the three persons of the Godhead. See discussion below, ch. 6.

17 Lampridius, *Hist. Aug. Sev. Alex.* 29.2.

18 Testimonies to the correspondence between Abgar and Jesus: Eusebius, *Ecc. hist.* 1.13; and Egeria, *Pilgrimage* 19. The legend of the portrait is recorded in the apocryphal *Doctrine of Addai* (c.400); text and trans., G. Howard, *The Teaching of Addai* (Chico: Scholars Press, 1981).

19 *Acts of John* 26–9, trans. G. C. Stead, *New Testament Apocrypha*, vol. 2, 220–1. Irenaeus claims to know of a gnostic sect that possessed a portrait of Christ and gives the image as evidence against them: *Adv. haer.* 1.25.6.

20 Eusebius, *Ep. 2 ad Const. Aug.*, in J. D. Mansi, *Sacrorum conciliorum nova et amplissima collectio*, vol. 13 (Florence, 1767), *PG* 20, 1545. A recent translation is available in C. Mango, *The Art of the Byzantine Empire 312–1453: Sources and Documents* (Toronto: University of Toronto Press, 1986), 16.

21 The authenticity of the Eusebian correspondence with Constantia has been challenged by Mary Charles Murray, who also gives a helpful summary of the manuscript tradition. See her article "Art and the Early Church," *JThS* n.s. 28 (1977), 303–45, esp. pp. 327–9. At issue (in part) is Eusebius' citation of the Transfiguration as proof that neither human skill nor ordinary materials could

capture mingled divine and human essence – an argument commonly made by iconoclastic authors. Many modern scholars have assumed the letter was authentic, however, and used it as evidence for their arguments. Among them are A. von Harnack, *Geschichte der altchristlichen Literatur bis Eusebius*, vol. 2.2 (Leipzig: Hinrichs, 1904), 127; J. D. Breckenridge, "The Reception of Art into the Early Church," *ACIAC* 9.1 (1978), 361–2; and M. Frazer, "Iconic Representations," in Weitzmann, *Age of Spirituality*, 514–15.

22  *Ecc. hist.* 7.18.

23  *Vita Const.* 3.49.

24  *Lib. Pontif.*, 34.9 and 13 (Sylvester), ed. L. Duchesne, *Le Liber Pontificalis* 1 (Paris: E. de Boccard, 1955),172, 174. Eng. trans., L. R. Loomis, *Liber Pontificalis* (New York: Octagon, 1965), 47–50.

25  See W. N. Schumacher, "Traditio Legis," *LCI* 4 (1972), 347–52.

26  On the place of philosophy in Christian theological treatises in the fourth century (esp. the Cappadocians), see J. Pelikan, *Christian Theology and Classical Culture* (New Haven: Yale University Press, 1993), 177–83.

27  R. F. Hoddinott discusses the identity of these figures in *Early Byzantine Churches in Macedonia and Southern Serbia* (London: Macmillan, 1963), 177f.

28  Gregory of Nazianzus, *Orat.* 40 (on the Day of Lights), 5–6.

29  Jerome, *Contra Joh. Hier.* 29.

30  The emperor was more commonly shown with a jeweled diadem than a halo.

31  Consult M. Collinet-Guerin, *Histoire du nimbe des origines aux temps modernes* (Paris: Nouvelles Éditions Latines, 1961) for more discussion.

32  See here Belting, *Likeness and Presence*, particularly chs 1 and 3.

33  See A. Grabar's discounting of the "Syrian type" in *Christian Iconography*, 120–1.

34  See Grabar's discussion of this possibility, ibid., 119–21.

35  This despite G. Snyder's assertion that "about the time of Damasus, the picture of Jesus shifted from the youthful wonder-worker to the royal or majestic Lord. At that time, Jesus shifted more to a bearded, dominant, elderly figure" a type to which Snyder refers as "the Byzantine Christ," in *Ante Pacem*, 165.

36  See discussion above (ch. 3) regarding the Orpheus/Jesus imagery and below regarding the feminine attributes of Jesus and their parallels with Apollo and Dionysus in particular.

37  This conclusion accords largely with T. Mathews' thesis as outlined in *Clash of Gods*, particulary ch. 5, "Christ Chameleon," 126f. Mathews also demonstrates a strong iconographic resemblance between representations of Jesus and the healing god Aesclepius, 69–72.

38  For discussion of the Peter/Moses conflation see R. Jensen, "Moses Imagery in Jewish and Christian Art: Problems of Continuity and Particularity," *SBL Seminar Papers* 31 (1992), 389–418.

39  This was the point made by Catholic scholar M. Dulaey, "Le symbole de la baguette dans l'art paleochrétien," *Revue des études anciennes* 19.1–2 (1973), 3–38; and refuted by Mathews, *Clash of Gods*, ch. 3, "The Magician," where he points out that early Christian iconography signalled Jesus' authority by showing him holding a scroll, pp. 59–41.

40  See L. de Bruyne, "L'imposition des mains dans l'art chrétien ancien," *RAC* 20 (1943), 113–266.

41  Images of Mithraic initiations are reproduced in M. Vermaseren, *Corpus Inscriptionum et Monumentorum Religionis Mithriacae*, 2 vols. (The Hague: M. Nijhoff, 1956–65), figs. 57–9. The one possible exception to the absence of magic wands might be the group portrait of philosophers from the Hypogeum of the Aurelii in Rome, who are shown with wands (possibly a gnostic image).

See N. Himmelmann, "Das Hypogäum der Aurelier am Viale Manzoni: ikonographische Beobachtungen," in *Akademie der Wissenschaften und der Literatur*, Abhandlungen der Geistes und Sozialwissenschaftlichen Klasse 7 (Wiesbaden: Franz Steiner, 1975), 17.

42  Justin Martyr, *1 Apol.* 22, 26, 30.

43  Origen, *Contra Cels.* 1.68.

44  Origen, *Contra Cels.* 2.49–51.

45  Athanasius, *De Incarn.* 46–9, particular text excerpt translated by A. Robertson in *Christology of the Later Fathers*, ed. E. R. Hardy and C. Richardson (Philadelphia: Westminster Press, 1954), 102–3.

46  Much recent scholarship has been done on the place of Jesus' miracles within the context of Hellenistic magical practices, and the early Christian apologetics on the matter. See D. E. Aune, "Magic in Early Christianity," *ANRW* 2 (1980), 1507–57; E. V. Gallagher, *Divine Man or Magician? Celsus and Origen on Jesus*, SBL Dissertation Series, 64 (Chico, CA: Scholar's Press, 1982); H. Remus, *Pagan–Christian Conflict over Miracle in the Second Century*, Patristic Monograph Series, 10 (Cambridge, MA: Philadelphia Patristic Foundation, 1983); and H. Clark Kee, *Medicine, Miracle, and Magic in New Testament Times* (Cambridge, MA: Harvard University Press, 1986).

47  This apparent substitution of halo for wand was pointed out to me by Linda Emery, in her letter to the editor, *Bible Review*, Aug. 1994 (in response to my article, "The Raising of Lazarus," *BR*, Apr. 1994).

48  See J. Wilpert, "Early Christian Sculpture," *AB* 9 (1926/7), 105.

49  Mathews, *Clash of Gods*, 126. Mathews' entire ch. 5, "Christ Chameleon," 115–41, addresses the issue of Jesus' feminine appearance. Also see R. Jensen, "The Femininity of Christ in Early Christian Iconography," *Studia Patristica* 29 (1996), 269–82.

50  Clement of Alexandria, *Paed.* 3.11, trans. S. P. Wood, *Clement of Alexandria: Christ the Educator of Little Ones* (Washington, DC: Catholic University Press, 1953). See also Augustine, *De oper. mon.* 39–40.

51  Mathews, *Clash of Gods*, 126–7. See also M. Delcourt's longer discussion of classical, early Christian, and gnostic literature on hermaphrodite gods: *Hermaphrodite: Myths and Rites of the Bisexual Figure in Classical Antiquity*, trans. J. Nicholson (London: Studio Books, 1961).

52  Euripides, *Bacchae*, lines 234–5, lets Pentheus speak of Dionysus as having "perfumed hair in golden curls." Both Ovid, *Met.* 4.13 and 20; Seneca, *Oedipus*, line 420, describe Apollo's feminine aspects while Diodorus, *Hist.* 4.5.2 comments upon Dionysus' ambiguous age and sex, saying that there were actually two Dionysi, the ancient one with a long beard, and the newer one looking youthful and effeminate. See M. Jameson, "The Asexuality of Dionysus," in *Masks of Dionysus*, ed. T. Carpenter and C. Faraone (Ithaca: Cornell University Press, 1993), 44–64; and T. Carpenter, "On the Beardless Dionysus," ibid., 185–206. Also see the discussion and footnote in A. Henrichs, "Greek and Roman Glimpses of Dionysos," in *Dionysos and His Circle: Ancient and Modern* (The Fogg Art Museum, Harvard University, 1979), 1–2; and C. Houser, "Changing Views of Dionysos," in the same volume, 12–24. For figures see K. Lehmann-Hartleben, *Dionysiac Sarcophagi in Baltimore* (Walters Gallery, 1974) and F. Matz, *Die dionysischen Sarkophage*, 4 vols. (Berlin: Gebr. Mann, 1968–75). For Apollo iconography see W. Lambrinudakis, "Apollo," in the *Lexicon Iconographicum Mythologiae Classicae*, vol. 2.1, 183–327.

53 One exception being that of the youthful philosopher-type now identified as Jesus but previously mistaken for a woman poet. See discussion in Mathews, *Clash of Gods*, 128 nn. 29 and 30.

54 This kind of argument is made by Mathews, *Clash of Gods*, 135–8.

55 In one Montanist oracle, attributed to Priscilla or Quintilla, Christ appears as a woman. See W. Tabbernee, "Revelation 21 and the New Jerusalem," *Australian Biblical Review* 21 (1989), 52–60.

56 Textual evidence for gnostic iconography includes Irenaeus, *Adv. haer.* 1.25.6 and Origen, *Contra Cels.* 6.24 and 38. While Irenaeus, however, gives no description of the images that the Carpocratians or Basilidians supposedly venerated, Origen actually describes a gnostic cosmological ideograph. Mathews, *Clash of Gods*, 138, argues for a possible gnostic source for the feminine attributes of Jesus, citing the *Apoc. of John* 2.9–14; and the *Trimorphic Protennoia* 4.4–26, both contained in the *Nag Hammadi Library in English*, ed. J. M. Robinson (San Francisco: Harper and Row, 1977). E. Pagels, *The Gnostic Gospels* (New York: Random House, 1979), 57–83; and W. Meeks, "The Image of the Androgyne: Some Uses of Symbol in Earliest Christianity," *HistRel* 13.3 (1974), 165–208 both explore the gnostic and Pauline understandings of God as mother and being "beyond male and female" in Christ. M. Delcourt also explored gnostic, orphic, and hermetic connection in *Hermaphrodite*, 75–84.

57 See P. C. Finney, "Gnosticism and the Origins of Early Christian Art," *ACIAC* 9 (Vatican City, 1978) and "Did Gnostics Make Pictures?" *Numen* 41 (1980), 434–54, for an excellent discussion of the problem of gnostic iconography. Finney concludes that gnostics made images but that they bore no resemblance to "orthodox" Christian images, and couldn't easily have been mistaken for them.

58 See Wilpert, "Early Christian Sculpture," 105. Like Mathews, Wilpert also attributes the modeling of Jesus imagery on Serapis iconography to the influence of gnostic Christians.

59 A useful parallel to this borrowing of imagery is the adoption of the image of Isis with baby Horus on her lap for iconography of Mary with the child Jesus on her lap.

60 See discussion of this image in ch. 3 above.

61 Mithras is also depicted as youthful, beardless, and with long flowing hair although otherwise his iconography, showing him slaying the bull, is quite distinct from imagery of Jesus.

62 See *Protrep.* 7, in which Clement says that Orpheus had it right – but not about himself. This for him is evidence that the Greeks had glimmerings of the truth, but they were too distracted by their idolatry to realize it.

63 See R. Brilliant, "Mythology," in Weitzmann, *Age of Spirituality*, 126.

64 See the discussion in H. P. L'Orange, *Apotheosis in Ancient Portraiture* (New Rochelle, NY: Caratzas, 1964), 28–94.

65 See discussion in E. Kitzinger, "The Cleveland Marbles," *ACIAC* 9 (1978), 673–5. The parallels between Alexander portraiture and the Good Shepherd was noted earlier by O. Wulff, *Altchristliche und byzantinische Kunst*, vol. 1 (Berlin-Neubabelsberg: Akademische Verlagsgesellschaft, 1914), 107. Kitzinger cites F. Dvornik, *Early Christian and Byzantine Political Philosophy*, vol. 2 (Washington, DC: Catholic University Press, 1966), 595ff., regarding a pre-Christian application of the Good Shepherd as a royal simile – an "epithet of the good ruler."

66 Origen, *Contra Cels.* 6.75–7. With regard to Christ's changing appearance, see also *Contra Cels.* 2.64.

67 Cyril of Jerusalem, *Cat. lec.* 10.5, trans. adapted (to use gender inclusive language) from A. Stephenson, *The Works of Saint Cyril of Jerusalem*, vol. 1 (Washington, DC: Catholic University Press, Fathers of the Church Series, 1969), 198. See also Acts of John 98.

## 5  IMAGES OF THE SUFFERING REDEEMER

1 On the two intaglio gems see *New Documents Illustrating Early Christianity*, ed. G. H. R. Horsley (North Ryde, Australia: Ancient History Documentary Research Centre, Macquarie University, 1981), entry no. 90.

2 Added to this list of early images is a fifth-century Sassanian seal with a crucifixion scene in the Metropolitan Museum of Art in New York. The well-known graffito that shows a donkey on a cross is illustrated in *DACL*, vol. 3.2, 3051–2; and discussed by W. Helbig, *Führer durch die öffentlichen Sammlungen klassicher Altertümer in Rom*, ed. H. Speier (Tübingen: Wasmuth, 1966). See discussion below.

3 See longer discussion below. One such example of an explanation for a lack of crucifixion imagery was proposed by E. Syndicus, *Early Christian Art*, trans. J. R. Foster (New York: Hawthorn, 1962), 103: "The primitive church did not locate the redemptive work of Christ so exclusively as we do in the Passion, but rather in his earthly life as a whole, in his teaching, his miracles, and the sacraments he instituted."

4 See R. Funk, R. Hoover, and the Jesus Seminar, *The Five Gospels* (New York: Macmillan, 1993), 6–8: "The church appears to smother the historical Jesus by superimposing this heavenly figure on him in the creed ... . In Paul's theological scheme, Jesus the man played no essential role."

5 See, for instance, *Ep. Barn.* 5–7; Ignatius, *Eph.* 18.1; *Trall.* 11.2; and *Phil.* 8.2; Justin Martyr, *1 Apol.* 6; for example. Of course, the New Testament itself contains a great deal of sacrificial language (2 Cor. 6:7; Col. 2; 1 Peter 1:17–21; Heb. 9:14).

6 E. Syndicus, *Early Christian Art*, 103–4: "Fear of profanation of the holiest may have contributed to this result ... the sublime idea of redemption could not be made into the act of execution with which fourth-century Christians were still familiar from their own experience." See also Milburn, *Early Christian Art and Architecture*, 109. F. van der Meer, *Early Christian Art* (Chicago: University of Chicago Press, 1967), 120–2 suggests that the image was either too horrible, repulsive, or undignified to depict before the late sixth century. Also see A. Kartsonis, *Anastasis: The Making of an Image* (Princeton: Princeton University Press, 1986), 33–9.

7 Sozomenus, *Hist. ecc.* 1.8.13; *Codex Theodosianus* 9.5.1 (316).

8 This argument was made by C. Pocknee, *Cross and Crucifix in Christian Worship and Devotion* (London: Mowbray, 1962), 38.

9 See M. Charles Murray, "Art and the Early Church," *JThS* n.s. 28 (1977), 304; and A. Grabar, *Christian Iconography*, 132, where he states: "It is often said that the image-makers did not dare to approach the subject of the crucifixion, but this is a gratuitous affirmation, particularly in view of the fact that the theologians of the period treated it constantly."

10 R. E. Brown, *The Death of the Messiah* (New York: Doubleday, 1994), 946f.; M. Hengel, *Crucifixion* (Philadelphia: Fortress, 1977), 23–63.

11 T. Mathews argues for a different interpretation of this graffito, however, by pointing to evidence that early Christians venerated the ass. See *Clash of Gods*, ch. 2, "The Chariot and the Donkey," esp. 48–50.

12 M. Shepherd, "Christology: A Central Problem of Early Christian Theology and Art," in Weitzmann, *Age of Spirituality*, 112. See also W. Lowrie, *Art in the Early Church* (New York: Norton, 1947), 110; and Syndicus, *Early Christian Art*, 103: "Pictures of the Passion and the Crucifixion did not begin late because Christians had to be gradually educated to regard the symbol of shame as the symbol of victory."

13 *Contra Cels.* 2.47, trans. H. Chadwick, *Origen: Contra Celsum* (London: Cambridge University Press, 1980), 102.

14 Minucius Felix, *Oct.* 9.4; 29.6–8; Tertullian, *Ad nat.* 1, 11–12; and *Apol.* 16.

15 E. J. Tinsley, "The Coming of a Dead and Naked Christ," *Religion* 2 (1972), 24–36. See also a response to Tinsley by P. G. Moore, "Cross and Crucifixion in Christian Iconography," *Religion* 4 (1974), 105–15.

16 Snyder, *Ante Pacem*, 14.

17 Ignatius, *Eph.* 18.1 (cf. Ignatius, *Trall.* 10); and Irenaeus, *Adv. haer.* 5.16.3.

18 Clement, *Protrep.* 11.114.1–4.

19 Tertullian, *De pud.* 22.4. See also Melito, *Peri pascha*; Origen, *Contra Cels.* 7.16–17; and discussion in Pelikan, *The Emergence of the Catholic Tradition*, vol. 1, 146–8.

20 The *"signum crucis"* was used on any number of other occasions. See Tertullian, *De Cor.* 3; Cyril of Jerusalem, *Cat. lec.* 13.36; and Augustine, *In Joh. ev. tr.* 118.5.

21 *Ep. Barn.* 8. On the relationship between theological and liturgical treatments, however, see J. Pelikan, vol. 1 of *The Christian Tradition: The Emergence of the Catholic Tradition* (Chicago: University of Chicago Press, 1971), 146: "There is reason to believe that the saving power of the suffering and death of Christ was more explicitly celebrated in the liturgy of the second century than formulated in its theology."

22 Hippolytus, *Ap. trad.* 4; Cyprian, *Ep.* 62. For more discussion see J. A. Jungmann, *The Mass* (Collegeville, MN: Liturgical Press, 1975), chs 2–3.

23 See J. Finegan, *Archeology of the New Testament* (Princeton: Princeton University Press, 1969), 220–60.

24 W. Baines, "Rotas-Sator Square: A New Investigation," *NTS* 33 (1987), 469–73; R. Houston Smith, "The Cross Marks on Jewish Ossuaries," *PEQ* (1974) 53–75; and E. Dinkler, "Zur Geschichte des Kreuzsymbols," *ZThK* 48 (1951), 148–72; and id., "Kreuzzeichen und Kreuz-Tau, Chi und Stauros," *JAC* 5 (1962), 93–112.

25 Compare Job 31:35 and Revelation 14:9 with the text from Ezekiel.

26 Finegan, *Archeology of the New Testament*, 343f.; Daniélou, *Primitive Christian Symbols*, trans. D. Attwater (Baltimore: Helicon Press, 1974), ch. 9; Dinkler, "Zur Geschichte des Kreuzsymbols." Also see Moore, "Cross and Crucifixion," 105.

27 Tertullian, *Adv. Marc.* 3.22; and *De Cor.* 3. See also Cyril of Jerusalem, *Cat.lec.* 13.36, in which the sign is called a "great phylactery" (*mega to phylacterion*). *Ep. Barn.* 9.8 also associates the letter *tau* with the cross.

28 Cyprian, *Ad Dem.* 22, trans. R. Deferrari, *Saint Cyprian: Treatises*, Fathers of the Church series, 36 (Washington, DC: Catholic University Press, 1977), 187.

29 See M. Guarducci, *I graffiti sotto la Confessione di San Pietro in Vaticano*, vol. 1 (Vatican City, 1958); and id., *The Tomb of St. Peter* (New York: Hawthorn Books, 1960), 94–122; W. H. Buckler, W. M. Calder, and C. W. M. Cox, "Monuments from Central Phrygia," *JRS* 16 (1926), 61–74; F. J. Dölger, "Beiträge zur Geschichte des Kreuzzeichens," *JAC* 1 (1958), 353–86.

30 See entry 336 in Finegan, *Archeology of the New Testament*, pp. 381–2; and an article by M. Black, "The Chi-Rho Sign: Christogram and/or Staurogram," in

*Apostolic History and the Gospel*, ed. W. Ward Gasque and R. P. Martin (Grand Rapids: Eerdmans, 1970), 320–7 for a fuller discussion of these papyri and bibliography. Also see E. Dinkler "Älteste Christliche Denkmäler," in *Signum Crucis* (Tübingen: Mohr, 1967), 134–78.

31 Clement, *Paed.* 3.11. See L. Eizenhöfer, "Die Sigelbildvorschläge des Clemens von Alexandrien," *JAC* 3 (1960), 51–69.

32 Hippolytus, *Antichr.* 59; trans. in J. Daniélou, *Primitive Christian Symbols*, 60. Compare Maximus of Turin, *Hom.* 50, (*De cruce Dom.*); and Gregory of Nazanzius, *Or.* 4.18. See also G. Stuhlfauth, "Das Schiff als Symbol der altchristlichen Kunst," *RAC* 19 (1942), 111–41.

33 See examples and discussion in Finney, *Invisible God*, 235–40.

34 Ambrose, *In Ep. ad Heb.* 6. An interesting thesis that attempts to explain the lack of textual parallels to the symbol of the anchor was put forth by C. Kennedy, "Early Christians and the Anchor," *BibArch* 38 (1975), 115–25. Here Kennedy argues that the anchor is a pun on the Greek words *en kurio*.

35 See Snyder, *Ante Pacem*, 14; New Documents in Early Christianity, no. 92; Finegan, *Archeology of the New Testament*, 378–9.

36 Justin Martyr, *Dial.* 112.

37 Tertullian, *Adv. Jud.* 13.19. Cf. Justin Martyr, *Dial.* 86.6. For lengthy discussion of the primary sources see Daniélou, *Primitive Christian Symbols*, chs 4 and 6.

38 Justin Martyr, *1 Apol.* 55.3–8; also *Dial.* 91.2 and 112. Tertullian, *Adv. Jud.* 10.

39 *Mart. Lyons*, 41. See also Ignatius, *Rom.* 5: "Permit me to be an imitator of the Passion of Christ, my God."

40 Minucius Felix, *Oct.* 29.6, trans. G. W. Clarke, *The Octavius of Minucius Felix*, Ancient Christian Writers Series, 39 (New York: Newman Press, 1974), 106–7.

41 Tertullian, *Ad nat.* 1.12.

42 Snyder, *Ante Pacem*, 14. O. Marucchi refers to the sheep as "the emblem of the believer among early Christian ideographic symbols," *Christian Epigraphy* (Chicago: Ares, 1974; a reprint of the 1912 edn, Cambridge: Cambridge University Press), 69.

43 See F. Gerke, "Der Ursprung der Lämmerallegorien in der altchristlichen Plastik," *ZNTW* 33 (1934), 160–96.

44 *Dial.* 40.

45 Tertullian, *Adv. Jud.* 10; see also Melito of Sardis, *Peri Pascha* 5.67.71.

46 Lactantius, *Div. inst.* 4.26.41–2. See also Paulinus of Nola, *Ep.* 32 to Severus: "Christ stands as a snowy lamb beneath the bloody cross in the heavenly grove of flower-dotted paradise." Paulinus' paralleling of the ram of Genesis with the Lamb of God is cited below, n. 55.

47 Paulinus of Nola, *Ep.* 32.10 (to Severus); *Lib. pont.* 34.9 and 13 (Sylvester).

48 *Quinisext. can.* 82, trans. H. R. Percival, *NPNF* ser. 2, 14 (1988), 401.

49 See R. Jensen, "The Offering of Isaac in Jewish and Christian Tradition: Image and Text," *BibInterp* 2.1 (1994), 85–110. See also H. M. von Erffa, "Abraham's Opfer," in *Ikonologie der Genesis*, vol. 2 (Munich, 1995), 145–88; and J. Gutmann, "Revisiting the Binding of Isaac Mosaic in the Beth-Alpha Synagogue," *Bulletin of the Asia Institute*, 6 (1992), 83ff.

50 The older interpretation is exemplified by A. Moore Smith, "The Iconography of the Sacrifice of Isaac in Early Christian Art," *AJA* ser. 2, 26.2 (1922), 159–69; and (more recently) E. Dinkler, entry 386, "The Sarcophagus of Junius Bassus," in Weitzmann, *Age of Spirituality*, 429.

51 I. S. van Woerden, "The Iconography of the Sacrifice of Abraham," *VChr* 15 (1961), 242.

52 Stevenson, *The Catacombs*, 68.

53 Snyder, *Ante Pacem*, 29. See also his discussion 51–2.

54 *Ep. Barn.* 7.3.

55 Melito, *Frag.* 9–11, trans. S. G. Hall, *Melito of Sardis on Pascha and Fragments* (Oxford: Clarendon, 1979), 75–7. See also Paulinus of Nola, *Ep.* 29.9, *Letters of St. Paulinus of Nola*, vol. 2, trans. P. G. Walsh (Ancient Christian Writers Series; London: Longmans, Green and Co., 1976), 112. Paulinus similarly connects the Lamb of God with the ram of Genesis: "The angel snatched up the victim and in its place set a hastily furnished sheep, so that God should not lose His offering, nor the father his son ... For the lamb which was to be later sacrificed in Egypt to typify the Saviour was thus already anticipated by a beast of its own species ... "

56 Tertullian, *Adv. Jud.* 10.6. See also *Adv. Jud.* 13.20–2, where Tertullian claims the bramble in which the ram was caught by the horns was a figure of the crown of thorns. Also see Irenaeus, *Adv. haer.* 4.10.1; Clement, *Paed.* 1.23; and Origen, *In Gen. hom.* 8. There are many other examples. See a longer analysis in E. Dassmann, *Südenvergebung durch Taufe, Buße, und Märtyrerfürbitte in den Zeugnissen frühchristliche Frömmigkeit und Kunst* (Münster in Westf.: Aschendorff, 1973), 185ff.

57 Ambrose, *De Ab.* 1.8; Ephrem, *In Gen. 1, liber ad Jud.* 10.77; Isidore of Seville, *Alleg.*; Chrysostom, *Hom in Gen.* 47.3; Paulinus, *Carmen.* 27, 616–17; Theodoret, *Quaest. in Gen.* 74; and Augustine, *Contra Faust.* 22.73 and *De civ. Dei* 16.32.

58 The readings at Jerusalem were probably similar to those found in Armenian lectionaries and include the Genesis stories of creation and the sacrifice of Isaac. See T. Talley, *The Origins of the Liturgical Year* (New York: Pueblo, 1986), 47ff. Regarding the Milanese Canon of the Mass and the *Sacramentarium Veronese*, see edn by L. C. Mohlberg (Rome, 1956), no. 1250; and a full discussion in B. Botte, "Abraham dans la liturgie," *Cahiers Sion* 5 (1951), 88–95.

59 Piacenza Pilgrim, Itinerarium 19. See J. Wilkinson, *Jerusalem Pilgrims before the Crusades* (Warminster: Aris and Phillips, 1977), 83. For further discussion see J. Wilkinson, *Egeria's Travels* (Warminster: Aris and Phillips, 1981), 154 and n. 8; and A. S. Clair, "The Iconography of the Great Berlin Pyxis," *Jahrbuch der Berliner Museum* 20 (1978), 23f.

60 On this group of sarcophagi see H. von Campenhausen, "Die Passionssarkophage: Zur Geschichte eines altchristlichen Bildkreises," *Marburger Jahrbuch für Kunstwissenschaft* 5 (1929), 39–68.

61 See above, n. 22 – taken from *Oct.* 29.6.

62 Tertullian, *Ad nat.* 1.12 (see entire chapter for more examples).

63 Lactantius, *Mort. pers.* 44.3–6. Although the date is disputed, the vision probably took place in the year of his victory, 312.

64 Eusebius, *Vita Const.* 1.26–9. The *chi-rho* first appeared on Constantine's coinage in 315, although there is evidence of the sign's precedent in earlier Christian and pagan contexts. See P. Bruun, "Early Christian Symbolism on Coins and Inscriptions," *ACIAC* 6 (1962), 528–34.

65 Eusebius especially notes that Constantine "henceforth placed the two letters chi and rho on his helmet." See A. Alföldi, "The Helmet of Constantine with the Christian Monogram," *JRS* 22 (1932), 9–23; P. Bruun, "The Christian Signs on the Coins of Constantine," *Arctos* n.s. 3 (1962), 5–35; and P. Bastien, "Le chrisme dans la numismatique de la dynastie constantinienne," in the exhibition catalogue of *Collectionneurs et Collections Numismatiques à la Monnaie de Paris* (April 1968).

66 The cross held by John the Baptist in the medallion of the Orthodox Baptistery in Ravenna may have been the addition of a later restorer.

67 See Egeria, *Itin.* 30–40. Receipt of one of the cross fragments at the Monastery of Poitiers in 569 inspired Venantius Fortunatus to compose hymns glorifying the cross: *"Vexilla regis prodeunt,"* and *"Pange, lingua, gloriosi proelium certaminis."* See F. J. E. Raby, *History of Christian-Latin Poetry* (Oxford: Clarendon, 1927), 88–91. For longer discussion consult H. A. Drake, "Eusebius on the True Cross," *JEH* 36 (1985), 1–22.

68 See the argument for this in J. Engemann, "Palästinische Pilgerampullen im F. J. Dölger Institut in Bonn," *JAC* 16 (1973), 5–27, esp. 25.

69 See a valuable and important discussion of pilgrim token imagery by G. Vikan, "Pilgrims in Magi's Clothing: The Impact of Mimesis on Early Byzantine Pilgrimage Art," in *The Blessings of Pilgrimage*, ed. R. Ousterhout (Urbana, IL: University of Illinois Press, 1990), 97–107. Also see C. Hahn, "Loca Sancta Souvenirs," in the same volume, 85–96.

70 See Egeria, *Itin.* 37.1 and 48.2. Consult Wilkinson, *Egeria's Travels*, 136–7, 240f. Also see the Piacenza Pilgrim, Itin. 20, in Wilkinson, *Jerusalem Pilgrims*, 83. Cyril of Jerusalem, Ambrose, and Melania the Elder among others reported the legend of the True Cross. For sources see H. Leclercq, "Croix, crucifix," and "Croix (Invention et exaltation de la Vraie)," in *DACL*, vol. 3.2 (1914), cols. 3045–139. Also see mention of Melania's gift of such a relic to Paulinus of Nola, Paulinus, *Ep* 31.1; 32.11.

71 For discussion of the influence of this hypothesized monumental mosaic on subsequent iconography see M. Frazer, "Holy Sites Representations," in Weitzmann, *Age of Spirituality*, 564–5. The theory was challenged by A. Grabar, *Ampoules de Terre Sainte (Monsa, Bobbio)* (Paris: Klincksieck, 1958), 45ff.; but revived by K. Weitzmann, in his discussion of the different compositions of crucifixion scenes on pilgrimage souvenirs including ampullae and reliquary boxes. See Weitzmann, "Loca sancta and the Representational Arts of Palestine," *DOP* 28 (1974), 33–55, esp. 40–3. Unfortunately neither Egeria nor Eusebius describe the apse imagery, although Eusebius, *Vita Const.* 3.31, describes other features of the building.

72 See Tertullian, *Adv. Prax.* 27–9; and Hippolytus, *Adv. haer.* 9.2.

73 Since it is nearly impossible to summarize briefly the fifth-century Christological controversies or the important primary sources, consult F. W. Norris, "Christ, Christology," *EEC* (1990), 197–206 for a succinct summary and basic bibliography.

74 Cyril of Alexandria, *Ep. 3 ad Nestorius*, trans. E. R. Hardy, in *Christology of the Later Fathers* (Philadelphia: Westminster, 1954), 351.

75 Hilary of Poitiers, *De Trin.* 10.23 and following.

76 See Tinsley, "The Coming of a Dead and Naked Christ," and Moore's reply, "Cross and Crucifixion," for a lengthy discussion of the relationship of Christology and iconography.

77 As described by Ignatius, *Trall.* 10.

78 Regarding medieval devotion to the cross see R. Kieckhefer, "Major Currents in Late Medieval Devotion," and E. Cousins, "The Humanity and the Passion of Christ," in *Christian Spirituality: High Middle Ages and Reformation*, ed. J. Raitt, B. McGinn, and J. Meyendorff (New York: Crossroad, 1989), 83–9 and 375–91; and E. A. Petroff, *Medieval Women's Visionary Literature* (New York: Oxford University Press, 1986), 12–17.

79 Julian, *Showings, the Long Text* 10, trans. and ed. E. Colledge and J. Walsh, Classics of Western Spirituality Series (New York: Paulist Press, 1978), 193.

## 6  BORN AGAIN: THE RESURRECTION OF THE BODY
## AND THE RESTORATION OF EDEN

1 Hippolytus, *Ap. trad.* 21.17.
2 See a very old, but still helpful article by H. B. Swete, "The Resurrection of the Flesh," *JThS* 18 (1917), 135–41. Also R. M. Grant, "The Resurrection of the Body," *JRel* 28 (1948), 120–30; J. G. Davies, "Factors Leading to the Emergence of Belief in the Resurrection of the Flesh," *JThS* n.s. 23 (1972), 448–55; A. H. C. van Eijk, "Resurrection-Language: Its Various Meanings in Early Christian Literature," *Studia Patristica* 12 (1975), 271–6. Books on the subject include M. E. Dahl, *The Resurrection of the Body* (Naperville, IL: Alec R. Allenson, 1962); J. E. McWilliam Dewart, *Death and Resurrection* (Wilmington, DE: Michael Glazier, 1986); J. Pelikan, *The Shape of Death: Life, Death, and Immortality in the Early Fathers* (New York: Abingdon, 1961); and P. Perkins, *Resurrection* (New York: Doubleday, 1984).
3 *2 Clem.* 26, in which the author sites Job 19:25–6 in support of the point.
4 On immortality of the soul in ancient thought see W. Jaeger, "The Greek Ideas of Immortality," in *Immortality and Resurrection*, ed. K. Stendahl (New York: Macmillan, 1965), 96–114.
5 See *2 Clem.* 8.4–5; Justin Martyr, *Dial.* 45; and Athenagoras, *De res.* 18.
6 Paradise as an "Edenic garden" is described in the Passion of Sts Perpetua and Felicitas. In some thinking, martyrs would be admitted to an earthly paradise, awaiting the end time, when the new paradise would be established. See Irenaeus, *Adv. haer.* 5.5.1 and 5.36.1; Tertullian, *De anima* 55.4; Origen, *De prin.* 2.11.6–7; and commentary in J. Daniélou, *Origins of Latin Christianity* (Philadelphia: Westminster, 1977), 394; and especially C. W. Bynum, *The Resurrection of the Body in Western Christianity, 200–1336* (New York: Columbia University Press, 1995), 43–51.
7 For instance see *The Treatise on Resurrection* (in the Nag Hammadi corpus); and *Gospel of Philip* 56–9.
8 Cf. the *Acts of Thomas* 27.
9 Cf. Irenaeus, *Adv. haer.* 5.9.1 and 3.
10 *De res.* 8–9, 62–3.
11 *De res.* 32, 57.
12 *De. res.* 8.3, and see discussion in Daniélou, *Origins of Latin Christianity*, 399.
13 Minucius Felix, *Oct.* 34; Irenaeus, *Adv. haer.* 5.14; Theophilus, *Autol.* 13; Tatian, *De orat.* 6; Athenagoras, *De res.*, perhaps the earliest entire treatise devoted to the subject (late second century – although his authorship of the treatise is disputed) says in ch. 7 that the body is changed in the resurrection.
14 Justin Martyr, *1 Apol.* 18–19, in which he asserts that we will be raised again in our very own bodies, even though they were dead and cast into the earth; cf. also ch. 52.
15 See the excellent discussion in Bynum, *Resurrection of the Body*, 27–34.
16 Origen, *De prin.* 1.8.4; 2.10.1–3; and 4.4.9.
17 Methodius of Olympus, *De res.*
18 Augustine, *De civ. Dei.* 22.11–22.
19 See E. B. Stebbins, *The Dolphin in the Literature and Art of Greece and Rome* (Menasha, WI: George Banta, 1929). H. Leclercq, "Dauphin," *DACL*, vol. 4.1 (1920), 283–96; L. Wehrhahn-Stauch, "Delphin," *LCI*, vol. 1 (Freiburg im Breisgau: Herder, 1968), 503–4; and Goodenough, *Jewish Symbols*, vol. 5, 22–30.

20 On the phoenix see the following ancient sources: *1 Clem.* 24–6; Tertullian, *De res.* 13; Cyril of Jerusalem, *Cat. lec.* 18.8; Eusebius, *Vita Const.* 4.72; and Lactantius, *De ave Phoenice.* On the peacock see Augustine, *Civ. Dei* 21.4. The images of the phoenix and peacock are well represented in Roman art of the same period, in which the phoenix was seen commonly on coin types associated with military victories while the peacock was a more general decorative and funereal motif. See R. van den Brock, *The Myth of the Phoenix According to Classical and Early Christian Tradition* (Leiden: Brill, 1972).

21 Paulinus, *Ep.* 32.17.

22 On the subject of the Dura image see A. Grabar, "La fresque des Saintes Femmes au tombeau à Dura," in *L'art de la fin de l'Antiquité et du Moyen Age,* vol. 1 (Paris: College de France, 1968), 517ff. See also, C. H. Kraeling, *Excavations at Dura Europos. Final Report 8, Part II: The Christian Building* (New Haven: Yale University Press, 1967), 76ff.

23 G. Schiller devoted the entire third volume of her *Ikonographie der christlichen Kunst* (Gütersloh: Gütersloher Verlagshaus Gerd Mohn, 1971) to the iconography of resurrection, including the triumphal images of the enthroned Christ as well as the empty cross, the empty tomb, and the ascension, judgment, and second coming of Christ. Also see J. Villette, *La résurrection du Christ dans l'art chrétien du IIe au VIIe siècle* (Paris: Henri Laurens, 1957).

24 See R. Krautheimer, *Early Christian and Byzantine Architecture,* 4th edn (New York: Penguin, 1986), 60–3 and 73–4; W. E. Kleinbauer, entry 582 in the *Age of Spirituality Catalogue,* ed. K. Weitzmann, 650–1.

25 See Gary Vikan, entry 453 in the *Age of Spirituality Catalogue,* ed. K. Weitzmann, 504–5 with bibliography.

26 K. Weitzmann makes this argument (the conflation of the two stories), "Eine vorikonoklastische Ikone des Sinai mit der Darstellung des Chairete," in *Tortulae: Studien zu altchristlichen und byzantinische Monumentum, Römische Quartalschrift* 30, Suppl.(1966), 321.

27 On the three women at the tomb see Villette, *La résurrection du Christ dans l'art,* 59–88.

28 See Irenaeus,*Adv. haer.* 5.5: if Elijah and Enoch were translated in their own bodies, surely we can be as well.

29 The two crucifixion scenes were discussed above, ch. 5; See *Age of Spirituality,* entry. 452.

30 See M. Frazer's introduction to "Holy Sites Representations," *Age of Spirituality,* 564–5.

31 See a brief discussion of many of these early images in Kartsonis, *Anastasis: The Making of an Image,* ch. 2, "The Prehistory of the Image," 19–39. The vision of Ezekiel was incorporated into the liturgy of Ascension Day in Eastern Syria, from which the Rabbula gospel originates. See *Age of Spirituality Catalogue,* 454–5. On the contrast between Eastern and Western images of the seraphim see R. Jensen, "Of Cherubim and Gospel Symbols," *BAR* 21.4 (1995), 42ff.

32 A similar composition appears on the doors of Sta. Sabina, which also shows Jesus in a mandorla and Ecclesia as an orant.

33 Extended discussion of the iconography and texts may be found in Dassmann, *Sündenvergebung,* 60, 70, 220–1.

34 See E. Dinkler, entry 375 in the *Age of Spirituality Catalogue,* ed. K. Weitzmann, 418; and a longer discussion by M. Sotomayor, *Sarcophagos romano-cristianos de España: Estudio iconográfico* (Granada: Facultad de Teologia, 1975), 32–43.

35 Justin Martyr, *1 Apol.* 52.

36 Irenaeus, *Adv. haer.* 5.15.1–2.

37 Tertullian *De res.* 29–30.

38 Jerome, *In Ezek.*; Cyril of Jerusalem, *Cat. lec.* 18.

39 As to whether Gregory sided with the Origenist "spriritural body" position or those detractors of Origen (Jerome and co.) who took a more materialist view, see Bynum, *Resurrection of the Body*, 63 (esp. bibliography in n. 12) and 81–6; Dewart, *Death and Resurrection*, 147–56; and T. J. Dennis, "Gregory on the Resurrection of the Body," in *The Easter Sermons of Gregory of Nyssa: Translation and Commentary*, ed. A. Spira and C. Klock (Cambridge, MA: Philadelphia Patristic Foundation, 1981), 55–80.

40 Gregory of Nyssa, *De anima et res.* Compare his treatise *De opif. hom.* 25.8–10, in which Gregory again cites the stories of the raising of Jairus' daughter and the son of the widow of Nain.

41 Irenaeus,*Adv. haer.* 5.13.1. Similar arguments concerning the physical resurrection were made by Tertullian, *De res.* 53.3; and *De carne Christi* 12.7; and Athenagoras, *De res.*

42 Gregory of Nyssa, *De opif. hom.* 25.11.

43 Cyril of Jerusalem, *Cat. lec.* 2.5, 5.9, and 18.16.

44 Augustine, *Tract. in Joh.* 49.20–5. See also Ambrose, *De repent.* 2.7.58.

45 Further discussion of the Lazarus imagery: R. Jensen, "Raising Lazarus," *BR* 11.2 (1995), 20ff.; and E. Mâle, "La résurrection de Lazarus dans l'art," *Revue des Arts* 1 (1951), 45ff.

46 On the general symbolism of nudity see J. Z. Smith, "The Garments of Shame," *HistRel* 5 (1966), 217–38.

47 Dassmann, *Sündenvergebung*, 222–32; 385–97; and L. de Bruyne, "Refrigerium interim," *RAC* 34 (1958), 112–14.

48 See W. Wixom, "Early Christian Sculptures in Cleveland," *Bulletin of the Cleveland Museum of Art* 45 (1967), 75–88k.

49 On the Endymion–Jonah iconographic parallels see Marion Lawrence, "Three Pagan Themes in Christian Art," *De Artibus Opuscula*, vol. 40, ed. M. Meiss (New York: New York University Press, 1961), 323–4. The prototype of Dionysus lying under the grape vine is also a likely model for the iconography of Jonah. See E. Strommel, "Zum Problem der frühchristlichen Jonasdarstellungen," *JAC* 1 (1958), 112–15.

50 See Mathews, *Clash of Gods*, 30–2.

51 Ignatius, *Trall.* 10. The first day – of crucifixion – corresponds to the Jewish day of the preparation, the second is the day of burial and is on the Jewish Sabbath. The third day is the day of resurrection – the Lord's day.

52 Justin Martyr, *Dial.* 107. Later John Chrysostom would also find a moral lesson in the tale, but one that could be used to exhort his congregation to obey God's commands as Jonah finally did; *Stat.* 5.5–17; 20.21ff.

53 Irenaeus, *Adv. haer.* 5.5.2. Here Irenaeus compares Jonah to the three young men, whose flesh withstood the fiery furnace and emerged whole.

54 Tertullian, *De res.* 58. A long, masterful study of the Jonah story in the writings of the early church was produced by Y.-M. Duval, *Le livre de Jonas dans la littérature chrétienne grecque et latine. Sources et influence du Commentaire sur Jonas de saint Jérôme* (Paris: Études Augustiniennes, 1973). See also Dassmann, *Sündenvergebung*, 222–32.

55 Basil of Caesarea, *De Spiritu Sanct.* 14.32.

56 Regarding the nudity of candidates for baptism see below, n. 65. On the womb-like aspects of the font also see discussion below or refer to the following ancient sources: Justin Martyr, *1 Apol.* 61; Tertullian, *De bapt.* 3; Cyprian, *Ep.* 73; and Zeno of Verona, *Inv. ad font.* 1 and 7.

57 Dassmann, *Sündenvergebung*, 258–70; 425–38. Daniel's clothing on the Junius Bassus Sarcophagus in the Vatican Treasury was the gift of later restorers.

58 Eusebius, *Vita Const.* 49.

59 Snyder, *Ante Pacem*, 49–50, sees the Daniel images simply as references to rescue from danger or threat from external powers.

60 Justin Martyr, *Dial.* 31–2; Irenaeus, *Adv. haer.* 3.21.7; and Origen, *De princ.* 4.5; *Contra Cels.* 6.45; *Ad martyr.* 3.3.

61 Irenaeus, *Adv. haer.* 5.25–6; Hippolytus, *Com. in Dan.*, esp. ch. 4.

62 Tertullian, *Scorp.* 8.7; *De idol.* 15.10; and Cyprian, *De lapsis* 19, 31; *Ad Fort.* 2, 11; *Ep.* 58.2; 61.2; and 67.8. Also see discussion in Daniélou, *Origins of Latin Christianity*, 321–3.

63 Gregory Nazianzen, *Or.* 48.74; Cyril of Jerusalem, *Cat.lec.* 5.4; Eusebius, *Or. Const.* 17; Jerome, *Com. in Dan.*

64 Hippolytus, *Scol. in Dan.* 10.16; trans. S. D. F. Salmond, "Fragments from Commentaries," Ante Nicene Fathers, vol. 5 (1865; repr. Grand Rapids: Eerdmans, 1950), 190.

65 See H. Leclercq, "Nudité baptismale," in *DACL*, vol. 12.2 (1936), 1801–5; and L. de Bruyne, "L'imposition des mains dans l'art chrétien ancien," *RAC* 20 (1943), 244–5, in which he claims that two elements are essential for the baptismal bath: the water and nudity. Ancient texts that give evidence of this include Hippolytus, *Ap. trad.* 21.3, 5, and 11 that describes candidates stripping and going into the water naked; and John the Deacon, *Ep. ad Sen.* 6; *Did. apost.* 16; Cyril of Jerusalem, *Myst. cat.* 2; Theodore of Mopsuestia, *Lib. ad. Bapt.* 4; John Chrysostom, *Cat.* 2.24; and *Ep. ad Innocentius.* See also Pseudo-Dionysius, *Ecc. hier.* 2.6–7.

66 This iconography changes in the fifth century, particularly visibly in the two Ravenna baptisteries – the Arian and the Orthodox.

67 On the size of Christ in baptismal imagery see E. LeBlant, *Étude sur les sarcophages chrétiens* (Arles, 1878), 27; J. Fink, *Les Grands Thèmes de l'iconographie chrétienne des premiers siècles*, trans. D. F. Bebuyst (Bruges: Biblica, 1966), 34.

68 Augustine, *Serm.* 228, trans. M. S. Muldowney, Fathers of the Church series, 38 (New York, 1959), 198–9. In his *Serm.* 376 Augustine speaks again of the "Octave of the Infants" and describes the newly baptized as *pueri, infantes, parvuli, lactantes* … (*PL* 38–9, 1670). See also Augustine, *Serm. ad neophy.* 1 (*PL* 11, 483); and *Tract. in ep. Ioah.* 1.6 (*PL* 35, 1982). The imagery of the mother font also adds to the idea that those baptized are as newborn babies. See W. Bedard's discussion of this in *The Symbolism of the Baptismal Font* (Washington, DC, 1951), 17–36, with bibliography and source texts. Also R. Jensen, "Living Water: Images, Settings and Symbols of Early Christian Baptism in the West," (Ph.D. dissertation, Columbia University, 1991), 361–4.

69 See Hippolytus, *Ap. trad.* 3; Tertullian, *De cor.* 3; and *Adv. Marc.* 3.22; as well as the *Sacramentarium Leonianum*, ed. C. L. Feltoe (Cambridge, 1896); English trans. in E. C. Whitaker, *Documents of the Baptismal Liturgy* (London: SPCK, 1960), 157–8. Also see *Ep. Barnabas* 6.8–17; and Clement of Alexandria *Paed.* 1.6.34–5.

70 John the Deacon, *Ep. ad Senarius* 12, text in A. Wilmart, *Analecta Reginensia*, Studi e Testi 50 (Rome, 1933), ET in Whitaker, *Documents of the Baptismal Liturgy*, 157–8.

71 The baptistery was designed to look like a mausoleum, but interiors were often decorated to reflect the rich plant and animal life in Eden (for example the Neonian baptistery in Ravenna and the baptistery of S. Giovanni in Fonte, Naples).

72 Theodore of Mopsuestia, *De bap.* 3. Evidence for the practice in North Africa comes from Quodvultdeus, *De symbolo ad catech.* 1.1; and Augustine, *Serm.* 216.10. See also Smith, "Garments of Shame," 224–33.

73 Cyril of Jerusalem, *Myst. cat.* 1.9, trans. A. Stephenson in *The Works of St. Cyril of Jerusalem*, Fathers of the Church series, 62 (Washington, DC: Catholic University Press, 1969), 153–4. Cyril connects the nakedness of candidates with the nakedness of Adam in Eden in *Myst. cat.* 2.2. Also John Chrysostom, *Cat.* 11.28–9; and Paulinus of Nola, *Ep.* 32 (ad Severum) 3.5. Commentary in Smith, "Garments of Shame," 222–4.

74 For detailed discussion of these images see R. Jensen, "The Trinity and the Economy of Salvation on Two Fourth-Century Sarcophagi," *JECS* 1999 (Winter), 529–49; and D. Markow, "Some Born-Again Christians of the Fourth Century," *AB* 63 (1981), 650–5, both with bibliography.

75 Another important iconographic parallel is in the scenes of Promethius creating a human being. For illustrations of this similarity see Gerke, *Die christliche Sarkophage*, 193.

76 Irenaeus connects the healing of the man born blind with the creation of Adam though the action of making clay. Thus the clay Jesus smeared on the eyes of the blind man pointed to the original creation from clay; *Adv. haer.* 5.15.2 and 5.16.1. On the healing of the paralytic see *Adv. haer.* 5.17.2. Also a sermon of Cyril of Jerusalem on the healing of the paralytic, ET in Stephenson, *Works of St Cyril*.

77 Irenaeus, *Adv. haer.* 5.16.3 and 5.19.1; trans. Ante Nicene Fathers, vol. 1 (1865; repr. Grand Rapids: Eerdmans, 1950), 544–7. The "recapitulation" of the sin of Adam and Eve, enacted by the work of Christ and Mary, was a theme expounded by Irenaeus in particular, although other Christian writers also worked with the parallels, including Tertullian and Ambrose. See Daniélou, *Shadows to Reality*, 40–7; and Dassmann, *Sündenvergebung*, 232–404. The iconography which shows Jesus standing between Adam and Eve seems to have a later parallel in the Byzantine image of the Anastasis, in which Jesus brings Adam and Eve out of hell. See Kartsonis, *Anastasis: The Making of an Image*.

78 The further possibility that the imagery is making an orthodox statement about the presence of the whole Trinity at creation and then again at the incarnation of the Second Person must be considered. See Jensen, "Trinity and Economy of Salvation." E. Struthers Malbon noted the Adam and Eve/Christ and Mary parallels in her study of the iconography of the Junius Bassus sarcophagus and made the parallel to Daniel's obedience, since he appears in the iconography of that monument as well: *Iconography of the Sarcophagus of Junius Bassus*, 59–68.

# SELECT BIBLIOGRAPHY

Beckwith, J., *Early Christian and Byzantine Art*, rev. edn (Harmondsworth: Penguin, 1970).

Belting, H., *Likeness and Presence*, trans. E. Jephcott (Chicago: University of Chicago Press, 1994).

du Bourguet, P., *Early Christian Art* (New York: Reynal, 1971).

—— *Early Christian Painting* (London: Weidenfeld and Nicolson, 1965).

Brenk, B., *Spätantike und frühes Christentum* (Frankfurt: Propyläen, 1977).

Daniélou, J., *From Shadows to Reality*, trans. W. Wibberd (Westminster, MD: Newman Press, 1960).

Dassman, E., *Sündenvergebung durch Taufe, Buße, und Märtyrerfürbitte in den Zeugnissen frühchristlichen Frömmigkeit und Kunst* (Münster in Westf.: Aschendorff, 1973).

Deichmann, F. W. *Ravenna, Haupstadt der spätantiken Abendlandes*, 4 vols. (Wiesbaden, 1969–89).

Deichmann, F. W., Bovini, G. and Brandenburg, H., *Repertorium der christlich-antiken Sarkophage*, i: *Rom und Ostia* (Wiesbaden: Steiner, 1967).

Dölger, F., *Ichthys: Das Fisch Symbol in frühchristlicher Zeit* (Münster in Westf.: Aschendorffschen, 1910).

Duval, N. et al. (eds), *Naissance des Arts Chrétiens: Atlas des monuments paleochrétiens de la France* (Paris: Imprimerie Nationale, 1991).

Elsner, J. *Art and the Roman Viewer* (Cambridge: Cambridge University Press, 1995).

Elsner, J. (ed.), *Art and Text in Roman Culture* (Cambridge: Cambridge University Press, 1996).

Engemann, J., *Untersuchungen zur Sepulkralsymbolik der späteren römischen Kaiserzeit* (Münster in Westf.: Aschendorffschen, 1973).

Ferrua, A., *The Unknown Catacomb: A Unique Discovery of Early Christian Art*, trans. I. Inglis (New Lanark, Scotland: Geddes and Grosset, 1991).

Finney, P. C., *The Invisible God: The Earliest Christians on Art* (New York: Oxford University Press, 1994).

Gerke, F., *Die christliche Sarkophage der vorkonstantinischen Zeit* (Berlin: de Gruyter, 1940).

Goodenough, E., *Jewish Symbols in the Greco-Roman Period*, 13 vols. (New York: Pantheon, 1953–68).

Gough, M., *The Origins of Christian Art* (London: Thames and Hudson, 1973).

Grabar, A., *Christian Iconography: A Study of its Origins* (Princeton: Princeton University Press, 1968).

—— *The Beginnings of Christian Art 200–395* (London: Thames and Hudson, 1967).

Gutmann, J. *Sacred Images: Studies in Jewish Art from Antiquity to the Middle Ages* (Northampton, 1989).

Kartsonis, A., *Anastasis: The Making of an Image* (Princeton: Princeton University Press, 1986).

Kitzinger, E., *Byzantine Art in the Making* (Cambridge, MA: Harvard University Press, 1977).

Koch, G., *Early Christian Art and Architecture* (London: SCM Press, 1996).

Lother, H., *Realismus und Symbolismus in der altchristlichen Kunst* (Tübingen: Mohr, 1967).

Lowden, J., *Early Christian and Byzantine Art* (London: Phaidon, 1997).

Struthers Malbon, E., *The Iconography of the Sarcophagus of Junius Bassus* (Princeton: Princeton University Press, 1990).

Mango, C., *The Art of the Byzantine Empire, 312–1453* (Englewood Cliffs: Prentice-Hall, 1972).

Mathews, T., *The Clash of Gods: A Reinterpretation of Early Christian Art* (Princeton: Princeton University Press, 1993).

Milburn, A., *Early Christian Art and Architecture* (Berkeley: University of California Press, 1988).

Charles Murray, M., "Art and the Early Church," *JThS* n.s. 28.2 (1977), 304–45.

—— *Rebirth and Afterlife: A Study of the Transmutation of Some Pagan Imagery in Early Christian Art* (Oxford: BAR International Series, 1981).

Oakeshott, W., *The Mosaics of Rome: From the Third to the Fourteenth Centuries* (London: Thames and Hudson, 1967).

Snyder, G., *Ante Pacem: Archaeological Evidence of Church Life before Constantine* (Macon, GA: Mercer University Press, 1985).

Stevenson, J., *The Catacombs: Rediscovered Monuments of Early Christianity* (London: Thames and Hudson, 1978).

Stuiber, A., *Refrigerium Interim, die Vorstellungen vom Zwischenzustand und die frühchristliche Grabeskunst* (Bonn: P. Hanstein, 1957).

Styger, P., *Die römischen Katakomben* (Berlin: Verlag für Kunstwissenschaft, 1933).

Syndicus, E., *Early Christian Art*, trans. J. R. Foster (New York: Macmillan, 1993).

Tronzo, W., *The Via Latina Catacomb: Imitation and Discontinuity in Fourth-Century Roman Painting* (University Park, PA: Pennsylvania State University Press, 1986).

van der Meer, F., *Early Christian Art* (Chicago: University of Chicago Press, 1967).

Volbach A. and Hirmer, M., *Early Christian Art* (New York: Abrams, 1962).

Weitzmann, K. (ed.), *The Age of Spirituality* (New York: Metropolitan Museum of Art, 1979).

—— *Ancient Book Illumination* (Cambridge, MA: Harvard University Press, 1959).

Weitzmann, K. and Kessler, H. *The Frescoes of the Dura Synagogue and Christian Art*, Dumbarton Oaks Studies, 28 (Washington, DC: Dumbarton Oaks, 1990).

# INDEX